FROM
Sex Appeal
TO SELF
APPEAL

Stripping Barriers to Recovery—
LEAVING ADDICTION, RETURNING TO BODY AND MIND
with A New Introduction by the Author

Susan Bremer O'Neill

ISBN: 978-0-9721046-1-6

Library of Congress Control Number: 2013907827

PRINTED IN THE UNITED STATES OF AMERICA

For all the lost girls and lonely women
who are looking for love
in all the wrong places—and in all the wrong ways.

ACKNOWLEDGEMENTS

First, I'd like to thank my parents who loved and supported me even when they didn't understand me.

I'm especially thankful for the women who have read this manuscript in its many stages and offered editing, content suggestions, and encouragement: Amy Farnstrom—you believed in me despite my own indecision and fear and pushed me beyond the first few chapters, Karrin Dalton for reading the first draft and gently suggesting that my sentences were a bit rambling, Carol Pinckney for not only reading the final draft but also for becoming one of my biggest advocates and helping me build the courage to publish, and Shirley Irving, Shanyn Avila, Molly Carlson, Oleta Kay Ham, Christine Baily, and Angie Mendoza. You are important women in my life. Marc Burgett, you were the sole man whom I entrusted with this very personal piece, and you helped me tremendously. You rock! Also, I'm eternally grateful for the thousands of women in my classes and workshops—you've not only inspired and motivated me to tell my story, but you've also taught me so much.

Most of all I thank my husband Joe, who, throughout the years, has stood beside me and not only listened to my reservations but also supported me when I couldn't support myself. For this I will always love you.

INTRODUCTION

Growing up female and living as an addict encouraged a separation from my physical body and emotions so complete and all-encompassing that it took something extreme and alien to most people to bring me back to myself. That something happened in 1995 when I began stripping, after I got sober at thirty-four.

Before this time, I was disconnected from and unable to know my own feelings and emotions, but I was hypersensitive to how others might see or think of me and how I should act accordingly. I lived in my head, concerned only with how others saw me. The disease of addiction dictates that the inner self is numb, therefore, the head of an addict is not connected to their body. I've heard many say this, and I have certainly experienced being one of the "Walking Heads." Also, my experience as a woman, teacher, and coach for women within and outside recovery, reinforces the fact that most women don't own their physical bodies or emotions. They too are Walking Heads.

Women aren't taught how to make friends with their female bodies or honor feminine thoughts and vulnerabilities. We're not given permission to be okay with our sexual beings much less to look at our anatomy for what it is. For many, their woman's body has become a foreign unsafe entity that isn't fully inhabited. Couple this with a lack of education about our craving for love, valuation, validation and the strong pull of sexuality, and we have a recipe for continual searching for acceptance and love outside ourselves. In short, we're trained to view our bodies as an "other." We focus on how it appears to others and how to please others with it.

ALL women I've encountered in my striptease classes and Self Appeal® coaching, whether they are recovering from addiction to a substance or not, need to recover their body and sexuality. In my experience, ALL women, at the very least, need permission to be in their own bodies—and enjoy them.

Life will present opportunities for every recovering person that they can use to re-educate and grow themselves up. In chapter two I write; "I believe there is a wisdom to life we cannot explain, but only, if we're lucky, pay attention to." I began to pay attention in the strip club just as anybody in recovery begins to pay attention in whatever circumstances they get sober. But just like merely stopping using isn't recovery, similarly, knowing you're a people-pleaser or that you give too much of your body and yourself away in search of love isn't enough to change your behavior either. Becoming aware of, or sober to, a disconnection from body doesn't mean it's fixed.

Recovery from any physical injury or disease is a slow process, but you can see it. Bones mend, crutches or other support apparatus are discarded, form and posture return, hair grows back. Having the disease of being disconnected from oneself, healing the mind in order to connect the body, is excruciatingly slow. You can't see it. You can't see neural networks being rewired, new ones established. It's a multi-layered process to recover one's physical body and body of emotions. Focusing on one's motivation, actions, and experiences is key to getting healthy. What you can measure and see is a slow change in attitude and action.

Once the addiction is stopped, there is a lifetime of learning how to live without anesthetizing oneself to your new reality. You have to shift and transform your misdirected thinking known in recovery circles as "isms." It's an on-going process to learn how to stay in your body and not leave. Within this recovery process, there is the potential to exchange one addiction for another (moving from alcohol to sugar for instance or from promiscuous sex to shopping). Also, quite often, once the sobering awareness becomes reality, you have to overcome secrecy and shame.

This book took me almost ten years from start to first publication in 2014. After I published it, my mother tried to read it (I'd warned her about some of the content) but couldn't, so I was again mired in shame not only about what I'd actually done but then also about what I'd written. Couple my shame, along with my lack of marketing skill and the few critical reviews I got that made me feel more shameful, and this book went into hiding.

Fortunately, I was able to continue my recovery of self. When I finally had enough distance from the initial shock of publishing and had received enough positive comments about the book, I reread it in hopes of creating an audio version. I was mortified to find errors. Errors! I, the perfectionist woman who never felt good enough had put something imperfect into the world which could invite criticism or worse, rejection. It wasn't right which meant *I* wasn't right. As usual.

Thankfully, despite being a woman in recovery from substance abuse and the "disease of please," I continue to grow in feeling whole, confident, powerful, nonreactive and unrestricted by my self-sabotaging thoughts. Today, four years from that first publication, I am more confident in my voice, my writing, my body, and my wisdom as a woman and ... I've fixed the errors! (Hopefully).

The recollection of significant events in this book is an attempt to show the patterns and changes in my recovery of mind so that others might be empowered to stay with and not escape their own shifting feelings and conflicting thoughts.

A part of me, the people-pleasing, ever-critical self who yearns to be loved for perfection, thought of editing and rewriting chapter one, as there had been some negative reactions to it, but I haven't. That is mainly because it's what I needed to write at the time, and I like it for that reason. It's good enough. It shows the pattern I was striving to illustrate. Humans, especially addicts, have patterns, usually chaotic and self-destructive.

All incidences written about are true (although names have been changed) and everything written is an honest account designed to help other women who wrestle with the same feelings. You may be a woman recovering from putting something into your body to escape your reality such as food, drugs or alcohol. Perhaps you're a woman engaged in an obsessive activity like exercise, shopping, or working too much that keeps you cut off from your body. Maybe you use men, sex, relationships or people-pleasing to gain approval and focus on something outside yourself to fill the void within. Whatever you are "recovering" from that keeps you from knowing your authentic self, I hope my story and the way I write it engages you. Whether it terrifies, shocks, entertains or simply provides you with an interesting glimpse into a world you know nothing about, I hope it prompts you to think and wonder about your own relationship with your body, your sexuality, and your self.

I wrote section one, *Beginning,* to highlight how an innocent child adapts through escape, then solidifies the habit of denial and distance from her feelings, her precious body and her God-given sexuality. Within this section, *Adaptation* and *Addiction*, chapters one and two, encompass my life from birth through the age of thirty-five. Some have said the paragraphs are jumpy, fast, and disjointed but that's just how life is for a child and an adult who lives in chaos. If you don't like that chaos or get too uncomfortable and just want the prurient details of being a stripper, skip to chapter three.

I started getting sober while working in a well-respected career, but realized I was miserable, so chapters three through eleven take you on my journey to gather self-respect and esteem in a most unusual way. Starting with the section of *Awareness*, the story slows down and specific examples are used because once substances that alter the mind are put away life does slow down. Also, more is remembered if you're not in a blackout. In *Understanding*, *Acceptance* and *Approval*, scenes and thought processes illustrate how I came more fully into and learned to love and value myself so I could love others and they could love me in return.

Your experiences may be different, but I'm sure that if you're a woman many of your feelings will be similar to those I've written about here. Recovery is an inside job, and it will be an amazing process if you have the courage to look at the patterns, stay in the interesting yet sometimes confusing act of self-discovery, and to not escape yourself, no matter what.

Please feel free to reach out with your own thoughts, stories, or if you just want to chat about your recovery of body, sex, and self. Go to susanbremeroneill.com and e-mail me through the contact page. It will be an honor to hear from you.

-Susan Bremer O'Neill

TABLE OF CONTENTS

From Sex Appeal to Self Appeal
Stripping Barriers to Recovery—Leaving Addiction,
Returning to Body and Mind

If there is ignorance around pleasure,
there will be ignorance around pain.

PROLOGUE

She stood.

He sat.

Her lithe, slender body towered above him in seven-inch platform spike heels and from his seated position appeared to be ten-feet tall. Her silky golden hair touched the top of her heart-shaped ass when she tilted her head back to expose her fragile throat.

She turned around to let him visually partake of her backside and he got lost in the heart and the hair and the way they all interconnected to form imagined perfection—all at his eye level he was seated so close. He wasn't supposed to touch though, there were rules against it, and this magnified her importance.

I saw her too.

Reflected in the mirror in front of me, this tanned seductress commanded everyone's attention. Her lined lips were filled with spiced cocoa and a honey cinnamon glaze—we wanted to eat them. Her eyes were two magnets with deep aqua centers, pools of serene glacial water we wanted to dip into and drink from. They reflected silver club lights and promised comfort, care, and the certainty that while resting in their thick-coal lining and night-black shading they'd provide solace.

She had the smooth calculated moves of a rose in slow summer bloom as her hands reached up and she stretched her toned muscles; her arms moved with the grace of delicate petals opening slowly. She wrapped them around herself as if they were a soft cotton blanket and we, every one of us in that darkened nightclub, wanted to be those arms. We ached to be close to the sensual hue of her body.

As the raucous singer from Puddle of Mudd belted out "slap my ass" from the song "Control," the knowing glint within her eyes sparked as she ran her hands slowly down the sides of her waist, then hips. What she wore was nothing larger than three strips of material with strings; the secret weapon, as she referred to it, because it was so close to wearing nothing.

This confident libidinous woman, Vixen, had been born inside and grown up within the strip club. Through applause and money she'd been trained to be the perfect image of unabashed sensuality they'd needed her to be. She'd become their idea of beauty and sexual prowess because she'd had none of her own.

BEGINNING:
SELF-DENIAL
AND NEGLECT

ADAPTATION

I was three years old when my family moved to Okinawa. By then we'd already moved four times.

I don't remember those moves, but in worn photo albums, two-dimensional snapshots are arranged in chronological order and help me reconstruct significant events. A black and white image of a stranger, whose scrunched up face is a shade of gray and whose disheveled hair suggests Albert Einstein tendencies, is proof I was born in Milwaukee. In a 2 x 2 monochrome square, I have concrete evidence that I wore baggy pants over diapers and that we lived in Washington State and visited Yellowstone National Park at a time when bears were allowed to walk right up to car doors. I search these flat images held hostage in time for recognition of the childlike innocence I'm certain I once possessed; what does the tiny blonde girl flashing the mischievous smile think as she stands next to a cinder block structure, our first home on a small island next to Japan?

Looking through these albums reconstructs moments of fearlessness lost to the complicated being I evolved into, like the time I held a live starfish from the Pacific Ocean while my mom sat on the sandy beach nearby changing my sister's diaper. Some pictures from my earliest years exist only through conversations related to me. One of these favorite memories is that I offered my long-coveted blanket to my new sister who had to sleep in a dresser drawer because we had no bassinet or cradle when she first came home from the hospital.

This life as a toddler produced static replicas of persons never really known to me: parents who are younger than I am today, and siblings new to the experiences of life. These reproductions trigger still more memories of an easy world before I became a slave to its ambiguous interpretations. A yellowed, torn still-life of my sister and I in matching dresses and Easter bonnets conjures a faint vision of a vast green field laced with the promise of colored eggs. My mother, an attractive twenty-something woman, models a bouffant hair style and wears a sleeveless Jackie O dress while she poses outside our army living quarters, a duplex, where our last name was stenciled boldly on the outside. At that house, our last place to live on Okinawa before we returned to the United States, my parents regularly played Pinochle with the people next door, and my sister and I dressed in authentic Japanese kimonos while the adults exclaimed how cute we were. When remembering this house, I also see myself watching the original *My Favorite Martian* on a black and white television, eating pink, blue, and green button candy off strips of white paper that we bought at an Okinawan store right outside the army base, and teasing two-year old Jimmy when he played with shovels and buckets in his sandbox.

One day while Jimmy's mom was in another part of their home that looked identical to ours, a few of us gathered in their bathroom. We stood around the toilet. Jimmy said he was going to prove that, indeed, a person could flush himself down. He stepped into the bowl. We strained our eyes to keep them open, unwilling to blink. He pulled the handle. The water surged in from all sides and swirled round his feet as we held our breath waiting for him to be pulled through the black hole to a place we were certain was smelly and vile.

Nothing.

"Liar, liar, pants on fire," the rest of us chimed.

He pushed the handle a second time.

Nothing.

"Liar, liar, pants on fire," we yelled with fervor as we rushed out of the bathroom passing his mom who was walking in to see what all the commotion was about. In the hurried retreat, I stepped on someone's foot. "Ouch," I heard.

Everyone else was barefoot, but I was wearing my coveted white go-go boots made popular by Nancy Sinatra's song, "These Boots Were Made for Walking." I felt like a princess in them, even after they turned from bright white to smudged chalky gray. At night I put them where I could look at them. During the day, I'd climb trees in them, admiring them as they hung off the end of my skinny legs, glimpses of nobility in an otherwise common leafy green. With them on, I could tolerate rough branches better than I would have been able to with tender feet, but when maneuvering all over the red and green swing set erected in our back yard, I had to be careful; the smooth metal was slippery. I'd hoist myself onto the horizontal support bar that ran between one set of the end poles that anchored into the ground and hold tight to one of those poles. This added four feet to my height; I could look down on the stylish boots and even the grownups, as I stood high above them.

These tangible Kodak images and their resultant memories are suspended in an era before the modern-day phenomena of people unscrupulously using video to chronicle other's foibles and pain. I'm betting no one in the past, at least no one in my past, thought to run for a camera during an argument or tragedy.

But happy times, like the happy memories between two people embattled in a nasty divorce, fade. And like those photographs, my memory is selective; my mind holds onto emotional illustrations that brought about painful feelings that have haunted me through the years. Although not always in the forefront of my consciousness, experiential snapshots have nonetheless shaped and molded who I am. Whether I wanted them to or not, they maneuvered their way into my barren expanse of gray matter before I had the opportunity to adopt the skills of adult reasoning and logic, and they still reside there today.

One of the earliest family portraits, taken before my father was to go to Vietnam, was wanted in case he never returned. We're a handsome family, young, pressed—my sister and I wear matching checked dresses with white eyelet lace. My sister's face reflects the silliness of being three years old without a care in the world and like a magnet draws our eyes to her golden hair. She sits on the lap of my mother, who is wearing a coral necklace and matching clip earrings that my father gifted her with on one of his return trips from the Orient. They show teeth in their smiles. I, on the other hand, sit on my father's lap, keeping my toothy smile to myself like he does. His eyes twinkle and reflect the pride of a young but capable solider, proud to serve his country, while my eyes neither twinkle nor smile. I'm formal, dutiful, proper—my hands clasped as if in prayer. Did I know he might not return? Did I know what war was?

I don't know the answers to these questions, but I do know that the child's mind thinks it can control outcomes. Perhaps if I was obedient and said the right thing, he wouldn't go away. Perhaps, if I made myself good enough, he wouldn't want to leave. Perhaps if I fell, he'd be there to catch me.

⌁

Breathing stops.

Body falls deeper, deeper, deeper.

Feet hit, eyes slam open.

Arms swing to the side—to the front—to the back.

Hand touches something hard. Grabs.

Arm pulls body around. Other hand grabs.

Lungs strain.

Hands pull arms, pull body, pull feet up, up, up the twelve-foot pole faster than the water is trying to expel me.

Head breaks through.

Lungs release, breath sucks in.

Bathing cap, required, is also being rejected by the hostile liquid and now sits like a globe on my head, a few capable hairs straining to keep it from floating away.

Droplets, like soldiers on reconnaissance, climb into my ears.

Heartbeat pounds my brain.

Eyes stinging, I search. Kids everywhere flail, dog paddle, hold onto adults.

I see the edge of the pool. I see my parents clapping on the other side of the chain-link fence that surrounds the swimming area. Their mouths are moving, but I can't hear what they're saying.

Instructor swings the pole, and me holding tightly to it, close to the concrete ledge. I take hold of it and hand over hand, pull myself along. I come to the stairs and climb out of the chlorine-clogged sea of aquamarine.

I shiver in the ninety-degree heat and walk as fast as my five-year-old legs can.

Breathing slows.

All the other students had hopped in, reached for the big stick, and then bolted out of the large blue bath twenty minutes ago, but I'd stayed in the shelter with my fear and desire to pee as long as I could. I yearned to be a good girl and jump like everyone else, it really did look easy, but the pool was bottom-less, the instructor a stranger.

Eventually, reluctantly, I gathered courage around me like a new white Easter coat buttoned tightly to hide a worn dress, stepped into the sunlight and away from safety, walked to the precarious edge of my resolve, stepped off the cement and plunged into the deep end.

With that hurdle overcome, I bolt away from the lapping lagoon, grab my towel in the women's changing room and run to my parents who've been on the outside looking in. My father scoops me up. You're a big girl now, he praises, his arms sur-rounding me.

My fingers lace themselves behind his neck, and I draw myself close to his sturdy chest. My blue eyes soak up the ap-proval emanating from the centers of his own cobalt eyes. I nestle deep in his arms.

But not every event in my memory was applauded.

I'm not sure whether it's an accurate childhood account or simply an older, socially-concerned intellect that fills in the picture in my memory, but mom's frowning face in the window back then was all I needed to tell me I was doing something I should hide when, while pretending to be taller than I was, I discovered a sensation I liked when I pressed my body against the swing-set pole. It felt so good in fact that I recreated it. I'd balance on the horizontal bar, stretch my short arms as far to the heavens as I could, grab onto the anchored post, then step off and let my legs dangle while wiggling my body around the pole centered between my legs. When I found the spot where the sensation returned and pressed hard, I could get the feeling back. I soon learned that if I kept my feet on the ground and used my legs to help push my body against the metal rod hard-er, I could intensify the warm feeling that began below, rose in intensity, and then crested to a euphoric calm throughout my entire being. I told my best friend and together we shared a secret, squirming around on the swing set. It felt good, and I continued to do it but with reservation and caution that no one else could see.

It was important to create good feelings because life pushed me out of my safe world where play and dinnertime was the routine. I don't have a picture of my first day of school, but I don't need one. I clearly remember waiting for the big yellow bus with my mom and sister and stepping up the huge steps after it stopped in front of us. Their faces moved slowly past as the bus began to roll forward, and I peered over the bottom edge of the window watching them get smaller. After that I sat quietly waiting for it to deposit me in this new place called school. Before he opened the door at our destination, the driver told us youngsters where to go after we got off the bus, but the other kids jostling around me and the scrubbed tile walls and bright lights inside the building were confusing.

A bell rang.

I stood in the middle of what became a vacant vestibule—alone.

Tears started burrowing for light from somewhere behind my eyes.

I didn't feel so big.

A grown up came and asked my name. She took my hand and led me to a room.

"Yes. My name is Sue Bremer," a boy was saying authoritatively as I stole in late.

"Is it really?" the teacher inquired, disbelieving.

"Yes," he repeated defiantly.

Tilting her head in my direction she bellowed, "What is your name," as I stood there in my fresh dress feeling soiled.

"My," I could feel the heat rise from my throat and fill my

cheeks. "My name is Sue Bremer," I managed meekly.

Everyone started laughing. The boy who'd been claiming he was me turned. It was Kevin from my neighborhood.

I stood stoic as the teacher finished grilling Kevin and told him to take the empty seat with his name on it at the end of a row.

She directed her attention back to me.

The seats were arranged alphabetically and I had to walk to the front of the class past all the small people who could barely touch the ground under their desk, while they snickered and smirked at what had just transpired their very first day of school. I sat silently staring straight ahead as the teacher tried to restore order in the room.

During recess, Kevin came over and smiled sweetly in my direction as a group of us sat searching for four-leaf clovers. Cross-legged, silent in my task of inspecting grass, I soon forgot the early morning episode. Other children had attested they'd found many clovers in that exact same patch of green.

Memories come more easily after this point in my life. School became familiar, and I settled into a comfortable pattern. On the bus I usually sat next to Doreen and even though Kevin rode the same bus, I didn't pay him any attention. One morning, he sat in front of us in a seat all by himself, his head low. Not too long after boarding, he peered around the edge of the seat, kept his brown eyes downcast, and held out to me a flower made of pink tissue paper. I took it. He turned back around quickly.

I cradled it gingerly in my hands.

When I got to my desk, I replaced the wilted clover I'd been hoarding with the delicate beauty. I took it home that night.

While playing hopscotch across the street from our house one afternoon, he approached sheepishly, rocked from side to side, bent down, then ran through the hopscotch squares picking up our stones. I chased him trying to get the pebbles back.

He stopped. A shouting match ensued. He taunted me while holding them out for me to take, but when I leaned in, he moved his hands behind his back.

"Give 'em back," I whined.

He smiled and brought his hands within my reach again. This time when I moved forward to snatch them, he angled towards me, and his lips touched mine. Startled, all thoughts of rocks vanished.

"Can I do it again?" he asked.

I saw his face coming toward mine, and I closed my eyes. When I opened my eyes, he was grinning large.

After that, he played hopscotch with us sometimes and occasionally shared a seat with Doreen and me on the bus. Many years later I'd refer to him as my first boyfriend.

It was on that same sidewalk another day, in the middle of throwing a stone from one hopscotch square to another, I saw Kevin's mom coming toward us. She was walking fast and her face was red.

He gave us the apologetic, I-don't-really-want-to-go look but turned back to her when she called his name.

Kevin was big, he stood taller than me in his bare feet, but that day, wearing cropped black shorts, exposing a hairless chest, he seemed extraordinarily small next to his mom. She crouched down in front of him, resting one knee on the pavement, placed both her hands on his little arms next to his sides and said something we couldn't hear. He turned and waved a limp goodbye.

I watched them walk away, their hands entwined, their backs getting smaller.

Mom told me later that day that Kevin's dad had been killed in Vietnam.

I never saw Kevin again.

Before I turned seven, my father went to serve in Vietnam for the second time, and my mom, sister, and I moved from Okinawa back to a small town in Wisconsin to be close to her family. Wearing junior-sized kimonos, we two blonde sisters were an anomaly even to our own relatives. It was fun at first, being someplace new and meeting and staying with grandpa and grandma and uncles and an aunt, but we were interlopers; it was a full house.

Attending the parochial school for first grade in this new town was as awkward as it was meeting and living with the relatives and as disconcerting as my first day of kindergarten. Every morning I'd remove my coat and boots, place them in the hall outside the classroom, take my place at the little wooden desk, lift the top and hide my home-made lunchbox and work-books inside, make sure my pencil was in its slotted groove, and sit patiently. I'd fidget in the warm room while the teacher finished writing on the blackboard. The bell would ring, and my agitation would grow. As the children quieted down, the teacher would open her slim book and start taking attendance. My body would tense, and I'd feel heavy in the seat, as if I were going to crash through it. My eyes, while looking straight ahead, not at anyone else, envisioned stinging black pupils boring into me. My stomach would roll. Hearing her start with the "A's," everything else in that room disappeared except my large ugly black glasses, awkward hair, home-made clothes, not-store-bought lunchbox, and weird name. "Brahma bull" some had called me a few times. She'd speak aloud the offending odd sounds that formed my name, I'd raise my hand, say, "here," and magically the world returned to normal. I could focus on something else.

For a while I focused on Sandy. Sandy wasn't new. She'd lived in the same house her entire life. She was familiar with the school, the other kids, and she had what I considered to be pretty, store-bought clothes that seemed to fit her round little body perfectly.

And I focused on learning. In school I could win the teacher's acceptance with excellent grades. There was no guessing as to what was right or wrong. If I spelled "catechism" right, I was given a gold star. At ten, when I read *Alice In Wonderland* and continued running across a word I'd never seen before, eventually slowing down long enough to sound it out, "li-no-le-um," and realizing it was the tiles and patterns on a kitchen floor, I was proud. There was only one way the word was right and therefore I was right.

It felt good to know the right way. I had a need to make order out of disorder.

About a year later and before I was nine, my father returned from Vietnam, and we moved to Fayetteville, North Carolina—our eighth move. Mom came with me the first day to enroll me in the new school, but after that, I had to walk a path through overgrown bushes behind the housing area by myself to get there. Bigger kids walked that same path, but I didn't know them. My legs trudged towards the beige columns and entrance walkway to get to a room where I also knew no one. The atmosphere of scrubbed and soiled kids, blackboard chalk and southern food I'd never seen before—black eyed peas, collard greens, and fatback—further alienated me. I'd find my class, get to my desk, and sit there like I was supposed to, hands folded in lap, earnest expression, neither full face smile, nor a frown—neutral.

One morning as the clouds poured, I made the walk to school sullenly with damp feet and a face on the verge of creating its own storm system. My legs were heavier than normal, but my vulnerable little body soldiered on through the bad weather. Passing through the houses and getting to the edge of the paved trail that wound behind them but still in view of the road, I saw a long blue car pull to the side. While the motor kept running, a large man in a suit and tie reached across the seat, opened his passenger door and asked, "Would you like a ride?"

Yes! I did want a ride. I did want to be somewhere warm and dry. But, and this was a very big *but*, I knew I wasn't supposed to ride with strangers. I shook my short pixie haircut from side to side as he proceeded to tell me that it was wet, and I should definitely take him up on his offer. He began to insist so much that I wrapped my arms around myself while trying to hold the umbrella upright and not have it jab the bushes which would make me fall, and ran the rest of the way to the school where everyone else knew each other and they served grits for lunch.

I didn't have to walk to that school alone for long though. My parents bought a house and we moved again.

New house, new school, new kids.

In this new place we became close friends with our neighbors. After school we'd get together at their house and watch *Gilligan's Island* and *Dark Shadows,* but one afternoon, intrigued by the word "strip," five of us gathered to play poker. We girls prepared by putting on necklaces, and the boys put their baseball caps and belts on. There we children sat peering over the top of our cards, seriously contemplating when to hold, when to fold, and how many cards to take. It was daylight, but the bedroom door was closed and curtains drawn. As each hand ended, good-natured moans erupted from the losers who had to remove a sock or shoe or something more essential like a shirt. This was the only time in my life I was happy to wear glasses. As more hands were played, the youngest boy, in first grade, was the biggest loser and sat with his bare chest showing then climbed under a blanket when he had to remove his pants to sit solely in his underwear. We earnestly dealt and gathered cards, trying not to let on how goofy we were really feeling as we made serious decisions about which article of clothing to remove next. We were called for dinner before anyone got completely naked and kept our poker faces on for our parents. We knew there was a difference between boys and girls, but most of us, except maybe Ed, who was older than me by two years, didn't really know what that meant.

Our play was normally etched out of the magnificent hues of childish innocence with such games as running races in the front yard after dinner and hide-n-seek, but it's out of that innocent life that adults grow. It was a scorching summer day when Ed and I found our way into the same hiding place while playing hide-and-seek. The dry air, heavy with pine needles in the ninety-degree heat was, at the very least, ten degrees hotter inside their small pull-behind camper parked in the backyard. Blacker than the room at night that had once frightened me into thinking monsters would emerge from under the bed, and noiseless, the surrounding world disappeared as our silent eyes adjusted our remaining senses to the intensity of the moment. The enormous quiet pressed us close to each other. Touching first our fingers, then our hands, then our lips, our competitions and contentious bantering disintegrated.

Bang! Bang! Bang! Fists and voices pounded against the aluminum siding.

We scrambled out quickly, our younger siblings' suspicions confirmed, as they chanted, "Sue and Ed sitting in a tree...."

"Shut up! Shut up! Shut up!" we yelled back as they ran and we chased.

We never ventured into the camper alone again, but sometimes when we'd play hide-and-seek we'd run towards the same hiding place and steal a kiss. We'd crossed over the line from playmates to something more, but I didn't know exactly what that something more was.

I was beginning to learn about attraction and dare I say it, what "love" involved in the adult world while living in that house, and I was also learning about death. Because we lived at the end of a paved road our area was a dumping ground for people who no longer wanted to care for their pets. We found a kitten then lost it to car wheels that sped by. We once took in a dog who it turned out had distemper and consequently died in our care, leaving the threat of disease to linger in our yard. We had two rabbits in separate cages, but one got loose, and we later found its headless body in the backyard. And although Ed's dad had survived Vietnam, he was no match for a brain tumor that got him sent home early from the battle zone. As his mind and motor skills declined, we watched his deterioration when one of the only tasks he could do was turn the jump rope for my sister and me. I cried at his funeral and better understood some of the mysteries of the world I was trying to navigate; dads either weren't around very often or they died.

I continued trying to make order out of disorder.

Some time after my tenth birthday, my father, a Special Forces Green Beret, a very tough man boyfriends would tell me years later, went to serve in Vietnam a third time so we returned to Wisconsin and the same small town we'd lived in previously. I returned to the Lutheran parochial school I'd attended in first grade so I was familiar with most of the students. For a short while I was the exotic girl-child who'd lived in faraway places, but that celebrity vanished quickly.

Standing outside our home one afternoon, one of my uncles rode by on his bicycle and said, "You're a whore." I'd never heard the word before, and since he was calling me one, thought I'd better look it up. I was an exceptional speller and while it took me a few times thumbing through the Webster's pages to learn how it wasn't spelled, I finally found "whore – noun, a promiscuous woman, a prostitute." I still didn't understand it so I looked up "promiscuous – adjective, indiscriminate in sexual relations." And I looked up "prostitute - noun, one who solicits and takes payment for sexual intercourse."

I didn't understand "intercourse" and thought about asking mom, letting her know what he'd called me, but the definition had "sex" in it, and I couldn't bring myself to ask. Besides, what if he was right? My swing-set feel-good play had evolved to the bedroom when I'd learned that as I lay on my hands clasped together, my body on top, I could bring about the feelings I'd produced while pressing myself against the pole. Had he seen? The child's overactive sense of responsibility kicked in, and I wondered what I'd done for him to call me that. Today I know that he probably just learned a new word and thought himself a big man for using it, but back then, just like I'd done with the laughing kids in kindergarten, I internalized his words and turned them against myself.

My father returned from Vietnam with a new duty assignment in the middle of the school year.

Fists clench. Fingers pulse white. Head throbs. Lips part, "I don't want to move!"

"You have to change your feelings," mom yells.

Trying to make order out of disorder.

Control, the illusion that we adults grasp onto to feel okay in a world that seems out of our control, is denied us as children. As a military child who'd moved twelve times before the age of thirteen, I lived in a tentative world. I couldn't control our moving around, or my father's uncertain yet eventual return from wars—first Korea, then Vietnam. I couldn't control the stares from the cliques of kids established in their lives before I arrived into their classrooms as the new science experiment to be dissected and scrutinized. With each new bedroom I helped decorate, with each new school I had to enter and introduce myself as the new girl in, I became conscious of feeling like an outsider. This wasn't a comfortable way to feel. So I quit. I never discussed feelings or natural substances that originated within, not sadness, loneliness, fear, frustration, anger, sexual urges, mucous, pus, shit, piss, nor blood. Therefore, during puberty, when my body was changing, it was natural to be detached, and I continued keeping the secrets of me, even from me.

The summer between seventh and eighth grade I attended a week-long church camp. A few of those days, after canoeing, craft making, nature walks and campfires, as I was getting cleaned up before bed, I noticed something in my underwear. Every night I saw the dark stain, balled up the soiled panties, threw them in my dirty-clothes bag, wondered briefly what was going on, put on a clean pair, and then forgot about it. I never confided in one of the other girls or told a counselor. After camp was over and I returned home, mom, with a pained expression on her face while standing in the middle of a dirty-clothes pile one morning, asked, "Did you start your period?"

I stopped, thought about it in an inquisitive way and finally said, "I guess so." I knew what a period was because we girls had gossiped and giggled about it, but I never associated that with what I saw materializing in my underwear.

Months earlier, before I'd gone to summer camp, I'd snooped in my parents' dresser drawer and found a cellophane-wrapped box containing a book and white-lace straps and was excited because I thought I'd soon be getting a bra. When it was discovered that I'd started menstruating, mom presented me with the pretty pink box delicately packaged. I was disappointed to learn it wasn't a bra, but instead a belt for holding kotex pads, wads of cotton that nestled between my legs. The pamphlet that came along with the belt was perky and showed pictures of the female reproductive organs, but it was all still a mystery to me. When mom asked me if I had any questions I said, "no," and closed the subject on what seemed to be a difficult matter for her and most definitely was for me.

Trying to make order out of disorder.

Months after my period started, a local boy was pressuring to "feel me up," and I was caught between what he wanted and my learned behavior of secrecy surrounding my body and feelings. Imagined consequences of rejection from the boy or disappointment and perhaps worse from my parents, filled me with dread. As mom and dad hovered, trying to help me determine why my stomach hurt, I couldn't tell them of my dilemma. A few days later in his friend's blacklighted basement lair, I drank the beer he offered instead.

We moved back to North Carolina.

Standing in front of an eighth-grade class already in session for a few months and again being introduced as the new girl, I silently spasmed. There was nowhere to hide. I took my seat and hoped for the day to end soon. The first few days in a new school, like the first few days of a new job when you're not expected to know company procedures, were usually okay. I wouldn't be expected to have homework done or to participate in discussions. The other kids would talk to me out of curiosity with direct questions like, "Where did you move from?" and "How many in your family?" hiding their real questions of, "Are you geeky or cool?" and "What can you offer us in exchange for our friendship?" After this initial inspection was over, the painful task of making friends would begin. Sitting alone in the cafeteria or standing alone outside during break magnified my isolation. If no one was looking at me, I wished they would so maybe I could glimpse a welcoming smile. But how would I return their gaze? And if anyone was looking at me, I wished they wouldn't because what was it they were looking at anyway?

Maureen was skinny with long brown hair and wore crisp white shirts and blue jeans. She wore silver necklaces and rings. Her friend Kristy was also tall, thin, had perfect posture and cascading red hair that touched her butt. Thinking of her to-day reminds me of the phrase "stick up her ass," but back then I thought she was cool. They both were. At first they accepted me, but usually without provocation, they'd gather in a group of two and laugh and whisper, and I just knew they were talking about me. When they would talk to me, I was attentive, agreeable, ready to do whatever they wanted.

One Friday night, Maureen invited me to stay over. I was in! I took my overnight bag to school and went home with her. Her dad was an officer, and their housing quarters were bigger and newer than our enlisted man's housing. Her room seemed like a grown woman's, with a vanity and mirror and hooks for different purses. She had a double bed. We ate a lackluster meal with some of her family members and then, as her parents relaxed in soft lazy-boys in front of the TV, she casually announced we were going out. Her curfew was late, 11 p.m., and I was amazed when they didn't ask, and we didn't offer, where we'd be or whom we'd be with.

We met up with boys older than us, one of them her boy-friend, and while feeling a bit like the younger sister no one wants around, I also felt divine. I was wearing one of her jean jackets and we were driving around unsupervised, drinking beer, listening to rock music. Later we stopped at McDonald's and even though I didn't have much money, bought a burger just to be with the crowd. I watched as Maureen wolfed down a burger, fries and a shake. Not long after eating but before we got back to her place, Maureen had the driver stop the car and she got out on the side closest to the curb. Within a few seconds, I heard her wretch. "She does that all the time," her boyfriend said.

Mom wanted me to invite her over to our house to recipro-cate, but I couldn't. We ate meals together as a family. I slept in a single bed. I had no friends to go driving with or to buy beer for us. Besides, more often than not, neither she nor Kristy was talking to me anyway. I later learned that they'd had a fight the weekend she'd asked me over to stay. They didn't fight often.

Cool was a dominant theme in my adolescence. Long hair was cool, embroidered dirt-encrusted jeans were cool, cigarettes and the smoke rings I practiced until I perfected them were cool, and drugs were cool because they led to lethargy and disobedience, which were definitely cool. Lindy, the next-door neighbor's eighteen-year-old sister visiting from Maine was cool because her teeth were worn down with nervous grinding from doing too much speed. Back then being cool was a goal, and I gauged everyone by it—and never seemed to be it.

During the summer after eighth grade, I hung out with my little sister, definitely not cool, at the Ft. Bragg pool closest to our housing area, so I didn't feel pressure from peers and wasn't concerned about an image. We'd spend our days trying to run on the cement without getting reprimanded as we jumped in and out of the silky water, dove off the boards, and talked with the young G.I.'s who worked as lifeguards. The pool was open to army dependents, as well as other enlisted personnel, specifically young men, who, more than likely, were still kids themselves but who lived in grown-up bodies and held grown-up jobs. An eighteen-year old Hispanic man from Chicago nicknamed Tonto approached me one day. I thought him cool because he wore one earring. I'd never known any guy with an earring. Between sparse bushes on sandy soil behind the pool he spread a blanket, and in the baking North Carolina sun we talked. "Have you ever tried dope?" he asked. I hadn't, and together we smoked my first joint. I felt nothing, which he said sometimes happened.

The second time we smoked, time stopped. When the marijuana effect hit me, I was leaning over the pool's water fountain, my hand on the lever, water running close to my lips.

A tingling sensation started deep in my heels and moved up my body followed by a lazy awareness that people were standing behind me waiting for a drink. I split. My body floated for a few hours on smooth, certain feet while my head existed in a plane far, far above them without a care or concern; moving, being new, and having teenage awkwardness vanished. The world was delicate and slow.

Like beer, the pot quieted my reservations. Though the situation seemed stupid and I felt uncomfortable, one afternoon I stood yielding while standing in a dusty cramped gymnasium utility closet filled with basketballs, volleyballs, and brooms when Tonto professed love for me and tried to get into my bathing suit bottoms. The closet in the gym built next to the pool was narrow, and I faced the door while he stood behind me. He fumbled around. I didn't really know what he was doing but his attempt was unsuccessful, for reasons my young mind couldn't grasp. I was relieved when we checked to see if anyone was playing basketball and when no one was, we left the closet.

Our short relationship ended when I came home from the pool one day with an engagement ring and ten-speed bicycle he'd given me. My parents made me return both items, said I couldn't see him anymore and that I was forbidden to go to the pool. I was angry. He'd professed love for me, couldn't they see that, and I wanted his attention—and the bike.

Trying to make order out of disorder.

At fourteen, I gave myself easily to a boy who was old enough to drive; I remember his car, a powder blue Ford Mustang. I remember his name—Martin—and will always remember a few key characteristics: Spanish, dark hair, large flat forehead, dark eyes, big frame. What I don't remember is losing my virginity, but circumstances surrounding that time lead me to believe it was at night on a blanket in the woods after drinking beer. I might have blacked out from drinking, or I might have just blocked it from my memory because I wasn't ready to "go all the way." I don't even remember how long we were boyfriend and girlfriend, but I do remember the feeling when I was with him of being accepted. I thought our love was destined to last forever, but before our relationship had an opportunity to evolve into whatever it may have, his father got Army relocation orders. Thus began for me a scene destined to repeat itself over and over with different men throughout my life. He became a voice on a wire. Unable to confide in anyone close to me, the only witnesses to my late-night tearful professions of undying love to Martin were the hurried-highway travelers, gas-station customers, and long-distance operators that connected North Carolina to California through the clinking of quarters in the pay phone.

By this time, I was entering my sophomore year and attending yet another new school, a senior high outside the army base. In an attempt to recreate that closeness I'd felt with Martin, I flung myself at a popular senior that lived down the street and rode the same bus. He wanted my body (I've since learned that teenage boys want every girl's body), and I wanted the acceptance he received from our peers. He got what he wanted in his bedroom one afternoon after school while his parents were gone, and I got another lesson in my sex education. I was ushered out the door because his parents would be home soon, and as I was walking home I pondered the wet fluid running down my leg. When I tried to talk to him the next day, he ignored me.

Although I only attended high school as a tenth grader for a few months, I now learned I was going to have to change high schools in the town of Fayetteville because we were moving to a newer section of the army base. My mother tried to soften my angst of having to uproot yet again by offering that

I could make a fresh start and meet interesting new people, but I was just numb. Instead of attending classes my last day, I sat in the woods outside drinking. No teacher missed me. I was in between schools, a gray area where academically I didn't exist. After first period started, friends helped me stagger to the bathroom.

Trying to make order out of disorder.

Not long after turning fifteen, a few weeks after we'd moved to the newer housing and I started the new school, I learned I was pregnant. I contacted Tonto, he was an adult I trusted even though I hadn't spoken to him in a while, and he took me to a place for a checkup where I could then get an abortion. A friend betrayed my confidence, though, and insisted I listen to her sister who pleaded with me to tell my own parents.

I did, grudgingly.

What had originated in me around this predicament—fear, denial, anger, and secrecy, continued in them. We never told the boy's parents. The dogma of the times, "a man will want to know you're a virgin before you get married," was repeated by my father as he sat with his arm around me. My body had betrayed me, and now it seemed like no one would ever love me.

David did. I met him at this second high school, and together we'd smoke pot during lunch breaks. He was gentle and artistic, played guitar, and had shoulder-length brown hair like Jesus, although he couldn't save me. Instead, he became another voice on the long-distance phone wire that eventually faded into a grab bag full of lost friendships and loves when, during that same school year, we moved a third time, this time to another state.

Trying to make order out of disorder.

Walking into the third school in my sophomore year after my father was transferred to Ft. Benning, Georgia, I could no longer pretend it was easy. I was lonely, scared, and angry.

Alcohol and drugs helped me quickly cover those feelings though, so being new looked tolerable. I had my own stash now and kept it close. Nothing could hurt me as long as I had my secret and looked good from the outside.

No more disorder.

My first full day at this new school, I ingested many white cross tablets, speed, but instead of helping me disappear and not feel scrutinized or different, they had the opposite effect. While walking out to the smoking area before school started, I felt my legs get shaky, my head get dizzy, and heard someone say, "That girl's going to fall."

I did.

Angelica stepped out of her group and ran over. She helped me up, introduced herself and invited me to meet her friends. Walking towards the school building for first period, a skinny male freshman with whom I later became friends gave me an accepting smile. Within a very short time span, I had spoken stoner code and was now one amongst my peers who could hold secrets. It didn't take me long to find friends who shared their liquor and drugs. And I no longer cared if teachers spoke my name out loud. Right after lunch I had sociology class and usually stoned, I'd often lay my head on the desk. "Bremer, pick your head up," the white-haired teacher who walked with a limp would demand. And I would—quite proud that I no longer gave a damn.

My emotional maturity was infantile and stunted, using substances thwarts growth, but my body had matured at a normal rate, so I used boys, powerful creatures I hoped would fill the black emptiness inside me, to anchor myself. With their attention I swiftly became connected. They kept me from feeling too lonely, scared, new, awkward, angry, hurt, different, lonely, lonely, lonely, new, new, new…. The girls were harder to get to know, but every boy liked the new girl, if only for a few hours.

I used my body to pay a debt—as if I owed something for any attention and love I received. Today they'd call it date rape. Only I was doing it to myself.

Memories run together now.

Danny and Linda both had long brown hair and had been boyfriend and girlfriend forever, or at least for a couple years, which in my mind was longer than forever. I envied her. I wanted her hair and her figure and her man—most of all her man. He looked like he possessed the universal key to happiness. I don't even know how we ended up together. In my fantasy he chased me, but however it occurred, my mind holds onto a few minutes when we were in bed together. I'm sure I knew he wouldn't leave her for me, but for a short time I hoped.

They got back together.

Harry was tall, well over six feet, with jet-black hip-length hair. He wasn't socially adept, so I didn't stay with him long. I was more concerned with how others saw him than with how I felt about him or how he treated me.

Debby and I smoked pot and roamed the streets carrying a cassette recorder blasting Bad Company's Bad Company. She would cut her arms and scratch her face, causing big welts. I can't remember what town I knew her in.

Marina's German mother cooked skinny frog legs in a large cast iron skillet. I have no recollection of her moving away and only know I was, "deeply disturbed, very upset" by it because my mother says so.

Linda's dad let her drive his '57 Chevy, today a treasure, back then, to us, a huge embarrassment. Sometimes she brought the Bacardi Rum and I brought the can of Coke to school so we could drink before first period. This gave us something to do when we had to evacuate the building because of bomb threats.

I still liked school studies. They made sense. I maintained

an A average; that was part of the game—focus, focus, focus—but going to school was uncool. In order to get out early, I skipped eleventh grade and took all my required courses including junior and senior English in my senior year. At sixteen years of age, recognized in the Honor Society, I graduated from high school. While at school, I acted casual although the impermanent trespasses upon my heart were anything but. Still, I maintained hope for something lasting.

Until Dennis.

I don't remember how I met Dennis. I wouldn't even remember where he fit in a timeline of the year 1977, but in my late thirties when I located him in Arizona and went to visit, he told me that he and I and Linda rode around together in her dad's Chevy. He also told me during that Arizona visit that I didn't have any goals when he knew me as a teenager.

When we met in 1976, I'd been attracted to his bushy hair tamed under a beret, his gentle demeanor, and his artistic talent. He was cool. While skipping school one day and hanging out in his room, I mentioned I really liked a charcoal drawing he'd done. He made a simple wood frame and surprised me with it as a gift. Reframed, it hangs in my home today.

His father got orders to move.

Although my high school graduation was happening before they were scheduled to leave, he told me he wouldn't come. I begged him, pleaded, and up until the last minute, hoped he'd show.

Then I persuaded my parents to let me stay out until eleven on graduation night. By nine thirty, friends poured me onto the front lawn after drinking 190 proof Everclear—alcohol so potent its sale is banned in some states.

Dennis came back months later to patch things up and offered this explanation as to why he wouldn't come to my graduation, "I don't like goodbyes."

It was too late.

I closed the front door on him as I permanently closed the door on my heart. I had a new boyfriend by this time, a laborer who had a hard time holding a job and who at one time dug graves for money. I now attracted brutish men I could simultaneously love and dislike. The fearless child in those early pictures no longer existed.

ADDICTION

*No matter how hard you try to free yourself,
until you see the value of freedom and the
pain of bondage, you won't be able to let go.*

Ajahn Chah
Food for the Heart

During fifth grade, the girl's basketball coach put me in the game, once. Never before having ventured on the court outside of practice, and having only practiced a few months, the real game was confusing and too fast for me. I ran with the opposing team members and headed towards the wrong end of the court as she yelled my name and gestured from the sidelines. She took me out after a minute and a half.

Similarly, my relationship reality had happened too fast. Every peer I trusted and confided in was yanked away prematurely. I was confused as to which direction to head to make relationships last, afraid they wouldn't last, and hurt when they, *always*, didn't last. Ticking down the seconds to the final buzzer, the imaginary game clock in my head urged me to run in quickly and follow others. Eventually, my heart benched itself, but my body kept wanting to get in the game. Not being sure of the rules, I pursued the seductive, destructive rock-and-roll dogma of sex and drugs, presuming life would be just dandy.

Along with my inner child, rebellious adolescent, contemplative adult (who does most of this writing) and future self who carries and nurtures the dreams of the collective me, there is still an adolescent male rock star that lives within me. Today, I temporarily escape adult responsibility through movies that include *Rock Star*, *Almost Famous*, and *Detroit Rock City*, but back then I wanted to be or possess one of the Male Rock Gods that appeared all powerful, standing on an elevated stage above me. As they slashed the guitars held to their crotches and whipped their hair around to the rebellious frivolity of the lifestyle, I worshipped them.

Sam, the brutish day laborer I was with after Dennis left, had long hair down to his ass like I did, and we dabbled with a few drugs together. After my dad retired from the military and my family left Georgia, moving back to the same small town we'd always returned to, I became homesick. Sam helped me pack all my earthly belongings and my two cats into my Ford Pinto and drove me back to Wisconsin to live with them. He moved on to Seattle where he'd been from. Our love, separated by distance, bloomed in the absence of love's inevitable daily afflictions. He asked me to marry him, and at eighteen, I was ecstatic. However, when I was stamping invitations, snug within the safe walls of my parent's home, I started having fitful nights filled with obvious realizations: he still couldn't hold a job and hadn't even bought me a ring.

I changed my mind.

The next man, (and I have a hard time calling the boys of my youth men, but they were legal adults) Kyle, didn't have the hair, but he had the pot and the powder, which gave him power. He also had a place to live in Rockford, Illinois, once he moved his girlfriend out. I was flattered.

I should have been suspicious.

It could have been a reaction to a nightmare that the waking mind snagged. Or, perhaps, I'd pulled all the covers, or I'd almost pushed him off the bed and he was, perhaps, just being reflexive. I could have even done the same thing myself. Perhaps I dreamt it. Whatever explanation, the first blow, in this case a swift kick in bed, was easy to ignore.

A few weeks later, I woke up an hour earlier than usual and was ironing my dress before work. Kyle, who'd continued sleeping when I'd first gotten up, now leaned on the door-frame between the living room and bedroom.

"What are you doing up so early," he asked between yawns.

"I've got a lot of work to do. I'm going in at seven."

His demeanor changed quickly as he hurled, "I know you're going to meet someone!"

Incredulous, denying his accusation, I retorted, "That's ridiculous. It's my job. I have a lot to do and Marjorie is going to open the office early."

He walked towards me and around the ironing board.

Slam!! The punch came low and fast. The iron fell to the floor. I doubled over, gasping for air.

He glowered. His skinny Doberman, who I feared but had learned to yell at and swat when I found him sleeping on the couch, usually hurting my hand, stood cowering in the living room.

"I'll drive you," he threw out over his shoulder as he walked back to the bedroom to get dressed.

Stunned silent, too surprised for tears even, I stayed down. I needed all my energy to breathe.

When I felt steadier I got up and continued ironing in our large sparse kitchen decorated with boxes that still needed to be unpacked.

"I'm sorry," he offered ten minutes later, and I wrapped my arms around him telling him it'd be okay. I'd help him learn to control his anger.

On the way to my job as a clerical assistant he said he needed the car, *my* car, to sell the remaining pot he'd bought a week earlier. "I'm going to get five pounds this weekend. We'll drive to Janesville."

My heart quickened.

Saturday, sitting in the spotless narrow kitchen with copper pots hanging from the ceiling in the restored farmhouse in Janesville, I listened as the two men, Kyle and Derrick, talked about hunting and motorcycles. Even though the sun's rays illuminated me, I felt as visible as the floor tiles hiding under the six-foot long solid-wood table.

Finally, after about half an hour, Derrick went to get the five-pound brown-paper package they'd agreed on earlier.

My heart quickened.

He returned with the package as well as a bag, mirror, and a set of scales. "This is pretty pure so if you cut it with Mannitol (baby laxative) you can stretch this eight ball to a quarter."

As their conversation floated to the background of my conscious mind, I sat. Mind darted. Pupils dilated. Blood coursed. Nerves twitched. Bowels moved. I excused myself to the bathroom.

Derrick laid out three lines.

He snorted one.

Kyle snorted one.

Then they passed it to me.

I took the rolled up twenty-dollar bill, placed it up to my right nostril, plugged the left with my index finger and breathed deeply as if my world depended on it.

My throat immediately started to drip with tainted mucous as I smoothed the mirror with one finger hoping to catch the remnants. I let the slow drip in the back of my throat lull me into passive complacency, dipped my finger into my drinking water and brought it up to each nostril, inhaling one last time to wash every possible granule into my nervous system.

Sunday, in our tiny rental home, we sampled more while Kyle made little packets. Then we jumped on his Harley to make deliveries.

The next morning, hung over and too tired from the late night, I called work saying I wouldn't be there.

They'd heard this before. "Don't bother to come in at all," Marjorie, the office manager, said.

I got a new clerical job right away.

When I showed up with a black eye, I told them it was from playing Frisbee.

Wham!

Bruised arm. Easy to hide.

As Kyle dealt bigger quantities, I became smaller. Surviving the holocaust of my day-in day-out life, I grew to resemble an attractive skeleton silenced by the ever-present party in our house. I'd stare through wide eyes as conversations like manic flies buzzed past and into each other across our wagon-wheel coffee table heaped with empty beer cans, overflowing ashtrays, and a mirror with dried saliva reflecting relentless tongues. Our magic fairy dust relieved the mental anguish of unrealized dreams and unfulfilled promises by people elevated not by accomplishments but by heads bursting with ideas void of action. It also quieted my stomach.

He scored heroin for a couple who'd drive hours one way just to shoot up in our bathroom.

Bam!

Black eye. Caught by a baseball.

The owner of the company I was now employed with, a tall graying Jewish man whose son I worked with directly, asked me to his office. "Sloan is concerned about you. He says you seem a bit harried and show up with bruises. Is everything all right at home?"

"Thank you, but everything's fine," I spoke meekly.

"If circumstances change, I'm here for you to come to. But if your attendance doesn't improve, we'll have to let you go."

"Thank you," I offered again, "I'll keep that in mind."

To aid sleep, I took Valium. To wake, I used more cocaine. To calm the shakes, I drank beer and smoked pot.

Every morning at the workplace diner, I'd stop in for my one certain meal, an egg sandwich to take to my desk. Most of my clothes had gotten so big they were form-fitted with safety pins.

The coke comforted me during the day when I didn't know what Kyle was doing in my house, with my car, with our mutual friend who also didn't work. Was he fucking her?

I gave him my paycheck to buy more drugs to sell. Where were the profits?

I ran.

But only in my mind.

"No one else will want you," he told me. "No one else will love you like I do," he told me. "I'm sorry," he told me.

And I believed him while I ached for his

c ...,

co ...,

coke ...,

and only that.

Trying to find help and answers I went to the church our family had so religiously supported all those years while attending mission church meetings in the southern United States. "You're living in sin," the pastor scolded.

Battered body, battered psyche, battered value system.

I mustered the courage to leave. With the help of a couple who'd been to our parties and in whom I'd confided, I started moving all my belongings one afternoon while Kyle was away. But he came home. And he was angry. I called the police. They came but didn't stick around. There's no law against being angry.

We put what we could into my friends' truck, and I went to stay with them for a few weeks. My stomach and heart were warmed by Earl Gray tea with milk and honey as we two child-like adult women talked. My beloved kitten and I shared their son's room. I worried he didn't know how to handle such a small fragile animal.

I found an apartment for me and my one sure love, Patches, my orange and white tabby, and on a dark night, all my possessions loaded into my Pinto, we drove over and moved in. I'd never lived alone. I introduced myself to the neighbor when the first thing I found, before I even turned the light on, was a dead rat on the stove. He removed it.

I continued unloading the car: a few blankets, towels, clothes, litter box.

On the final trip from the house to the car, I saw a lump in the road.

I returned to my neighbor's.

Yes, he'd take care of it the next day. He got a brown paper bag and scooped my squashed dead cat off the street.

I spread blankets and a pillow in the bathtub.

I met another guy who took me to a rock concert on the Mississippi River featuring the rock band, Head East, and who said, seriously, that he wanted to keep me barefoot and pregnant. He gave me big green pills. I took the Quaaludes (that's what he said they were) and slept for two days.

I called work. They had no choice, they claimed, but to fire me.

All this time Kyle had been calling. "Let me come over."

I hesitated.

"What are you going to do for money? You can move back in with me."

I relented.

He came over.

He was remorseful. He was always remorseful. He bought me a new kitten. And brought a gun for me to keep. It was a sketchy neighborhood.

I wanted his coke. He wanted me. I drove to his house— my old house. I couldn't afford the long-distance phone bill so I called my parents from his place. "Tell them we're getting back together," Kyle urged.

"Do you want to come home?" my dad queried.

"Yes!"

Within an hour my parents left their home in Wisconsin to drive the five hours south over the Illinois border to get me. In darkness we loaded my dad's truck with as many of my possessions as we could fit, then drove the five hours back, arriving home around three in the morning.

Mom bought me a new pair of pants—the smallest size I've ever worn. Within two weeks I'd outgrown them.

I shook whenever I knew Kyle was visiting his family in town.

The drugs had quieted me. The hits had quieted me. Then I had quieted me. I'd learned to strangle my own voice so well in fact that when I was twenty and Kyle came back to town and wanted to have sex and I didn't, I couldn't open my mouth to let the words out. I could have shattered the windows of his car if only I'd have opened my mouth and let out the deafening, "No! No! NO!" that, with force like the strength of ten strong men on one end of a tug-o-war rope, I held restrained within my brain.

It wasn't until my forties, when I attended self-defense classes and part of the training was to shout "No" loudly as well as forcefully using my entire body, that the tourniquet that had constricted my vocal chords began to loosen. In that class, in my assertive defense, I fought off the men dressed in padded suits that were simulating attacks on all us women. I barked "No!" and punched the visceral remains of all the past abusers still lodged within my psyche. I fought against and defended myself for the first time from all the unkind words, unwanted advances, inappropriate suggestions, derogatory remarks, physical punches, unprotected sex, contemptuous looks, and lecherous stares I'd allowed to pass without comment or retribution for over three decades.

In my youth though, I simply returned to a world I knew how to navigate. At twenty-one I enrolled in a laser technology program. It wasn't that I loved science or even held a fascination for anything remotely associated with physics; the school was just close to my parent's home. I was told it was the toughest field of study in the institute, hardly any women enrolled in it, and that upon graduation, the jobs available paid more than any other course.

It was a challenge.

I excelled.

Many years later I would realize that one of the reasons I put myself in a position to compete with men was because I'd felt so utterly helpless around them. I'd kowtowed to their ideas and demands of me. I didn't know how to talk with them. I didn't know how to secure the love and acceptance I secretly yearned to have, so I determined to beat them. I gloated when my test scores and papers ranked higher than most and openly battled for highest grade-point average with the smartest man.

However, the predominant conflict was within myself. I needed men in order to feel whole. I was nothing without an other, a mirror in which to reflect some sense of placement and therefore peace, but at the same time I loathed my dependence and lust for their approval. I determined need for men to be a weakness, and I rejected and denied my longing for them physically and emotionally. Instead, they became the enemy whom I chose to seduce when it was convenient for me. I had sex casually, and my focus on my studies allowed me to act as if it was enough. I took the reins and let the men know I didn't have time for more. I still felt devastated when they didn't want more than just sex, but I was ashamed of what my body ached for and afraid of what my heart craved. I hid in my head and used school studies to distract myself from myself. After two years I graduated with honors, the only woman amongst fourteen men out of a starting class that held four women and thirty-five men. On paper I looked good.

I accepted a job at a national scientific research facility and was excited to move west, to the land of golden sunshine and movie stars. Contrasted to my imagination, I was sorely disappointed to find myself in a dingy hotel room in a small cowboy town where there were security bars on the cashier's front-desk window. There was no ocean in sight.

In the drug store that first full day in California, when I had nothing else to do but explore my new town and find a permanent place to live, everyone was staring at me, or at least I imagined they were. I felt like a Cyclops from a strange land, Wisconsin, somewhere east of the west coast, full of dairy farms (I have relatives who owned farms) and I was naked, unacceptable and new …, new …, new …. It was kindergarten all over, first grade revisited, fifth grade relived, seventh grade resurrected. I retreated with my wine and food to my hotel room and television.

I wasn't alone long though.

I'd long ago abandoned my parents, "don't take a ride with strangers" rule, having hitchhiked numerous times as a teenager, and one lonely afternoon while walking, a swarthy attractive man in a sexy yellow corvette pulled alongside. At first I declined his offer for a ride, but when he circled back around, promised he wasn't an ax murderer, and flashed a white grin that accentuated his tanned skin and dark curly hair, I got in. We went to the store, bought items I needed and liquor (what else would you expect by now) and went back to my one-bedroom apartment that I'd lived in for a few months.

Self-honesty forces us addicts to admit that though we never recapture that initial euphoria of the first high, we hope. We crave. Lust rules.

While not as sophisticated as cocaine, if anyone can call any drug sophisticated, he brought out something white and plentiful. Methamphetamine. Powder. Power.

A few weeks later he brought his belongings over.

He asked me to marry him, and I was in love with the idea of being in love and blinded by not only the drugs but also by an overdeveloped and misplaced sense of obligation; we were already living together. When the intoxication of having everyone gather in my honor and of wearing the symbolically virginal white wore off, I started to have doubts about my love for him. (Did I even know what love was?) I reluctantly realized that he too, just like the men in my recent past, couldn't hold a job, but this time I'd already bought the dress and sent the invitations.

Immediately after returning from our honeymoon drive back to California from Wisconsin where we'd had the church wedding and reception, my subconscious desire not to be married spoke through my genitals.

Someone else's answered.

Clandestine daytime trysts in motel rooms with an

exotic-to-me, sophisticated (if anyone can call a man banging someone else's wife sophisticated) foreigner with a sultry accent alerted my sense of monogamous propriety. I knew there was a problem, if I was newly married, yet cheating. My father said that if I'd made a mistake, fix it.

The relationship had already gone on longer than all my previous ones and for me, forever had the lifespan of about a year. I left my husband after six months of marriage and moved into my own apartment.

My grandmother was angry. "She sure is a good actress," she told my mother. Although never spoken to me at the time, I learned later that the men I worked with were also angry.

By this time, I was twenty-six and suddenly there was no one else around to distract me from seeing myself in the mirror each morning. There was no one else to reflect back to me an idealized image of who they thought I was. There was no one else to focus on. I wasn't angry, but I exercised like crazy.

Still, my husband was angry.

After he'd pound on my new apartment front door, yelling, I'd pound my feet on the stairstepper exercise machine. After he'd chase me down, follow and pass me as I drove, yelling from the window of his curvaceous '77 corvette, I'd follow the lead of bodybuilding experts.

I'd head to the gym after work and spend three hours a day forcing my muscles through repetitive exercises to exhaustion before I went home and collapsed, too tired to think about the fact that I was alone. Six days a week I'd put my headphones on and stretch and pump my flesh to the count of fifteen while secretly comparing myself to every other woman, and some-times man, in the gym. I compared myself in order to feel stronger, slimmer, more disciplined and therefore superior. I had to appear better at something in order to feel better at any-thing. I grew my hair long and kept it blonde. I put myself on a pedestal using modern-day externally manufactured criteria. But no matter how young I was, no matter how attractive or how much I exercised and how little body fat I had, I wasn't good enough.

My brain treated me like the white elephant in the room that no one saw or talked about; however, my body knew there was something amiss. It tried to get my attention. While eating one evening my right arm went numb. I couldn't keep a fork raised to eat. I was right-handed.

Every possible medical test was ordered: cat scans, head and spinal MRI's, an eye exam; a brain tumor was eventually ruled out. But for a period of time—much, much too long—the words, "multiple sclerosis," rained down on me and buried me in dread. After months of pokings, proddings, and imagings, the verdict was merely stress. Unfortunately, the prescription for me to begin biofeedback training was as cataclysmic as if it had been cancer needing radiation and chemotherapy for the cure. I was told I'd have to slow down and listen to my body, become a friend to myself. But I wasn't somebody I liked. I didn't want to get to know me, and I didn't know how even if I *had* wanted to. Instead I missed and was late for appointments so often the biofeedback practitioner scolded me until I quit entirely. It wasn't until years later that I recognized my arm only went numb when I was alone on the weekends and had to endure my own company. I was like the relative I couldn't stand to be around and wanted to ignore.

Lift weights. Diet. Cycle in place, going nowhere real fast.

I had to find another distraction. I couldn't exercise *all* the time.

We caught each other's eyes while at work one day. He resembled Kyle in appearance: dark hair and eyes, similar square body.

He offered to cook me dinner.

He had a home, albeit a rental. He had animals that looked

well fed and cared for. He had a roommate. We had salmon and rice and vegetables.

There was a phone call. He cut it short.

He was attentive and pleasant, and I didn't have to rescue him. I didn't have to pay his bills or make his meals.

He ushered me out the door with a kiss rather early.

A few weeks later we went for a motorcycle ride. He'd taken care of everything: packed a lunch, brought water, even supplied the joint we smoked before taking off with his friends.

I hadn't been on a motorcycle since leaving Kyle seven years earlier, and while George's bike wasn't a sleek Harley Panhead with purple custom paint and chrome like Kyle's, it was black, slick and smooth. The roar of the motor and the speed with which he drove it, along with his black leather jacket and chaps, satiated the wild child within me who, if she couldn't be a male rock star, felt she should have at least been born earlier so she could have been a hippie and attend Woodstock. She'd been living by the '60s free-love philosophy, and here was a new opportunity to be unrestrained in that good Michael Jackson, *I'm Bad* kind of way. Holding George from behind, feeling the wind buffet and rush around me and being so close to danger, indeed death if something unexpected happened, being so totally out of control, was invigorating. He wasn't what I would call a sexy man, but his control was, and I let my body relax into his power.

After our ride he just assumed we'd have sex. I didn't argue. I let him own me as if I was a romance-novel heroine who in a sweaty, steamy scene abandons all reservation and surrenders herself completely to the mysterious stranger. Like the high-powered executive who makes tough decisions and has complete control all day needs the dominatrix's whip and command to balance his life, I, too, gave over control but for different reasons. His command of my sexuality let me explore my body in ways that were unfathomable to my conscious mind.

He said he'd call again.

And he did—just not right away.

It was a week. Why hadn't he called?

I eventually called him.

He cut it short.

When he finally had time again, he took me to dinner where he paid for one of our entrées with a buy-one get-one-free coupon. *How delightfully frugal*, I thought. *How gauche*, I thought.

"What have you been doing?" I asked casually, careful not to seem too eager.

He'd spent time with his mom, a small, yet strong woman who not only raised him on her own, but who'd built a thriving business at the same time. His eyes glistened as he spoke of her strength; she'd survived major surgery a few times. How sweet, I thought. He adores his mom. I wanted to meet this woman he idolized.

I wanted to be a woman he idolized.

He took me home to his bed again and this time, afterwards, I asked, casually, careful not to seem too eager, "What are you doing tomorrow?"

"I have a date," he boldly pronounced.

My heart sank.

"I date other people. Is that a problem?"

I split.

Yes, it was a problem. My body craved him all for myself. Yes, it was a problem because I was now attached (having sex bonded me), and I felt betrayed.

"No," I lied. My mind wanted to remain open. And he was a challenge. My mind wanted to win.

By the time Kyle had shown his violent temper, I'd been seduced by the cocaine and too hooked to reason. Now I was ensnared by George's sex. It was a sport he'd perfected. He knew how to take from me essence beyond my usual release. Underneath his body I was like a puppet and I imagined, no, *knew*, our physical consummation was the ultimate sign of love. After all, sex for me was the basis of a relationship. They all started with sex and then, if I was lucky, and I hadn't been so far, but it was just a matter of time, the relationship of my dreams would evolve.

Then he brought the white powder.

The methamphetamine left an acrid rotting smell in my nostrils that even while reminding me of mummified decay from the inside out, I couldn't get enough of. The crank kept me thin. The man, tempered with the tension of the sex and who he was or wasn't also sleeping with, kept me on edge. Giving up control to him I had no time to focus on me.

I snooped in his dresser drawer one December afternoon before Christmas when he left me alone in his room and found a list with five women's names, an item written next to each one. My name wasn't on the list.

I loathed myself for looking.

I loathed him for being a playboy.

I put a pretty smile on when he came back.

Sometimes I'd drive by his house and when there was a car in the driveway I knew wasn't his or his roommate's, visualized myself knocking on the front door, loudly. I imagined cursing him violently when he came to the door, then pushing past him into the house and confronting the other woman.

But I never did. That wasn't acceptable, lady like, or endearing.

Instead, after drinking champagne at a holiday party one evening, I phoned, something I never normally did. His roommate answered. "No," George wasn't home. Who was he with, I wondered, as I burned inside. It was late, after nine.

I asked his roommate if he wanted to go dancing.

He did.

We drank.

Driving home on the freeway after leaving the nightclub, George, on his motorcycle, rode up to the side of his roommate's truck. We waved at the man dressed in black wearing clear night goggles and a quizzical look.

His roommate drove me home and didn't leave.

The next day he had to.

The roommate called a few hours later and said they'd talked. He wanted to know if I'd go out again some time.

"Maybe," I said.

We never did.

A few months later George called. I knew then that he loved me even though he never said it.

In preparation for our dates, I'd shower away my inhibitions as I resigned myself to all-night partying and taboo ecstasies. The tap, tap, tap on my consciousness from memories of warm oils, scarves, toys, and clean sheets, like the ritualistic tap, tap, tap of the blade on the mirror, quieted the impassioned reservations about some of our activities. I went along sexually because when I wasn't with him, I wondered who was. And it was habit. I'd always gone along. By day I was too tired to give a damn that my mind and heart were ignored. Our only real dialogue was sex.

What we were doing was under cover of night and secretive. But display-stand magazines, along with telling me I wasn't slim enough and how to lose those last pesky pounds, also told me, in broad daylight, that I needed to be a better lover and how to be bold and brazen as a sexual woman. They were showing me thin models with their midsections exposed or entire bodies covered only with strategically-placed accessories. Glamorous images stared suggestively back at me from the glossy pages and movies like *9 1/2 weeks* titillated my sexual curiosity. When a friend talked about the Exotic Erotic Ball in San Francisco, I wanted to parade my body, be wanton, revealing. After all, I'd been punishing myself into acceptable show shape through compulsive exercising and restrictive eating, and at twenty-seven I wanted to be just like the women the media and magazines flaunted.

George wouldn't go. He had a moral problem with it. He probably slept with someone else that night.

For the Ball, I wore a gauzy beige dress from a second-hand store that I'd cut to expose my body in crucial places: my navel, my muscled left buttock cheek, a right thigh daringly close to my pubic hair, a left nipple. To hide myself on the long walk from the parking lot to the coliseum I wore a make-shift coat; an old dress I sacrificed by removing the arms, zigzagging the hem to above my knees, and tie-dying it to a molted brown.

I wanted to be daring and decadent, but the methamphetamine and liquor I ingested in order to have the courage to participate in this lascivious spectacle had its usual numbing affect on my brain and now body also. I stood fixed and silent listening to the committee of voices arguing in my head. Like a hung jury, a unanimous decision wouldn't be reached as to how, why or which way I should move. People in varying degrees of costume and dress, or lack of it, strolled past our group as my brain, like a rolodex, shuffled through magazine articles, past present and future boyfriends' opinions, childhood parochial school teachings, drug and alcohol induced rationalizations, and my own distorted musings as to what strangers and my family and friends might think of me. The judge, as usual, decreed me, my body, and my sexuality wild, wrong, bad, ugly, and fat. I remained rooted in one place all night and didn't take my coat off for the entire evening.

I'd been existing in a chaotic blitz, as if I was a tumbleweed rolling along, sucking men, bottles, straws, mirrors, and dumbbells in to fill the vacuous hollows that supported my frame. To an outside observer it would seem like I had a choice in these activities, but I didn't. They just became a part of who I was. I didn't question them just as I had never questioned why I had arms; they were a natural part of my being. But these external supports no longer helped me play hide-and-seek with myself. When these outside distractions left for intermission, clear pictures of my behavior ran like matinee movies in my mind. And while my job had anchored me and provided grounding for five years, the longest time I'd ever lived in one place, coworkers and friends had seen me terminate a young marriage, told rumors about me sleeping with the boss, been privy to my slurred speech, and, I'm certain, perpetuated rumors of my sexual promiscuity.

I longed to start over. I wasn't aware of this yearning to start fresh, nor did I know about the internal scrutiny I was feeling from myself and others; I just had a pining for something new.

I returned to what was familiar.

At twenty-eight, I ran away from George, as well as the old place, old friends, old me. I fled to a new state and took a job as a traveling laser service engineer.

The next three years were a blur: Minneapolis one year; engaged and living in Delaware for one year; disengaged and living alone in Detroit for one year. Each week during those three years I was in a new city in the United States or Canada to fix and install laser equipment.

I was an anomaly; a woman service technician. The company that hired me thought I had the qualifications, but I hadn't used my electronics knowledge and troubleshooting skills for five years and didn't feel competent. However, I read the technical manuals about the laser and machining workstations I was supposed to be working on despite being confused and also disinterested. I didn't care how they worked, but fixing them was my job. And disturbingly reminiscent of all those times I was the new girl, I was again being examined too closely. Customers stared at my femaleness, yet ignored me during serious discussions with my male counterparts about their electrical and optical problems. Coworkers as well as customers scrutinized my technical skills, or what I presumed to be, the lack of them.

To stifle my lack of enthusiasm for my work and the unceasing surveillance in my mind, I turned to a new drug.

At my new Minneapolis desk, I ate all day long: doughnuts, vending machine Oreo cookies, bags of Fritos, pretzels, popcorn and McDonald's Big Macs, fries and shakes. I felt conspicuous and tried to hide this overconsumption but reasoned that since I wasn't heavy, no one noticed. I ran five miles at the gym every night and lifted weights. I kept a supply of laxatives in my bathroom.

For the first few months I traveled and worked with experienced technicians who could teach me about the systems. While in Delaware on one of these trips, a senior coworker and I were fixing a laser system for a man named Anthony, while Anthony was fixing his eyes on my toned body. After the second day we were there, Anthony and I met in a park after the workday ended. When my colleague and I finished repairing his CO_2 laser and left the state, Anthony began courting me over the phone.

We'd never even been in the same room together other than professionally, so the first time he jumped on a plane to come visit, I wondered about sex. He was staying at my place. It never occurred to me that I could have asked him to stay in a motel or sleep on the couch. Late one Saturday afternoon in my apartment, high with anticipation and alcohol, we sat on the floor slowly touching, allowing our fantasy of what we wanted our relationship to be outweigh the reality of what it was, in its infancy.

I've heard some say that you should have sex quickly in the beginning of a relationship to ease the tension of guessing what it might be like, and that made sense then, but today it sounds absurd. I gave away to someone I barely knew the most intimate part of who I was, as I'd done so often before.

Our tearful goodbye was exacerbated by every separation I'd felt in my entire life, and even though we planned to be together in a couple weeks, it felt as if we were never going to see each other again. On the way home from the airport, I raced to the grocery store and bought a quart of mint chip ice cream and a box of sugar cookies. I sat alone in my new apartment, in my new city, with my new television. To quiet the insecurities about the coming work-week where I might be expected to actually fix something, and to quell the loneliness that was magnified after dropping Anthony off at the airport hours earlier, I ate myself to sleep. The delicious desserts filled my belly until my mind felt nothing—no past—no present—no future. Sweets for oblivion.

I'd extricated myself from feelings for so long, I no longer heard my body say *full, stop eating, you've had enough.* I continued running the track five miles a day when I was in town, going in circles, nowhere, and lifting weights for another two hours just to keep my weight down. Along with the plethora of fears that subconsciously motivated me, gaining weight was at the top of the list. Now I also carried Dexatrim.

The romance was magical, as if we went to Disneyland every other weekend. Our tangible worlds were less mundane cooing into the phone wires about impending physical and material delicacies we'd enjoy together. Perpetual holidays were contrived through ecstatic airport kisses, daylong fiesta-style sex, and elaborate visions of what our next reunion would consist of. Our weeklong vacation to Cancun was the honeymoon before the marriage. After Anthony and I would part, although my tears were tempered with future plans, I faithfully turned to my other love—food.

Feelings of inadequacy harangued me before arriving at a client's business to fix or install their Nd:Yag laser system, and I crammed doughnuts, chips and anything else I could eat with my fingers into my mouth while driving and consulting maps to my destination. Loneliness plagued me in restaurants, so I gorged in the privacy of my room. I tried to vomit once because I'd eaten so much my stomach ached, but I couldn't. I called and cried to my sister instead. "Everyone overeats occasionally," she soothed, but I knew this wasn't occasional, and I knew it wasn't normal.

One weekend Anthony brought an engagement ring.

Then he left again.

Pastries with soft white centers smiled up at me from behind a glass partition on a cold winter day in Buffalo when I stopped at a bakery. They looked so cute. And sweet. I wanted to take all the cannolis home. I bagged a few. Later, as I stood listening to the customer in the welding factory, my stomach ached from eating four in my car on the way to the work site on top of the granola, sausages, and buttered toast I'd wolfed down at the hotel breakfast bar. "Yes," I knew he needed his system as soon as possible. "No," I didn't know what was wrong yet. "No," I couldn't stay over the weekend. "Yes," Armando, his manager, could watch and assist if necessary.

My mother could see my frenetic pace and motivations. In her later-to-be-revealed-to-me infinite wisdom she yelled, "You're running away from yourself," when I told her I was moving to Delaware to move in with Anthony, but I disagreed vehemently. Like everything else in my speeded up world, I never examined my swift dependence and reliance on someone

I barely knew; I truly thought I was running *toward* love. He was my fourth man in what was to be a string of five live-in lovers in ten years.

Anthony didn't have powder or fast vehicles, he drove a Toyota Corolla, but he did have muscles. His exercise fanaticism was just as great as mine. He'd even get angry with me for not going to the gym.

By this time my compulsive exercise, overeating, diet pill and laxative-using routine was causing a plumber's nightmare. My bowels didn't know when to let go or hold on just like my mind didn't know how to control what I was doing to my body, so I sought psychological help. Gaining weight was the one thing I feared most in life. When the therapist said I had bulimia, (even though I didn't purge, I exercised my food away), I was happy that I could be figured out.

But Anthony and I couldn't figure each other out. We were both too hard physically as well as emotionally. He enjoyed my seeming independence when I flew all over the United States and Canada fixing and installing laser equipment, but wanted me to be more domesticated at home. I also enjoyed my independence but wanted a man who could let me be fragile. Neither of us had softened enough to realize these truths much less put voice to them.

After ten and a half months living together, the imagined looks from our common-wall neighbors who I knew heard our loud fights, reflected the obvious; we weren't going to survive as a couple. Having signed a twelve-month lease though, we felt trapped. We stayed together sleeping in separate rooms until he got custody of the sofa and I took the dining room table to Detroit where the company's main office was located.

Uncertain of my actions once I'd start, I'd stopped drinking alcohol when I was alone, especially in cities where I didn't know anyone, which was basically any city, including the one I lived in. I'd learned that I couldn't even trust myself when going out to dance in a nightclub, the one activity that usually ensured I'd stay semi-sober. One evening I ended up in bed with someone, who, when we got naked, I learned had a squishy ass. My rigid criteria for a relationship lambasted my sober mind the next day for this obvious transgression, not the one-night stand mind you, but for having it with the man with the flabby tush.

So I ate and exercised more. And carried my diet pills and laxatives. The few anorexic, bulimic, and women-dealing-with-food-issue meetings I attended couldn't do much to arrest my compulsivity, but they did give me someplace to go when I was occasionally home.

It was while lugging my big gray toolbox around the North American Continent and on and off airport conveyor belts that I became envious of the beautiful women I saw wearing dresses and high heels and getting attention and assistance from men. I yearned to be them; beautiful and helped. I yearned to be another person with a different life. I was tired of running from state to state and hotel room to hotel room, *to* men and *away* from men. Like a rubber band, I had allowed myself to be stretched in accordance with what I wanted to what I thought other's wanted, *from* what I thought they thought *to* what I knew they thought, only to be confused and rejected and snapped back again by what society dictated and other's whims and coercions and my pleadings and obsessions.

I was doing what I read and heard would help me be an independent, happy, fulfilled woman. I was pursuing a career and supporting myself, but after a harrowing two weeks working in Watts, a depressed area of south Los Angeles, the energy needed to keep the confident façade up at all times, especially with myself, vanished. That week I'd remained composed and didn't flinch when it was suggested I not leave the customer's building, even if just to go to the fenced-in parking lot by myself, because it was too dangerous. Determined to keep up my exercise, after the front-desk hotel clerks were robbed at gunpoint, I continued to run up and down the fire escape stairs ignoring my fear that *anyone* could enter the stairwell, fanatical that I not gain any weight, even at my own peril. The only night I was brave enough to venture outside the hotel for dinner and go to a Wendy's close by, the multitude of black faces reinforced my dominant feeling of being different not only from everyone else but also from the parts of me that projected self-assuredness. I was drained.

In an aisle seat on a plane bound for Detroit one Wednesday night a short time after working in Watts, going home from someplace I don't remember, I watched other people piling past me on the way to their seats. At my eye level, I saw only asses: big ones, little ones, skinny ones, cute ones, ugly ones, covered in polyester, jeans, corduroy and flannel, some covered with sport coats. I couldn't look away. Besides where was I supposed to look? At the seat back in front of me? At the empty seat to my side that I hoped wouldn't be filled but was probably going to be by some fat ass that would flow over into my space? I wanted to scream at all of them, "Get your ass out of my face!"

They were all full of shit.

And I was full of shit and fed up with a life I didn't want; a life that was groundless, literally; my ass was always on a plane.

After the two-hour flight, I stood impatiently waiting in the aisle for the door to open as asses squeezed all around me.

Keep it in. Keep it in. Normal people don't yell at the top of their lungs.

I relieved my bladder in the bathroom outside the terminal gate, but there was no relief for my mind.

The shuttle bus driver stepped down the stairs to help me get my toolbox, luggage cart, and overstuffed garment bag on board.

Tip the nice man. It's expected.

As the bus wound its way through the hopeful cars waiting for owners, I saw my familiar, though not ideal, vehicle. I'd bought the truck when I was driving my ex-husband's smooth corvette.

I barreled along the freeway in my tan and blue Ford Ranger, mouth gaping, hungering for the solitude of familiar objects I knew waited patiently for my return. The darkness of my heart was hidden from the other drivers in the pitch-black night. At my core, I wasn't a truck person. I wasn't a technical person. I wasn't a happy person.

"Arrrrgggghhhhh!"

Louder, "Aaaarrrrrggghhhh!!"

Louder still, "Aaaaaarrrrrrrrgggggggghhhhhhh!!!"

My throat ached.

My lungs heaved.

Non-waterproof day-worn mascara streamed.

It'll be okay. My home. My bed. Soon. Two days left of the week. No time to send me out on a plane to a strange city again.

Park.

Rest.

I walked into the corridor that led to four identical doors opening to four identical apartments that housed neighbors I'd said "Hello" to so seldom I could count the number of times on one hand.

Unlock door. Enter.

Solitude. At last.

Blinking light. *Great. Someone wants to talk with me.*

Play.

"Susan, it's Myron. We have you reserved on Continental flight 3693 leaving tomorrow morning at eight."

I kicked a hole in the wall.

After one year living in Detroit, yet traveling so extensively I never even slept in the same bed long enough to dirty the sheets, I ran back to California, back to my familiar job, and moved in with George whom I'd run away from three years before.

I'd won! He'd missed me too! I was the first woman he'd ever lived with.

I was home.

This revived California relationship lasted one year. His dichotomous view of my drinking, opposing it when it didn't suit him, in other words, when he didn't need me in an amorous, pliable mood, was bewildering. And my memory was short. The reality of what a long-distance relationship actually was, compared with the fantasy of what two people wanted it to be, as experienced when I moved in with Anthony a few years earlier, had been forgotten. Mine and George's fantasy, built through long-distance phone cables and occasional visits, was far different than the reality of what living in the same house was like. Mixing not only booze but also powder into the relationship made a volatile combination of dissatisfaction coupled with sleep-deprived misunderstandings and unspoken hurts, fears, and angers.

I believe there is a wisdom to life we cannot explain, but only, if we're lucky, pay attention to. Though I still wasn't conscious of my motivations and reactions, the arduous circle of chaos within my mind, coupled with running in circles on tracks, continuous loops on departing and returning flights, and driving through rental car return mazes, got my attention. The bedlam within that hadn't stopped me when my arm was going numb, had finally, perfectly, exhausted me so thoroughly all I wanted to do was to settle down and get a cat. I needed a living body to love me and be there to anchor me. Society said I needed a tax shelter, so I bought a house. It was the fear of disappointing my parents because they'd lent me the down payment for my home and the unconditional love I felt for my kitten that raised my consciousness, caring, and maternal instincts far beyond my capability to be responsible to myself.

I wanted counseling. I'd seen one or two therapists while I was navigating around the United States and while never sticking with any particular one, knew it was a place where I could go and have someone listen to me for an hour.

I contacted my insurance.

Taking health store diet and pep pills every day didn't feel normal to me, but the insurance medical evaluator didn't ask me how many capsules filled with guarana or ephedra, which was banned by the FDA in 2004, I was taking on a regular basis. I didn't think she was going to ask either, so I lied about the amount of alcohol I was drinking. I told her I was drinking wine every day. I wasn't. I had never been an every day drinker, but the similar mindset of using a substance to escape was obvious to me. Then she told me that before the medical system could help me they had to evaluate me. I made an appointment. Before I could get to that appointment, I started a second job, part time, that I was excited about.

A month previously I'd wandered into a gay and lesbian bar with friends and was captivated by one of the male go-go dancers as I watched him shimmy on a box. I'd talked to him after. "Do you have any women dancers? Can anyone do it?" He said he'd seen me dance from his box and that he'd put in a good word for me with the management.

I cut an old pair of jeans into short shorts, bought some cheap high heels and found a pink tank top I'd accidentally shrunk. I took some sunglasses and went for my first night to dance on top of a box.

I was nervous and bought a drink to help calm myself. A kind woman ten years my junior offered to buy me another drink and said she'd escort me from the dancers' box to the dressing area and back again. I hung on her arm feeling important as we made our way back and forth at the beginning and end of each half-hour set.

The night was a blur: base pumping, rotating lights, dancing me, drinking me. Another drink took the edge off. So much edge had been taken off my nervousness in fact that at the end of the night I had my shorts around my ankles and the escort's head between my legs. When the other dancer, the same man I'd talked to a month earlier, walked in the shared dressing room, I felt the all-too-familiar shame and humiliation I felt every time I blacked out.

Three days later I went to the insurance-mandated psychiatric appointment and was given questions similar to those found here:

1. Can you drink large amounts of alcohol without becoming "drunk?"
   Why would you want to? Isn't that the point?
   "No."

2. Do you drink to feel good or to make you function better?
   Do you have a better reason?
   "Yes."

3. Have you ever become "drunk" suddenly and without warning?
   Yeah, after about five drinks I'm suddenly drunk. What a stupid question, seriously.
   "Not sure."

4. Have you ever passed out or experienced memory loss due to drinking?
   Doesn't everyone?
   "Yes."

5. Have you ever become violent or agitated while drinking?
   Only if someone takes away my drink or car keys.
   "Yes."

6. Do you drink to escape pain, either physically or emotionally?
   Duh, again. Is there another reason to drink?
   "Yes."

7. Do you engage in binge drinking? (5 or more drinks in a sitting)?
   Who knows? After five I lose count.
   "Yes."

8. Do you ever have to drink to get through the day?
   On vacation and weekends I drink to start the day. Isn't that what weekends are for?
   "Yes."

9. Has drinking ever negatively affected your family relationships or friendships?
   What relationships, seriously. Oh, do you mean in the past as well? Drinking helped me endure many relationships.
   "Yes."

10. Has drinking ever negatively affected your school or job performance?
    Not applicable. I've never drank during work. During school I had high honors. Does not showing up for work due to hangovers count?
    "Maybe."

11. Do you have a history of alcohol or other drug problems in your family?
    Yes, I've been giving you my history and I'm part of my family. Also, I think my uncle, when he was young, got in fights while drinking.
    "Yes."

12. Have you ever tried unsuccessfully to stop using alcohol?
    I can stop anytime I want. I did it yesterday and also last week. But then I realized it's hard to escape emotional and physical pain. Oh, do you mean before I pass out?
    "Yes."

13. Do you ever take a drink as a morning "eye-opener?"
    If you don't get up until afternoon is it still considered a morning eye-opener? Also, see item #8.
    "Yes."

I tried to make a joke of it but was compelled to answer honestly. My reality had never been more black and white.

I made the commitment to attend outpatient drug and alcohol counseling every night and on Saturdays for eight weeks. Similar to all those people who were angry with me when I left my husband, now *I* was angry. No booze. No pills. No pot. No powder. Not even any men.

In a group session one evening, I was complaining about my job and droning on about how life wasn't fair. I was discontent, but I was also lucid and my head was clear. A female counselor spoke up and said the words that, unbeknownst to me at the time, gave me one of the keys to help unlock my self-made prison: "I challenge you not to be a victim."

AWARENESS:
BEFRIENDING
THE SELF

A man could not connect himself to a woman without a body.

Joyce Carol Oates
Wonderland

ENCOUNTER

*The talk of those without experience is like the
empty wind whistling about your ears.*

Lama Yeshe
Becoming Varasattva

The second time I was scheduled to go-go dance, a month after the first, I thought of not showing up. I was afraid rumors of my sexual indiscretion had circulated, but my sense of responsibility said I had to—they were expecting me.

I arrived at the club early and when the bartender didn't make reference to my first night's antics, I calmed a bit. I ordered a soda then hid in the makeshift dressing room, a section next to the club entrance partitioned off with long black drapes. Sitting alone in the closed-off area, I talked myself through the anxiety of not only dancing in public, which I'd never done sober, but also dancing on a box in front of people. *I told them I would. I'm here. I might as well do it*, ran through my mind that searched for courage. The other dancer came in and I apologized for my behavior the previous time. "Already forgotten," he cheered as he waved away some of my butterflies with a sweeping hand gesture.

At ten o'clock I walked my shy, shaking body out of the dressing area with wobbly yet determined legs and went to the three-by-four-foot wood stand at the edge of the dance floor. I grabbed onto the vertical metal bar, pulled myself up, stood for a few seconds, surveyed the early sparse crowd, then caught the tune the deejay was spinning and hung onto it as it jerked me around clumsily. I had no idea what I was doing. I was making a spectacle of myself, inviting attention, allowing people to watch me, something I'd recoiled against when I was a traveling service technician. I was more aware of my body than I'd ever been.

I looked over the bouncing heads bobbing and jigging below me, unwilling to see if anyone was focusing on me. Fortunately, it didn't take long for the pumping music and heat of the circulating bright lights to push my body into familiar Michael Jackson and Madonna imitations. Self-consciousness about my sober dance moves disappeared. All that was left was Whitney Houston singing "I'm Every Woman," and a floor full of women dancing with each other alongside men dancing together. My attention shifted from above their heads to their faces. Some winked, some gave approving nods. One brought a one-dollar bill and stood in front of the box, smiling. I knelt down and she placed it in the side of my shorts. I stood back up on my pedestal—higher than I'd ever been. I beamed when one of the guys said, "You're so hot, I'd switch for you honey." Before I left, I made a three-month schedule with the manager.

For the few hours I danced, I felt free. The departure from my regular suburban-town sightings was exhilarating; slim effeminate men wearing skin-tight leather pants and mesh tops, women wearing muscle shirts and chains as if they belonged to a women's biker gang were as different as I'd always felt; unusual, in direct opposition to my usual routine. I adored the men kissing each other, the women kissing each other. I felt they were my people; people living their lives in some state of societal normalcy by day, untamed and bold in their expression of themselves and their sexuality by night. I was happy when I danced. The movements my body now made to the rhythms were automatic, choreographed by some inner woman who no longer felt self-conscious about who she was or what she looked like. The moves were easy, honest, and I learned to make them seductive. The energy I expended to keep up three half-hour shifts of non-stop hard-driving dancing was enormous, and afterwards I went home, fell into bed, and had nightmares of being in bondage and tied up in my usual conservative life. It didn't pay much, but I didn't need the money. I needed the distraction. I craved it. The power I'd given away to magazine models, starlets, advertisers, pot, powder, or even men, for the short amount of time I danced, I now took back.

Between a gyration with one hand held high clutching the upper bar and the other hand moving out over the crowd as my body too swung away from the stage one evening, my eyes locked onto a dark-skinned woman of Asian and Puerto Rican heritage whose spiky black hair made her taller than everyone else. I kept my eye on her as she danced. She had similar qualities to the men I'd always been attracted to: dark hair, authoritative air (I learned she was a security cop) and a round body like Kyle's. When my first shift was done, I walked through the crowd to return to the dressing area and change out of my sweaty outfit into something new. Our eyes met. Throughout the rest of my shifts our eyes sought each others' frequently. When I was done and changed into clothes that weren't soaking wet, we made pleasant introductory statements in the parking lot while I secretly thrilled with the thought of kissing her full lips. We made a date. I stepped in closer. She did too. I returned her kiss boldly then drove home in silence wondering what it all meant.

For a few short months, I called her my girlfriend and she introduced me to lesbian friends and dance clubs in San Jose. Although my best friend in technical school had been gay, I'd never seen the rainbow-colored flag much less an entire neighborhood where people openly had same-sex partners, so one Saturday afternoon she escorted me to San Francisco's Castro District. We ate dinner in a restaurant on Church Street and looked into shops while holding hands. I felt rebellious, liberated, scared. *What would my family say? How would I explain this? Was I really a lesbian?* There was that couple from Los Angeles I'd met in a San Ramon dance club about six months earlier who I'd shared champagne with in their room, but despite the man's stunning long blonde hair and movie-star good looks, I'd been more attracted to the woman. I drank a lot that night to get over my nervousness about being with someone of the same sex, but now my clear sober mind couldn't move beyond my sexual inexperience; I couldn't reciprocate my girlfriend's physical attentions.

I had more than enough practice with men however, and Marcos, who I also spied while go-go dancing, had youth, (ten years my junior) tattoos, and jet-black hair to his waist that intrigued this high school girl who'd never gotten to keep her long-haired soul mates. He possessed sexual brazenness I'd never encountered (or perhaps I was just more acutely aware of simply because I was sober), and he extracted from me a sexually-charged persona I'd never met. I believed him when he said I was sexy. When he brought out a camera, I was eager and tried to mime erotic pleasure. I look at the pictures now and see a woman with a pained expression wearing too much makeup and a photographer who had no sense of how to capture lines and angles, but at that time I found the suggestive play titillating. Our flirtation and lustful innuendo spilled out of the bedroom and into his hair stylist's chair. Cutting my hair one afternoon while I was grumbling about my Lab job he nonchalantly said, "You have a great body; why don't you try stripping?"

My curiosity was piqued.

I got the San Francisco Chronicle and searched the Help Wanted Ads. A few places advertised *"showgirls needed, no experience necessary."*

On a quiet Tuesday night, I gathered my new adventurous self and off we went to visit the Lusty Lady, a peep show in San Francisco. The neon sign that blinked *All Nude* and the jeans-clad man with the weathered face at the entrance didn't deter my enthusiasm. Curiosity and purpose propelled me forward even while a few men walked by and gave me suggestive looks. I stepped cautiously and made my way slowly into the dark hallway until my eyes adjusted to the dim lighting, then turned right like the front-door man said to do when the corridor branched in three directions. Slim doors were lined up next to each other so I chose one in the middle. I looked carefully before I entered the small room that couldn't have been any bigger than two-feet wide by five-feet long. A bench hugged the left side of the area that felt extraordinarily confining, a cubby hole. I noted the box of Kleenex attached to the wall. I put a quarter into the slot by the window. When the mechanical curtain went up I saw a large well-lit room with girls clustered in the center. All were nude except for high heels, hats, gloves, or waist chains. One started moving toward me.

The curtain went down.

I put two more quarters in quickly.

The curtain went up.

She stood close to the window, looking at me, smiling. I wanted to blurt out: Do you enjoy working here? How much money do you make? How long are your shifts? Instead I smiled politely and too embarrassed to make eye contact with a totally naked woman, looked past her. The other women looked lethargic and distracted. Some kneeled along the opposite side of the room with their backs to me, their fronts exposed to someone else who I presumed was sitting in a booth identical to mine. I slogged out of the room, unable to picture myself being one of a group of girls enclosed in a glass booth, waiting.

I next went to a Gentlemen's Club on Montgomery Street that besides advertising showgirls also claimed to offer a four-star dining experience. A large man in a tuxedo opened one side of the ornately-carved, double-wood door for me. An attractive woman sat behind a well-lighted glass case where shirts and miniature-sequined cones with tassels were for sale. When I said I just wanted to look around because I was considering working there, she let me in without paying the twenty-dollar cover charge. The top of the stairs opened to a mahogany and brass bar. I found a stool and sat sipping seven-up while surveying the main floor.

Crystal chandeliers hung high above customers in suits who occupied white-linen draped tables. Women wearing evening gowns and cocktail dresses were everywhere, their faces and jewelry twinkling with reflected lights. The activity and rich details of the surroundings were enthralling. Some women walked around and stood at tables briefly, then left. Some walked to a table and sat down for a few minutes before leaving. Some walked to a table and sat down for a short while then stood, took their dress off and danced in front of the table. Some just sat and ate or drank, while others still, who were sitting at tables, would get up, walk with a man into a back room, only to return to the table together after a song or two or three. Every few songs, two new women would come onto the main stage, an elevated three-foot pedestal visible from anywhere in the club. They would dance around for three songs, then leave. The men looked up to them with rapt attention. Their focus on the women was like manna to my female soul; at the Lab I felt invisible as a woman wearing jeans and a hard hat like one of the boys.

I lied to a Lab coworker and his wife one evening while their kids played innocently beneath our feet, about why I wanted to use their video camera. I took it home, set it up, took my clothes off, and pranced around gracelessly. I felt foolish and thankful no one else could see, I had no idea how to move, but the exercise served its purpose. After viewing the video a couple times, deciding I looked okay and checking, double checking, and triple checking that I'd erased the footage so I could return the camera and tape, I made the decision to audition.

They only held new-girl try-outs during the day shift, so I called in sick to the Lab and drove back to San Francisco. I met the housemom and followed her around on an introductory tour of the club with another woman who was also auditioning. (Typically the housemom is a retired dancer, has a designated chair in the dressing room and works for a small club salary and tips from the girls. She collects nightly stage fees, ensures that the women sign contracts for management, supplies tampons, chocolate, tape, safety pins, and an ear whenever someone needs to lament or bitch.) During our walk through the subdued daytime atmosphere, the housemom introduced me to the deejay using the stage name I'd chosen that I'd always liked because of its exotic-to-me sound. I gave him three CD's I'd brought and told him which songs I wanted played in their specific order. "You'll get a ten-minute warning before your turn to go up," he assured me.

After that we'd gone downstairs, and I put on the same pink top I used for go-go dancing and a one-piece short-short jean jumpsuit I'd purchased years earlier from Fredericks of Hollywood but was never brave enough to wear in public. Under that I wore the mandatory t-back bikini bottom and bra and required pasties that I'd bought at the club. Then I sat with the other girl and listened to the housemom talk about the rules and the contract we needed to sign each time we worked.

Distracted by the paperwork in front of us, I was calm like I am the first day of any new job while filling out IRS forms, learning company policies, and being oriented to surroundings and products; I didn't need to be responsible for anything. Suddenly though, infiltrating my composure, a voice boomed through the speaker from the upstairs main floor, "Next up on stage is Jasmine."

Adrenaline surged.

"I thought I was going to be given notice," I shouted as I ran to the counter where I'd put my belongings.

"You'll be okay. You have time," the housemom said as I searched the mirror for mascara lint and lipstick smudges on my heavily-made-up face and looked at my chest to see if my nervous heart was pulsing through my jumpsuit.

I ran upstairs.

I stood by the side of the stage ignoring the urge to run to the bathroom. When the girl that was up there offered me her hand to help me up the steps, I clomped on. In a heroic attempt to feign ease, I pasted a smile on my lips and started moving my feet and body the same way I did as a go-go dancer; my arms gyrated to the beat while my torso and legs kept frenetic rhythm, and I shimmied my butt back and forth. My mind tried to keep myself steady, notice customers, look happy and sure of myself, step back and forth between the mirrored panels that separated the two sides of the stage, count songs, and remember what article of clothing was supposed to come off when. I tried getting my jumpsuit off at the end of the first song but my spike heel caught the hem of the right leg. I lost balance and keeled over a bit but steadied myself before falling close enough to the varnished floor to kiss it.

During the beginning of the second song I stood swaying in my new underwear wondering what to do next. I looked behind me to the three-step stage entrance and standing there like some encouraging soccer mom on the sidelines of the big game was the housemom mouthing, "You can do it. You can do it." She took her index fingers and pulled the sides of her mouth up.

My grin returned.

For the third song, I was supposed to dance topless and then, literally, the last minute, remove the pasties and expose my nipples while staying away from customers who might walk up to tip. (Nobody tipped my first day.) Kneeling, smiling at the two men I could barely discern at two distant tables, and remembering to keep my hips circling, my hands fumbled. Exasperated after unsuccessfully tugging at the sequined cones, I looked down, saw sticky glue tentacles holding tight the covered fabric that sheltered my shrinking nipples from the bright lights, and felt absurd. Then the base boomed, lights flicked, and I tugged a bit harder. POP—one was off. My fingers moved to the other breast. POP—the other one was off.

The song ended.

On unsteady legs I tottered to the stage entrance, grabbed my clothes I'd haphazardly thrown, clutched the garments to my breasts carefully so as not to lose any, and followed the housemom back to the dressing room leaving my bare backside with a strip of material running up my butt, the last scene for the customers. I was hired (which isn't really hard to do as long as you don't injure yourself or maim anyone else while getting used to prancing around in stilettos). Jasmine was born.

The next dancer on the stage, after her three-song set, brought me my forgotten pasties that I had to reattach. "Most women cut the tassels off," she told me.

My job would be to perform, but no one cared if I made any money. As long as I showed up when I said I was going to and paid my stage fee (which they waive the first day), club management wasn't concerned with how much I did or didn't make. I only made sixty dollars that first day, pretending to know what I was doing while undulating and weaving in front of a very drunk man, but it happened fast—three songs—nine minutes max. I scheduled myself for weekend night shifts.

Like having a stall in a trade show where people wander past and inspect the company products for sale, the stage was my booth to show my wares in order to sell private dances where I made the bulk of my money. Ambitious to get it right, I watched the girls who I thought were sexy and successful. I was captivated by Stormy whose turn on the stage, highlighted with hard-driving rock music and pulsing white light, produced an aura of dark seduction as she stood towering above our heads wearing only black boots and shorts. Men approached the stage and flung money that rained down upon her. Madeline's approach was softer. Her show featured soulful rhythm and blues that accentuated unyielding submission to her own subtle caresses of her curvy petite body. Mimicking these women who attracted the most attention, I learned to dominate a stage and command favors through using my hands to roam my skin. This was unnerving at first, even torturous. The impropriety of letting strangers, no, not *letting* strangers, but *doing it for* strangers, willfully, inviting them to watch what for this religiously-indoctrinated girl had once been taboo even for herself, produced the same shameful awareness that occurred when I dreamt I was in public, naked. My thoughts of leering eyes were soon subdued by the environment; it was normal to touch one's self in the strip club, and although it took time to become comfortable manipulating voyeur's concentration in this way (they would associate their hands with my own) it eventually became second nature.

I also asked the men what they came into the club for. They told me they came for attentive company, sexual intimation, and fantasy. They're the ones who told me that the cocktail dress I wore my first few days, the one I thought perfect for being a showgirl because of its high feather neckline and the fact that I'd worn it for my sister's Las Vegas wedding, imagining all showgirls to be like Las Vegas showgirls, covered too much; the hemline barely exposed my knees.

And I perfected the air dance. We weren't allowed to touch the customers, other than hands, knees or shoulders, and the customers definitely weren't allowed to touch us so I developed the strength in my legs that held me upright and stable even when bending backwards or squatting. My legs got so strong I could hover right over a man's lap as if at any minute I'd sit down on it. Other girls were rumored to break the rules but I wasn't going to. That wasn't the kind of person I was. I didn't care when I saw other girls making more money. The job was fun—it wasn't my sole support. Also, it was already beginning to pay me more cash than I'd ever had before.

Within the first year, after I'd begun consistently making three-hundred dollars a night, I began to need not only the attention, but also the money. Stuffing the green bills into my small purse became intoxicating. The bejeweled bag I carried would bulge with ones and twenties, and when I felt I could take a break in the downstairs dressing room, I'd empty it into my padlocked locker. I'd return home after a night, tired, yet exhilarated, take any hundred-dollar bills I'd gotten and add them to a pile in a lockbox in my closet. I'd never seen a hundred-dollar bill before I became an exotic dancer. I reminded myself of an unkempt elderly miser. Every time I added to the pile I counted each and every hundred-dollar bill anew.

Nine months after I started working, around Christmas when I had time off from the Lab for the holidays, the housemom asked me to come in for the day shift because she needed more girls. To make up for the fact that this shift could be unusually light for customers, the stage fee we had to pay was reduced to twenty dollars, at night it was sixty-five. I figured I could make a couple hundred if I was lucky.

John and his partner came in around 4 p.m., during the middle of my dominatrix set. Sometimes the black boots, vinyl gloves, and whip scared them away. Sometimes it brought them closer. John had been brave enough to walk to the stage and let me wind the whip around his neck. He gave me twenty dollars and asked me over to his table. With the stage costume off, I became sweet Melissa again (for a very long time I gave them a fake real name when they asked for it instead of telling the men my real name), and we exchanged light, good-natured flirtatious bantering. I took him into the VIP Room, a large back room that held at least twenty chairs and was monitored by a bouncer at the entrance. He'd given me a couple one-hundred-dollar bills as soon as he'd sat down. I'd never seen hundreds doled out so easily.

We laughed.

We joked.

I pretended I was attracted to him.

When he offered me money for sex, I wasn't surprised. A lot of them did.

When his offer reached five thousand I was tempted but still hesitant. He showed me pictures of two small blonde boys on tricycles to prove he was a safe guy—a family man.

"I'm not a truck driver or sleazy. I'm a professional," he'd said.

Excitement versus morality played tug of war within my head. Money—a lot of money. I'd just bought a new car. I could get a car cover, floor mats, an alarm system, a vinyl bra for the front .... Christmas was here ....

I searched his green eyes. His face wasn't unappealing. He didn't have acne. The light beard was slightly gray, something I thought distinguishing in a man. His eyes were kind of cute when they wrinkled at the corners. His hair was short, exposing his ears that weren't deformed or hairy. His body—hard to tell for sure under the coat and slacks—didn't look overweight.

Amidst the indistinct shadows of the nightclub, I could almost see myself enjoying sex with this man. I'd heard rumors that some of the other girls from the club were doing it. And he'd told me about the evening he'd spent with a different girl from this club a few months ago. "We made love," he boasted. *Yeah right*, I thought. *You had sex.*

"I'm a really nice guy."

"I'm a really nice guy."

"I'm a really nice guy," he professed over and over.

I brought my breasts within an inch of his face.

"You smell delicious," he purred.

I shook them slightly so my flesh gently touched his cheeks. I turned around, and leaning against the brass pole in the middle of the floor, arched my back so my butt was high and firm. I petted my outer thighs and slowly turned to face him. I smiled my luscious red-lip stripper smile. Beneath the face makeup and the browns and blues of my eye shadows I hid my real motivation; the money that was being offered to me here in one afternoon would take me two months to earn working forty hours a week at the Lab.

I laughed.

I thought.

Morality pulled hardest.

I reluctantly declined.

Then he offered dancing.

Just dancing.

Just dancing for one hour for two-thousand dollars.

Car payment, medical bills, financial cushion, school tuition, I thought.

"Okay," I'd agreed. "One hour of nude dancing for two thousand."

We quickly formulated the details. "I'll pick you up two blocks down Broadway on the left hand side of the road. Be ready to get in as soon as I stop so no one will see us," I'd urged. "I'm driving a blue Honda Del Sol."

"I'll be there holding a briefcase and smiling," he'd whispered while handing me another hundred-dollar bill.

I'd made nine-hundred dollars in six hours, seven of that from him in the last one-and-a-half, and he promised another two thousand if I met him outside the club walls. I walked quickly, almost ran, through the club to the dressing room.

All I'm going to do is dance. I'm not getting any weird vibes from him, I told myself.

I packed my costumes, curling iron, makeup tubes and brushes swiftly hoping none of the other girls noticed my rushed actions. I hoped they didn't notice me freshening my makeup. I hoped they didn't notice my lingerie under my torn faded jeans and sweatshirt. I hoped no one would see him getting into my car. (We could be banned from working for leaving with a customer.)

~~~~

"Room 112 at the end of the hall," the desk clerk informs while handing John the keys.

The corridor is generic. If the doors didn't have numbers I wouldn't be able to tell one from the other.

He opens the door and flips the light switch next to it. The forest-green, low-pile shag carpet is illuminated by splashes of yellow light outlined by two worn lampshades. The coverlet on the hard double bed tries to brighten the room with its big floral patterns of pinks, yellows, and blues, but the cigarette burn holes belie its cheery facade. In the corner sits a plain wooden chair with a thin green cushion and a small wooden desk. A worn Gideon Bible and creased stationary lay on the desktop.

Bible. God. Church. Mother. *What would she think?*

I put it in the desk drawer.

The TV, suspended from the ceiling and anchored to the wall, does not have a radio.

Shit. No music.

"Do you want some cocaine?" the stranger in the suit who I'd tried to convince myself I was attracted to asks as he weaves from side to side chopping white lines.

"No." As an afterthought I add, "But thanks anyway," watching my tone. I don't want him to feel rebuked.

A few years ago the cocaine would have been welcomed. I could snort a few lines, have a few drinks, and the room, this night, this man, me, would have an inconclusive haze enshrouding it. I couldn't do it now though. Money and attention were my new drugs.

In the club I'd been brazen, brassy, bouncy, but now, hiding in the disinfected bathroom, I reluctantly remove my clothes. It's so quiet I hear my own short breaths, and I remind myself to breathe deeply. I neatly fold and place my jeans on the counter. My sweatshirt, also painstakingly folded, is placed on top of the jeans. I stuff my socks into my worn cowboy boots. I notice the scrubbed white tile, prepackaged soap and shampoo, the sanitary paper covering the toilet, the white shower curtain and tub. In the sterile stillness I'm afraid to make a sound. My hands are shaking so violently, it's as if I've snorted the cocaine.

I summon my courage and pry myself away from the confining yet private sanctuary. I walk hesitantly to the foot of the bed wearing only my club costume of push-up bra and t-back bottom.

"That looks like a comfortable spot for you to watch from," I say, thankful he's seated at the head of the bed far away from me. On the thin Ramada bedspread he lays reclining as if he's a Greek God and the harem parade is about to start. The dollar signs in my eyes fade as I take in his balding head, plain white boxer shorts, gray hairy chest, potbelly, and skinny legs.

"You can start anytime," he coaxes.

My thoughts hunker around in my mind. "I'm really nervous, maybe we can start with the lights way low," I implore.

"You can turn the lights down to start, but after you feel more comfortable can we turn them back up a little? I want to see what I'm paying for." Adding, he soothes, "But only to the degree you feel comfortable."

As I start to dance, agitation mingled with a Guns N' Roses song, "Welcome to the Jungle," ricochets around my brain. While Axl Rose croons about night games in my head, my reasoning mind recognizes,

I don't know this man I'm not in love with this man
I'm not even in like with this man

Overriding the practical points the imaginary band chorus is making about disease, somewhere in the recesses of my awareness I realize,

this man is somebody's husband somebody's
father my body is sacred

My skin starts to sweat. My throat feels like a steel door has closed inside it, and I struggle to get air into my lungs. My head floats next to the ceiling, and I watch foreign flesh move.

this is me I don't know this man this is stupid there's not even any
music this is harder than I thought how can I keep this up for an
hour

He slithers a little closer to the end of the bed where I stand dancing to the music within my head. I remove my bra exposing the breasts he's already seen at the club. I cup them, massage them and lick my nipple. Slowly I play with myself, not wanting to hasten what I know he expects next.

As Slash's guitar wails on my gray matter and the catchy overplayed tune easily rolls off my neural network, I hum the refrain softly as my own refrain continues.

I don't know this man it's probably only been a
few minutes but it seems like thirty

I don't know this man okay two-thousand dollars
this will be over soon I don't know this man

I feel really stupid, I can't find a rhythm without music,
I wonder how long it's been

"The underwear, remove your underwear," he commands extending a hand as if to help me remove my last piece of clothing.

I laugh timidly and back away.

He removes his dick from his undershorts and starts fondling himself.

"Is this okay? I just want to participate in my own way," he offers as I swallow the lump rising in my throat.

NOT REALLY, I silently scream.

"Sure," I manage to eek out.

I continue dancing, turn my back to him and start removing my t-back panties bending over and showing him the honey pot he's come to see. I don't want to look in his face.

The rock group I imagine keeping me company is still trying to distract my head from my reality.

Torn between wanting to keep my backside to him forever

---

yet wanting to face him because I'm uncertain of his actions, I turn back around and see he's moved to the end of the bed close to where I'm standing. I lift one leg onto the bed, angled outward, to give him a good show.

"Just let me touch your legs a little," he whispers like a deprived child.

I let him touch my legs as his breath becomes shorter, faster. My skin begins to twitch. His cold hands were just on his member.

"Come. Come here closer," he begs as his eyes start to roll back into his head. "Give me a hug."

I imagine the smell of him.

Axl, Slash, and all the Guns N' Roses guys begin a cacophony about jungle and death and screaming.

Hovering somewhere above and behind my shoulder, my brain sees for the first time that this man could overpower me. All the news reports I'd ever heard about strangled, bloated, bludgeoned, battered, bruised, dead women start a cacophony within my head. Dirty, dingy, dark, damp, depressed, desolate hotel rooms also conjure stark images, and it's as if I've been awakened from a deep sleep.

My head returns to my body.

In a panic I grab my purse and grope inside it for my pepper spray while keeping my eyes on him. "I, I can't do this. Stay away from me."

I clutch the yellow canister in my right hand, poised to spray, and keep one eye on him and the distance between us as I stumble about quickly gathering my clothes with my left hand.

Jolted, he slides back to the head of the bed. His lips, which had been parted longingly, clamp shut. His eyes widen causing his forehead to crease in exclamation. "I'm sorry. I didn't mean to scare you," he apologetically murmurs as he positions himself back in his boxers. "I really wasn't going to hurt you,

I just got carried away," he stammers as he draws his knees up into his chest and wraps his arms around them.

I dress quickly. With each garment I feel more protected.

Watching me put on my old faded jeans and too-large black sweatshirt, his eyes narrow, face reddens, and, walking to the table where the money lays, he sarcastically snaps, "I suppose you still want the money!"

I want to run, to breathe fresh air. I want to shower. I can smell his skin and I want to wretch. I'm still fearful. He could force me. But I too am angry; that he's so rich, that he acted so nice, that he showed me pictures of his kids, that he kept on and kept on, that I'm so broke. "You can keep the money. I don't want your fucking money," I blurt through sobs.

Again, his expression shifts, his eyes close, and his face softens. As he starts to dress, I hear his barely audible, "You can have the money. You probably need it worse than I do."

We finish dressing in silence.

"Will you drive me back to the City?" he eventually asks.

Having to care whether he's coming or not irritates me as we walk to the dark parking lot.

We had traveled across the San Francisco Bay Bridge to Berkeley because there was a big convention in town and there weren't any rooms available in the City. During that drive the gaiety of our flirtation had subsided but I'd still been spirited by the thought of the money. That enchantment, like dynamite eradicates rock, is now disintegrated. We sit side by side in my compact car while noxious memories like dust fumes suffocate me. Laboring for clean air, I force myself to cross miles that head away from the safety of my home in Livermore so John can retrieve his car in San Francisco. I'm grateful I have the road and traffic to concentrate on and look straight ahead, reticent. We exchange inconsequential pleasantries: the fog, the weather, the water, as if two strangers passing time on the bus forced together by circumstance.

"It's getting too late to go somewhere, and I have to be up in the morning. I suppose I could go home to my wife."

"Yeah, you should go home to your wife," I say.

When I recounted to my therapist what happened in the motel room, she was afraid for my safety, but I still didn't see the depth of my own disregard. Like a harried rabbit darting across the road before the speeding car can run it over, I'd played chicken with my life before. When I was a teenager, I continued to hitchhike even after I narrowly escaped, sliding my arm out of my coat, from a man who viciously grabbed for me when I started getting out of his large front seat. When I was a young adult, I'd occasionally meet someone in a bar and leave with them to the parking lot or all the way to their home or mine. Writing this now, as a mature married woman in the safety of my home, I'm reminded of the 1977 movie, *Looking for Mr. Goodbar*, that I didn't watch until the 90's, and my heart palpitates with fear as I realize how close my life could have come to imitating the movie's ending. Not that I was looking for Mr. Goodbar. I'd been searching for Prince Charming. I'd grown up with fairy tales like *Sleeping Beauty*, *Cinderella* and even modern-day *Shrek* where princesses are rescued and the couple lives happily ever after.

But life doesn't resemble fairy tales. Knights didn't ride on white stallions any longer or carry shields and javelins. Would-be rescuers now drove Mercedes or were chauffeured in Limousines and instead of arriving chaperoned at your front door in the revealing light of day with their engraved announcement card to spend time in conversation, courting, they arrived cloaked in the secrecy of night and carried American

Express cards or better yet—cash. While my unconsciousness was just as deep as Sleeping Beauty's slumber, my resting place wasn't a beautiful castle, and my hopeful lover in the motel room jarred me awake by wanting more than a kiss!

I promised my therapist I wouldn't place my life in jeopardy for money again, but I did continue to put myself in situations that could have been fatal. Even in my mid thirties I still succumbed to the arrogance of youth and stupidly thought nothing would happen to me—if I considered safety at all. My mind was focused elsewhere. I *really* thought that *Cosmo*, *Vogue* and *Shape* held the answers: happiness would be gained through attaining more money; I'd have true love of self by being thinner and sexier; the perfect man would make all my dreams come true. The strip club was ideal for me to try and attain these misguided goals. I was making cash money, being told I was beautiful, sexy and svelte, and each night I was prowling for that perfect man.

Before I could embrace my ideal man in the present however, I had to make peace with my untarnished male ghost from the past—Dennis. The hole in my heart he'd left when he refused to attend my high school graduation eventually filled with every boy, then man, I felt abandoned by. In a valiant effort to heal this void, I located him in Arizona using a detective agency, (this was before we could search for people through the internet) called him up, then flew to Flagstaff for the weekend.

I didn't recognize him. He was much shorter than I remembered. His radical long hair was gone. He wore coke-bottle glasses. He still partied and seemed proud of the fact that he hadn't changed much since high school.

Back home, alone again, I convulsed uncontrollably like a mangled beast, unable and unwilling to stop the pain of unrequited love that for over eighteen years I'd excelled at stuffing inside; body flat, hands curled, carpet indents on my face, animal noises escaped from deep within my belly. With no one to look good for, no place to go, nothing to medicate myself with, I let loose the anguish that had defined and dogged me an entire life. I yowled, panted, pounded, kicked, growled, snarled, and wailed.

Eventually, I slept.

When I woke up, I felt drugged.

A few days later my heart felt lighter than it ever had.

My mind and body felt unshackled as well. Every night I worked, I was Cinderella at the Ball, twirling in a world full of laughter and sensual permission. I could set my own schedule and talk to whomever I picked. The control I wielded became an aphrodisiac, and for the first time I could remember since reciting to my parents a rhyming poem I'd written in grade school about finding a solution to pollution, creative self-expression burst forth in the music I chose, the costumes I wore, and the movements I made. Cavorting in pretty dresses to loud rock music while being told I was beautiful and being handed money wasn't work.

What *was* work was pulling myself out of bed at six a.m., throwing on old jeans and driving to a place where I sat in resilient anonymity performing the same tasks day in and day out. Shot preparations for the giant NOVA laser system were conducted by several teams at Lawrence Livermore National Laboratory. Each group of specialists had specific tasks and checklists to complete that were independent of another group's. After I finished my required job tasks, I'd sit at my computer console and wait for others to finish their preparations so we could fire the laser and conduct experiments. In this spare time, I began writing thoughts and poetry about feelings emerging within me. I was experiencing a newly inspired artistic way of being in the world as a direct result of my night work, and restlessness consumed me during the day.

I was told to quit writing. "Sit patiently," I was directed by managers.

This frustrated and angered the rebellious teenager within me who enjoyed being unleashed and unrestrained. I screamed in my car during lunch. I dozed during breaks in the women's bathroom. I agonized. I hated. I didn't know how to merge my two worlds, and the defiant adolescent seesawed with the compliant adult until one dismounted and the teeter-totter crashed hard to the pavement.

I kept the job I enjoyed.

Then, petrified, like a piece of wood that's been buried in the forest beneath rock for millions of years, I wanted to pull the covers over my head and become a fossil. Nothing looked familiar. I had no medical insurance, no worker's compensation, no sick pay, no paid vacations, no paid holidays. My financial security was now based on competition. Every night that I worked alongside my large-breast constituents, I compared my small, natural breasts. While doing the personal dances I could wear bras with lots of padding to create the illusion that I was larger than my A cup (we were required to keep our tops on when we danced for customers), but when I was on stage and took my top off, I felt inadequate. Just as I noticed the conspicuous attention men paid *all* women with large breasts, I now saw that within the club, larger-breasted women sold dances. Laura, a bubbly blonde woman like myself, was one of these women. She also owned her own bachelor-party business that, from her descriptions, sounded safe, fun, and lucrative. To work for her though, I needed two items—business cards and larger breasts.

I didn't hesitate.

Laura picked me up and brought me home immediately after implant surgery. She was too busy to stick around for long, but before she drove back to San Francisco, she offered,

"You can have him redo them," as if my breasts were a pair of pants I could exchange. And before the surgery I'd boasted about my brazen escapades so when a couple of male friends I used to work with from the Lab came over a few days later, I felt obligated and lifted my shirt reluctantly. What once had been private and personal now became discussion and fodder for others' approval—or disapproval.

I wasn't proud, and I wasn't happy. I'd been ripped open, had two saline sacks placed under my skin and had been stitched back together almost without a trace. (The insertion points were underneath my arms). Nipple eyes, heavy with pain, stared back at me from the mirror and questioned my decision. My breasts were hard and painful to touch and my chest looked distorted; the skin had been stretched too tightly. Because I couldn't lift myself from bed to get up to use the bathroom those first nights after the surgery, I lay tearfully calling to a friend who slept peacefully upstairs, certain I'd made a huge mistake. Again, I was jolted aware of my body. This time though I couldn't just grab my pepper spray and cover myself for safety.

After a few weeks, the soreness went away and my skin pallor returned. The doctor instructed me to move the saline pouches in the pockets he'd created under the muscle, but I couldn't—it was too painful. One healed too high in my chest and although others don't notice, I'm always aware of it. I'm used to them now, fifteen years later, but initially I was self conscious of my size and everywhere I looked I noticed women with small, natural, perfectly-formed breasts; growing into C-size bosoms would have been less jarring than waking up with them. I only wore tight clothing at work.

Although I felt uncomfortable outside the club because I was proportionally different than other women, inside, my new breasts brought me confidence. I changed my padded bras to string bikini tops that barely covered my nipples, and when I approached a man I made sure my breasts were at his eye level. I'd bring them close to his view, allow my perfume to tickle his nose, and whisper, "Would you like me to take off my clothes and seduce you?" (To do the dances, we removed our dresses.)

My tips went up. (It wouldn't be until years later that I'd finally understand that women who projected confidence, no matter what their breast size, did quite well.)

To get business cards made, I had to have pictures taken and it was in the photographer's studio, surrounded by pictures of David Bowie, James Brown, Mick Jagger, and the young Jackson Five to name just a few celebrities he'd captured on film, that I felt important. Laura showed up to tease my hair and make sure we got pictures of big hair and big boobs— what she said men looked for when hiring strippers for bachelor parties. Contrasted to the anxiety I'd felt as a laser technician—microscopically dissected by customers—I welcomed this intense focus on my body. I was amateurish and awkward in front of a camera, but the composed man behind the lens coaxed and cajoled the girl within who liked playing dress up.

"Stop."

"There."

"Tilt your head."

"Move your arm."

"Jut your chin."

"Look here."

When he said, "Beautiful," "Great," "That's it," I felt gorgeous.

Laura paid for this initial photo shoot since I was an employee of her business. That would have been the extent of my affair with modeling, but before I left his studio after looking at proofs from that first shoot, the photographer offered to take more pictures for merely the cost of film—no fee. "Play," he called it. "Bring lots of outfits."

Sometimes for the stage I'd begin a three-song set completely covered to dispel nervous jitters, so for this second shoot I began by wearing a man's suit I'd purchased at a local thrift store complete with hat, dress shirt and tie. I was stiff, but the all-too-eager-to-please girl within me soon helped the sexy woman emerge; my inhibitions fell away as the coat came off, tie loosened, hat was tossed, and shirt was unbuttoned. The woman who'd never felt pretty enough or good enough, was suddenly extraordinarily special without having to be in competition for grades or men or money or attention. All I had to do was stand, move slowly, hold poses. As I performed the seductive moves I'd been perfecting on the stage, the shirt slid from one shoulder, lips parted, eyes half closed, and pants unzipped and slipped lower until I was comfortable in merely a t-back and loosely draped dress shirt.

The minuscule piece of glass between the photographer and myself afforded me the illusion of distance, just as the girls and employees of the club helped me feel safe and separated from customers even when only inches apart. With blinding bulbs pointed in my direction the photographer disappeared from behind the lens into a black void while his voice pulled visual orgasms from me. When he directed me to tilt my head back I felt the searing heat on my taut neck. I felt the grace and elegance of my shoulder as it bent forward slightly to catch the scorching rays.

We decided I should put on the black motorcycle jacket, thigh-high boots and leather gloves next. He snapped a few pictures, then commanded, "Remove your panties."

My gloved hand took their place.

"Sit on the helmet," he directed as I continued to shield my crotch. We took a few shots that way, then "Stand," he voiced and "Put the helmet on." The full-face helmet gave me anonymity, so when he suggested I remove the hand from my crotch and place both hands at my sides, I felt covered. I stood, leathered fists on hips, open waist-length jacket exposing merely the center-line of my chest, nothing on below the waist. His lens picked up every detail.

It was ten o'clock at night and the studio was silent. The rock music we relied on earlier to help me stay in an alluring mood was no longer necessary. As he'd done before, the photographer walked into the dressing room to look for more clothing options. "Let's do something with these," he suggested walking out with rope and nipple clamps in hand.

I'd been exploring my sexuality and it's that experimental girl who put the items into the bag to bring to the shoot, but it was late, I was tired and no longer enthusiastic. Yet similar to how I'd always weighed boy's, then men's desires heavier than my own, I took his feelings into consideration. *He's doing all this for me—for free.*

"Okay," I spoke.

He changed the backdrop to a charcoal gray canvas while I stood on the side wearing the man's suit coat for cover.

"Let's use the mask too," he offered.

When I wore the mask on stage I pulled my hair in a ponytail so I did that in the safety of the dressing room as I scanned my face. *He's been a gentleman all night. He hasn't made a pass to do anything other than photograph me,* I told myself.

But I don't feel comfortable.

"Are you almost done in there?" he called.

I put the mask on and walked out to the shoot area.

"You put the clamps on," he said.

With the suit coat on still, I attached one then the other to my erect nipples and the metal chain swung between my breasts.

After he loaded his film, I removed the coat, then stood

naked wearing only the black feather mask as he wound the rope around my body.

He took one picture with the mask on, then asked, "Do you mind if I take the mask off?"

In the quiet of the studio he walked very close to my nude lassoed body and taking care not to disturb a single hair from my tight ponytail, removed the mask and exposed my face.

"Can I use the tie to blindfold you?"

I'm cold.

He stepped back. Click, click, click, I heard the camera.

"Angle your head down."

Click, click, click.

The room became as still as a winter night fleeced in new snow when no sane human ventures out in the storm, instead opting to stay inside where it's dry and safe.

But I wasn't dry—my body was clammy.

I couldn't quite describe what I felt then. I was more confused than safe. I was caught somewhere between compliance and uncertainty, between terror and resigned calm, between awareness and denial. There was no sudden flash of dread as there'd been in the motel room. But, my screams, if there had been any, would have been silent outside the studio walls. My eyes, would have been wide, my body lifeless.

I was relieved when he suggested we stop.

I put my clothes on quickly.

The words to describe the way I felt at that time wouldn't come until I watched *8MM* starring Nicholas Cage years later. In that 1999 movie, he works as a private detective hired to determine the authenticity of what appears to be a snuff film, and his search takes him to and through underground sex for hire and sadomasochistic venues. It's a dark movie, both in theme and cinematography. Like a lazy, albeit energized, fire, this film evokes the same slow-spreading heat that creeps along my limbs when I read about some sinister atrocity perpetrated on another human; isolation—evil—blackness. Today, I realize that back then, blindfolded—roped—clamped—isolated, my feeling was of being stained.

Excluding the bondage photos (which I still find hard to look at) when I returned to see the proofs a week later, I was surprised. I saw beauty others had told me about but I'd denied. Prior attempts to see myself were braided with my mind's distortion of religious condemnation for the sinful body, a cultural obsession with flawless perfection, and polite societies' denouncements of strippers. In those black and white and color pictures I existed outside myself—the only place I'd ever looked for answers—the only place I'd ever thought valid.

I'd been on the stage a year and a half by this time and could easily manufacture sexy impersonations, but the photographer's patient persistence pulled from me real feeling I could now see. I was no longer simply a reflection from an admirer's eyes. I was concrete; my sensual body real. *I'm sexy*, I thought as I scanned high cheekbones, a slim waistline, tailored legs, perky breasts, a genuine smile, inviting eyes, and a demure presence revealed through the soft hue of photographic filters. *I'm beautiful*, I allowed myself to think briefly, secretly, before the judgments and insecurities stole in and took up their vigil on the outskirts of my reasoning. In those two-dimensional images, I met a woman who'd been elusive to me.

The first step to having friends is to meet them. In this visual recognition, I began to circumvent validation I'd once found only externally, through boys and men, then through praise, applause, and payment from customers. A small seed of self-awareness was planted, that if nurtured, could grow into self-acceptance. I could now begin to befriend my body—myself.

We humans incline towards protecting friends.

CONNECTION

The real in us is silent; the acquired is talkative.

Kahlil Gibran

When you've been in enough of them, all airports start to look the same. So do the weary travelers shuffling through their corridors. But once, when I was a traveling service technician wandering between airport gates, a woman walked past me and grabbed my attention as abruptly as if she'd pulled my hair and yanked my head around. First, I heard the click of her pert black leather boots. Next, I witnessed her determined stride, and my focus shifted quickly to her matching knee-length black skirt and bolero jacket accessorized with a wide brim hat, fingerless gloves, and sheer black stockings with a seam up the back. After she sat, she meticulously crossed her legs, as if rehearsed, and even though her makeup was impeccable, took out her compact in a swift move flashing dark red fingernails. She dabbed her lips with an even darker ruby lipstick.

I couldn't take my eyes off her.

Her matching black luggage pieces fit snugly on top of each other for easy maneuvering, and the large thin artist's portfolio she'd cradled under her arm perched itself with casual poise on the companion chair next to her. From where I sat wearing my conservatively conforming grey slacks and burnt-sienna blouse keeping the eye that wasn't on her on my nicked grey toolbox and mismatched luggage, I felt inferior to her in every conceivable way: appearance, stature, economics, education, and career. I concealed a few small sheets of bad writing somewhere in my purse.

This woman looked like the women I'd secretly always wanted to be like. Their lives looked interesting and effortless, and I imagined the magnitude of the love they received. I wanted to be one of them—someone prettier, smarter, richer. But I'd grown up with what in my generation were standard things parents told their kids: "Children should be seen and not heard," "Don't call attention to yourself," "What will the neighbors think?" These phrases and thoughts were so firmly embedded into my psyche and so thoroughly a part of the internal dialogue churning through my head, my eternal chatter, that I instinctively thought it sinful to call attention to one's self in any way. Yet everywhere I looked, the message was otherwise. And this message is louder today than it was in the late '80s when I envied the woman in the airport and in 1995 when I was a new exotic dancer. Today I know that celebrity and money don't guarantee a happy life, back then I felt they did, and that I was nothing if I wasn't being admired and lusted after.

The other message so thoroughly embedded within my DNA structure that it feels intrinsic to my nature was, "good girls don't." Although I'd been sexual often, I thought my sexuality bad. Unknowingly, I'd banished it to what Carl Jung calls our Shadow, our not-recognized desires. Basically, it was a part of myself I denied and tried to will away. In "Finding the Shadow in Daily Life," from the anthology *Meeting the Shadow,* William Miller explains it simply, "Shadow is all we wouldn't dare do, but would like to do." Sigmund Freud referred to it as the repressed side of our personality. This unconscious exclusion of aspects of ourselves that are unacceptable and displeasing to our family, peers, and society, goes into what Robert Bly, in the same anthology, refers to as an invisible bag each of us drags behind us that we begin to fill as children. These shadow selves do not disappear, nor do they lie dormant but instead creep out to embarrass or shame our ego, the self we present to the world. Bly states that the bag continues to fill until we're young adults, around twenty. After this time and for the rest of our lives, we continually try to retrieve lost parts of ourselves from these bags, in order to be whole people, instead of mere fragments of the people we really are.

Like I'd done unsuccessfully for many years before getting sober—promised myself I wasn't going to use alcohol and drugs—I'd also tried to stop being promiscuous and having casual sex. I wanted to be a good girl, chaste and valued as the parochial-school teachings and church decreed. But everywhere I looked, sexuality was used to market happiness and success and being sexually appealing was lauded as a fundamental goal to strive for. And just like alcoholism, that is said doesn't disappear when the drinking stops but instead lies in wait and gains teeth like a ferocious tiger ready to spring once the alcohol is consumed again, denial of and disconnection from my body and fear of its inherent needs and desires didn't make the urges or the associated behavior go away. My repressed sexuality hadn't magically disappeared with the thought that I wanted it to be contained, but instead crept out when my conscious mind wasn't keeping a tight rein on it.

Also in *Meeting the Shadow,* "What the Shadow Knows: An

Interview with John A. Sanford," Sanford posits that archangels will thrust us into situations where we will be confronted by our dark side. What we do in that situation is up to us. Without clearly understanding the underlying motivations behind why I was attracted to the strip club initially, it was merely fun at the time, I was drawn into an arena where I perceived my body and sexuality was valued, something I'd never done for myself. Within the club, I stood face to face and shook hands with my dark side, and I decided to hang out with her. The strip club provided a protected venue and erected boundaries around my licentious expression that I'd never been able to set for myself. Under dark cover of the club, I felt energized and glamorous every time my erotic self came out to play. Now I was one of those beautiful women. I *was* Cinderella at the Ball. And the more sensuality and sexual intimation I oozed, the more money I made.

Before quitting the Lab, the transformation that occurred when I ran home at 4 p.m. after working eight hours, jumped in the shower, grabbed my bag of costumes and makeup and stopped at the Shell Station for a large coffee to drink on the hour drive into San Francisco, was as complete as if a fairy godmother had waved a magic wand. I became invigorated and sparkled. My dirty pulled-back daytime hair was now clean, loose, and shiny, and the uncertainty of the night was filled with fanciful dreams of great amounts of money, charming secrets, and ever-lasting love. I never knew what magical prince might arrive to save me from the drudgery of my usual, scripted day. In every night there were many first dates, and as with any new relationship everyone was on their best behavior. We laughed. We joked. I danced. They paid. At the end of the night, at the imagined stroke of midnight, I turned back into conservative fully-clothed Susan, bone-weary yet fulfilled from her many first dances at the Ball.

The strip club was a microcosm of the world where women

preen and men take care of them: some customers bought dinner for us in the club, some men met women outside the club to take them shopping, some men paid for breast implants and other cosmetic procedures women professed they needed. It was also a world where instead of the male having the privilege to choose, a belief I'd grown up with, I had the opportunity to select. Like any male/female relationship there was the seductive, I-like-you-do-you-like-me dance—a dance I'd never taken the lead in—but as my strip club persona grew stronger, so did my ability to make the first steps. I never had to wonder or wait anymore. It was ladies' choice all night, every night. As this new liberated woman flourished within the strip club walls, so did my courage outside the club.

For a person who never had a defined self and who wanted to be someone else, Halloween was the perfect time of year. I could be anyone, act any way I'd like. The event I associated with lascivious rebellion, the Exotic Erotic Ball, happened every year, and after I'd been dancing for some time, my sober boyfriend who lived across the street in a rented townhouse identical to the one I owned, said he'd go with me. While he enjoyed being fully clothed and made up to be a scary wolfman, complete with fake blood spilling down his flannel shirt, my outfit was more risqué: black lace body stocking, thigh-high black leather boots, black thong panties, and no bra. I teased my hair and spray painted it purple and painted my entire face with white and heavy eye shadows so that even if you knew me—you wouldn't know me—as was proven when I ran into somebody I'd worked with from the Lab who was there observing, not costumed.

Unlike my first experience at this Ball eight years previous where I stood rooted in one place like a hopeless weed, with my new-found courage and the scary Wolfman as my protector, I possessed the bravado to wander all over the coliseum where the event was taking place. I was immortalized in many attendees' pictures and was interviewed by a major cable news network. They wanted to know what impelled me to be an exhibitionist.

Exhibitionist?

Flattered to be noticed, I answered. "During the day I'm a buttoned-up conservative woman, and I don't dress provocatively. Exposing myself isn't something I *need* to do. I'm just a regular person who's merely having fun and being free of societal restraints in an acceptable place. I'm sowing oats." Throughout the night, however, and for days later, I defended myself to myself to quell my own self-doubt and rising judgment.

Unfortunately, just as an angry spouse or family member who is ignored or who can't verbalize their feelings might become resentful and passive aggressive but seem copacetic on the surface, I, too, existed with my body in silent conflict that no one else could see; I continued my long-established pattern of food restriction, binge eating, and excessive exercise. Others couldn't detect this secretive battle though, externally I looked trim and toned, so armed with new breasts and business cards, I looked ready for bachelor parties, my new second job. Laura told me what the guys would be looking for when we showed up: big hair, big boobs, high energy, and whip cream games. During the first few parties I worked with her to learn the timeline of events, how to play the sexually suggestive games, the tricks of illusion that helped men think they were getting more overt sexuality than they actually were, how to defend against the occasional wise guy or trickster who tried to touch more than he was allowed, and of course the sole reason for our doing this work, how to make the most money. After training with Laura during three parties, I was seasoned enough to take along a male bouncer and be on my own.

Normally, the men sat as we stood and explained how the

party would evolve, but during this first solo party south of San Francisco, the longhair, blue-collar, shirtless bachelor with tattoos insisted on standing beside me as I addressed the group. Irritated, yet polite, I let him. Then, instead of sitting and letting me perform, something they'd already paid for when they'd booked the party, he wanted me to go straight to the games that cost extra. This would have been okay, after all, it would have been more money for me, but he was so drunk that instead of allowing me to explain the games he kept picking me up, spilling beer on both of us. At first, although exasperated, I was diplomatic. I really wanted to put on a good show especially since it was the first one without Laura. I held onto my composure, joked sweetly and had been a good sport through the bachelor's inebriated shenanigans, but inside I felt angry, disrespected, and scared. The only reason my anxious unease was manageable was because the other men at the party tried to help me keep him in line.

Eventually though, I had to exercise the option we warned them about if they got out of hand.

"We're stopping the party now," I said with authority. No one questioned my decision. Some of the men even helped the bouncer and myself gather the lights and props I'd brought. But when we walked to the front door, it was locked.

One of the men scurried to get the key from the bachelor (it was his house).

Relief nudged my panic aside.

However, alarm surfaced again when we were backing out of the driveway. The bachelor came to the porch yelling and brandishing a shotgun.

Looking back on it now, this was just as dangerous as being in a motel room with one person. But like the time I was shot at in Columbus, Georgia, because my boyfriend was yelling racial epithets, I laughed it off as an adventure, and not the real threat that it was. Since those youthful days in the South, my body had aged almost eighteen years although my maturity hadn't. When getting ready for future parties, I overrode my weariness, choked my nervousness back into my belly, and allowed the camaraderie and illusion of safety (my bouncer was a large man) to override my hesitation and dread.

More often than not the parties went well, I told myself, as I relived the fun I'd had while being with Laura. In those parties, I laughed freely and was amazed at how well men behaved when a naked woman stood in their midst. Compared to how I felt when I was scientist Susan wearing clothes and interacting with men at the Lab, like a menial peasant woman hungry for recognition as they ogled, commented on, and assessed well-manicured women who toured the laser facility, I felt satiated and full when at the parties. If they were good they'd get to see me, maybe touch my legs, arms, back or stomach, maybe glimpse a portion of my personality, real or fictional.

꒰ꕤ꒱

One late evening in Santa Cruz, a graying man answers the door of a quiet split-level bungalow. "Hi, you must be Vixen," he says, "I'm Frank, come on in." (Laura told me her boyfriend had always liked the name Vixen and I used it for the bachelor parties, later adopting it as my stage name at the Gold Club.)

At the table are three more men: one balding, one gray, and one with salt-and-pepper hair. Four more walk into the kitchen and everyone introduces themselves. I guess they're all in their forties.

"Who's the bachelor?" I ask.

"Nobody's a bachelor," the short bald man at the table retorts while staring at me through thick plastic glasses. "We're just here to have a party."

Frank leads the bouncer, Dave, and me to the back of the

house. My short heels sink into the plush carpeting as we make our way to the bedroom. The exposed wood beams and pillars are charming, but the house is devoid of any personal knick-knacks that give a home character. Instead, suitcases and piles of clothes from the men's holiday week are scattered about the periphery. Donna, Laura's co-owner in the business, is standing half-naked in the bedroom trying to determine what costume she's going to wear. "There's champagne if you want it," Frank directs. "I'll leave you two to get ready."

"These guys look dead," I lament to Donna, "I'm pooped." I'd already done one party in San Mateo with Laura and then rode over an hour with Dave. It was almost midnight and my feet hurt.

"All we have to do is a quick show and we're out of here," she reassures me.

Bachelor parties are usually five to thirty men with ages ranging in the twenties and early thirties. Based on experience, I know older men typically sit stone-faced in their chairs and are shy. They stand out from the rest of the men with their gray hair, wrinkled faces, and lack of enthusiasm, and they position themselves around the edges of the room close to the door-way for unobtrusive viewing and quick escape if attention is directed their way. When they're approached and singled out to play a game, they either never try to touch us inappropriately, or they became monstrous octopi with tentacles emerging from everywhere that have to be fought off. Usually, there are only one or two of them, the dad or grandfather of the bachelor, and while the young men are gung-ho and willing, the older men sit reluctant and have to be urged when someone pays for them to play a game with us. Tonight there's a whole houseful!

I have a light string of five red bulbs on wood bases that we set around the room on the floor, and Donna has brought red bulbs for the lamps in the room. Dave goes into the living room and starts setting up the lights.

We each select a costume, dressing in layers to prolong the striptease part of the show. We look like good cop/bad cop: me, blond and innocent in my cheerleader's outfit with white lace anklets and her, brunette and tough with black leather boots carrying a black whip.

I walk out to the kitchen where the eight men are gathered around the table smoking dope, "Are you guys about ready?"

"Yeah, we're ready," Lionel, the tallest, slimmest man offers as he introduces himself. "We've been ready all year."

"Why are you all here?" I inquire, trying to get an understanding of the men and gauge how the night might unfold.

"We're old college buddies," Herman, the shortest roundest one replies. "Once a year we get together and have a party. Last year, Joshua was getting married, and we had such a good time at his bachelor party that we decided to have another party— just for the fun."

"I'm a computer consultant from Russia," Frank responds, "Greg here is an accounts executive manager at a bank in Denver, Ralph is an accountant from Tucson," and he continues to rattle off where all the men are from.

"That's cool," I answer, realizing my fatigue while shifting my weight from one foot to the other to stop them from hurting. I also conjure a conservative image of each man at his job all the while calculating how much money I hope to make.

Donna calls them down the two stairs to the sunken living room where our makeshift stage is set. Herman and Greg bring a couple chairs from the kitchen and the rest of the men take places on the two couches hugging the walls. I check the tape in the boom box while Donna walks around the room teasing the men with her whip. Dave sits on the floor in the corner where no one really pays any attention to him.

After that first show without Laura, I never again had an incident where men became too unruly and I felt my safety was threatened, but Dave was a big man, five-foot, eleven inches and two-hundred pounds of muscle and he acted as a deterrent, just in case. If the men were anything other than obedient and respectful, it was usually only drunk and obnoxious.

In the middle of the room, surrounded by somber-looking middle-aged men, I explain the show. "We're going to dance to three songs where we'll come to you. There will be a lot of touching but please don't touch our breasts or pussies or we'll have to stop the show."

"And I'll have to spank you," Donna adds, brandishing her whip. A few of them nod in agreement. A few of them offer that they wanted to be spanked.

"We'll strip to nude and dance," I continue, "then we'll explain the interactive games to see if anyone wants to play." In three short months I'd learned to rattle off the party description as easily as it'd been to announce the, "Clear the laser bay" spiel I'd repeated at the Lab on average four times a day for at least six years.

Beers by their sides, some look eager, some look resistant.

I start the music on the portable boom box, and the first song blares into the black room illuminated by red bulbs. Our job is to make the party happen. No matter how tired we are we have to summon energy similar to the force of Mount Vesuvius and erupt into fireballs of motion and movement. Like any performer putting on a show, we hope to get enthusiastic responses to fuel and feed our energy. I quickly jump onto Joshua's lap, my legs straddling either side of him and though still fully clothed, I clutch his head to my breast. The men howl approval as Sly and the Family Stone belt out, "Boom Shaka-lacka-lacka," from "I Want to Take You Higher," and the pounding notes bounce around the room. One of the first things we always do to liven up the men and get them into the party spirit is to get their shirts off. We tell them, "It's not fair if we're going to be the only ones naked," and now I whisper into Joshua's ear before I pull his t-shirt over his head and glasses, "Put your beer down." Donna is pulling Greg's shirt off at the same time. Then I turn around and squirm on Joshua's lap amidst shouts of, "Yeah, yeah," from the other men and, "higher," on the boom box.

I whip off my tight blue-sequined top (still wearing the bikini top) and fling myself at Herman. *If anyone is going to protest having his shirt removed*, I think, *it'll be Herman, he's the most overweight*, but to my delight he pulls his own shirt off and sits grinning like a proud Buddha. With one foot on the floor, I raise my other leg and balance my foot on the seatback behind his neck. I pull his head close to my bikini-clad crotch, putting my skirt over his head. The men's yells reverberate louder.

I unbutton the wrap-around skirt, fling it into the corner, and move to Lionel. Lionel is wearing silver-wire glasses that I remove from his face and shove into the front of my bikini bottoms for a few brief seconds. "I'll never wash those glasses again," he boasts as the men scream. I hand his glasses back to him and move on to the next man.

Donna and I continue around the room dancing, taking the men's shirts off, paying each one attention. When all the men are sitting without shirts on, and their adrenaline and excitement levels are high, we remove our bikini bottoms and, as if we had practiced and choreographed this routine, we lay on the floor spreading our legs and gyrating in unison. The men can't really see much, it's too dark, but our naked reality permeates the room and the men are satisfied to fill in the blanks of our anatomy with their fantasy. We dance and pose and wriggle our way through "More Human Than Human," by White Zombie, and Billy Idol's "White Wedding."

At the end of the three-song set we stand naked, sweaty, and breathless in the center of the room, and I describe the tipping games as Donna demonstrates the actions.

"Now it's time for the interactive part of the show. We'll make a whip cream trail around our boobies and on our inner thighs which you can lick off." Donna uses the canned whip cream to simulate where the whip cream will go. "We'll massage hot oil into your chest first with our chest and then in the sixty-nine position sitting and sliding with our pussies." Donna lays on her back as I get on top of her showing the positions of the bodies. The men jeer and joke and jab at each other. "Then we'll do the grand finale, which we won't tell you about, but you'll have to experience. All these games will cost twenty dollars a piece or one-hundred dollars total for each man."

Usually only one or two men want to do a couple of the games, but typically everyone is forced, by their buddies paying for them, to play at least one.

"We're going to go put on our game attire, and we'll be right back." Our game attire consists of thigh-high boots to shove the money into so we won't lose it or have it stolen. (I learned that once the girls were at a party where they collected money, put it in their designated dressing room, and then when they were doing the games the men snuck back into the room, stole the money, and paid for more games with the stolen money.)

Back in the bedroom my high-energy façade quickly fades as we speculate how much money we'll make and how much longer we'll be there. I don't have to do anything the next day so the late hour doesn't bother me, but by this time I'm so tired I don't care if anyone is interested in playing.

When we return from the back room, men are scattered all over the house drinking and smoking pot. We gather them back to the living room.

"I think we should all give them one-hundred dollars a piece and each of us does all the games," Frank declares. They all shout in agreement and start taking money out of their wallets as Donna and I stand smiling at each other.

I forget my fatigue.

"I think," Frank continues, "that since the girls are naked, we should be naked too, or at least almost naked." He pulls off his pants and stands in the middle of the room in white jockey shorts.

"I agree."

"It's only fair."

"Off with the pants," we hear from all around the room and suddenly all the men are standing in their white briefs flinging their clothing into the corner of the living room. Herman runs up to his suitcase, pulls a pair of briefs out, and puts them on.

I'm reminded of the strategy for getting past the nervousness of making speeches, *imagine your audience in their underwear*, and am amused and not at all intimidated by eight powerful men in their skivvies.

I put on the music.

As the dark rock licks of Metallica introduce "Enter Sandman," Lionel gets up and starts doing what he calls the Mashed Potato. He extends his arms outward, fists together, then makes clockwise circular motions in rhythm to the music. We all start doing it. We all ten synchronize our arm movements and in perfect unison look like some x-rated version of a dance band, an eclectic performance piece one would expect to see in experimental theater; two naked women in thigh-high boots and eight executives in their underwear all standing in a circle doing the Mashed Potato with hard rock music blaring in the background. I hoot with laughter while marveling at the unpredictable situation.

Donna nicknames the men, The Nasty Boys, and they accept the label with enthusiasm chanting, "The Nasty Boys, The Nasty Boys."

But we still have work to do.

We pick two men and tell them we're going to race to see

who can finish the cream first. We have each man kneel before us and we paint a whip cream loop around one breast extending to our navel. We cover our nipples. When we yell, "Go," the men have to lick all the whip cream. Stewart wins but has more whip cream on his face than in his mouth. Don is a more discriminating eater and though finishing last, doesn't have one spare ounce on his face. It doesn't really matter who wins, there isn't any prize, but the men like the competition. In turn, each man does the whip cream game, except Frank and Herman. We have to join them on the sidelines Mashing before we can get them to do the game.

Then I take Frank and Donna takes Herman. Side by side on the floor, on the black fur throw I use for just such occasions, we lay them flat on their backs and squirt baby oil onto their chests. They close their eyes and grimace because it's cold so we soothe, "We'll warm it up." We lay on their bodies, face to face, and started massaging their chests with our chests. Donna keeps falling to the side of Herman because he's so large she can't stay on top. After about forty-five seconds of this we turn our bodies around, sit on their chest and massage the oil back and forth, back and forth, sliding all over them with our bottoms for another minute.

Next, I apply extra red lipstick to my lips and get a black marker. Luckily, all the men have on white underwear. I apply red lipstick kisses on Frank's underwear band. Then, as he lay there oblivious of the next antic, I pull down his shorts and reveal his limp penis. I'd seen Laura do this at a party once and it'd gotten such a good-natured howl from the crowd I incorporated it into my show. As everyone looks on, I put two dots for eyes and a smiley face on the end of his penis with the black marker, pick up the shrunken member with the marker and bounce it up and down exclaiming, "Mr. Happy. Mr. Happy." The other men thunder with laughter and, usually, the man reddens, but Frank just lays there smiling. After a short length of time, I pull up his underwear and whisper, "the worst is over." I roll him onto his stomach. I then rip down his shorts again, exposing his bare buttocks, and with my handy marker draw a bullseye on his butt. Unbeknownst to Frank, because he can't see what I'm doing, I pull out a concealed dildo and hold it in my hands poking it into his butt cheeks to simulate anal intercourse. Butt cheeks usually tighten and the unfortunate participant fights to roll himself over, but not Frank. He just lays there laughing.

This is the grand finale. All these men have paid for this but how many will actually let us do it? Usually we can get one man to play the last game, perhaps two if someone wants to pay their buddy back for being teased in this way, but never more than that.

But this night, to my surprise, "I want a Happy Face, I want a Happy face," is echoed by all the men in the living room. Maybe it's a male-bonding thing. Everyone will have this experience and they'll be sworn to secrecy and therefore more connected than before, kind of like young boys becoming blood brothers. Maybe it's just a way to counteract their dreary, conservative career personae, but these men have surpassed the typical bachelor-party behavior of being embarrassed and ashamed at exposing themselves in front of their friends and have challenged my perceptions of older men.

Donna and I move from man to man performing oil massages and yes, Happy Faces and bull's-eyes all around. Frank and Herman continue to do the Mashed Potato on the sidelines and occasionally I stand and do it with them, laughing all the while.

The whole show and games take us two hours. We laugh, talk, do the Mashed Potato, and never once feel like we're doing anything out of the ordinary; just ten adults partially and fully nude having a good time. Before we leave, at their request, we take a picture of them all in their underwear, and Donna and I even join in for one, fully clothed. I also leave them the tape of rock-n-roll music they aren't familiar with, for a souvenir. We leave the Nasty Boys, invigorated yet dog-tired, each with two sets of Happy Faces, one on their face from their unusual Full Monty experience, and one drawn on their body.

* *

In these parties, as well as in the club, I was meeting this sensually playful side of myself I'd never known. It was a new relationship and most new relationships start out great. It's not until you spend time together that you begin to see things you don't like about the "other." My lascivious dark side was being released from my shadow bag and magnified in front of my eyes like the holograms I'd designed in laser electro-optics classes. I could look at myself from all angles. Initially the bachelor parties were wild and titillating. They were dirty in the that-gets-me-excited way because they felt so culturally taboo, but quickly they became grueling and too revealing.

Oftentimes we'd do back to back parties like the night in Santa Cruz. I'd nap in the middle of the afternoon trying to store energy for the night, then, hyping myself up with large cups of coffee, transform myself with makeup and hairstyle into Vixen, bachelor-party Diva. Focusing only on the dollar amount I could make, I'd have energy to perform the first show but we'd arrive at the second place exhausted, with oil in our hair and whip cream residue on our bodies that couldn't be entirely wiped away with sanitized baby wipes. Although we'd be met with an enthusiastic welcome, it was a chore to summon more energy when there wasn't any left.

I began to loathe some of the antics we'd engage in to make as much money as possible. Laura introduced and pushed the crowd to pay for dildo shows after all the other games had been played in order to squeeze every last dollar out of the men. We wouldn't tell them about this menu item at the beginning, then they wouldn't spend as much on the other games, but they'd usually scrape together more money for this, even after they'd professed they didn't have any. While I was willing to stand naked in a group of men wielding control, I felt conspicuously exposed inserting a rubber device into my vagina and pretending to like it. I was being the "bad girl," something my shadow side hungered for, and I was giving up parts of myself for acceptance, something the teenager within me had learned, but soon found that what I was going along with merely for money was repugnant to the slowly burgeoning consciousness of the adult within me. The first time felt naughty and tolerable, the novelty of it overriding my internal critic, but this act went beyond merely showing my body. This act felt dirty, as in distasteful, so I felt dirty. And sometimes the woman I had to work with seemed dirty, as in foul.

I liked working with Laura, but we were two blondes and every now and then the men requested a blonde and a brunette so Laura paired me with Donna as she had the night we had fun with the Nasty Boys. Laura mentioned once that Dona had in the past used heroin, and I wondered if she still did. Her face was no longer lively and attractive; occasionally her skin had a sickly pale or green tint. The men noticed this as well. I was embarrassed for her, and for myself for being her partner, when she had to beg and manipulate the men into playing games with her when they were drawn to me instead. Also, the men were offered and some paid in advance, for a girl on girl show so we had to pretend to be into each other. Though we never actually made skin to mouth contact, it's easy to hide what's going on with long hair in a dimly lit room, I didn't want to be anywhere near Donna's body, especially her nether region.

It took five months before I had my fill of the parties and the mayhem that came with them and quit. But before I did, I was fully exposed to an aspect of my subconscious I tried very hard to ignore—an innate desire to be one special girl for one special guy.

One evening while I was slithering around naked, dripping with baby oil, on a man who was soon to be married, I found myself wishing I could be the intended bride instead of the bachelor-party girl. This thought startled me, and I tried to will it away. I forced my smile to be bigger. I laughed harder. I tried to count the money I'd made so far. I looked over at Laura, grateful not to be alone. Yet my customer-service experience kicked in and forced me to look into his eyes again. That's what helped make money—the personal contact. Doing this I felt saddened with the realization that I was nothing but a freak show to him and his group. I was the girl they wouldn't take home to mother. Although we never had sex during parties, I was the proverbial girl they'd fuck but not marry. I didn't have their respect.

But then I didn't have my own.

I couldn't esteem, appreciate, or honor someone I didn't know. Externally I looked like a centerfold—the media-hyped image of perfection—internally, I was still disconnected, unacceptable, fearful, angry, shameful, guilty, and chaotic.

Although I'd briefly glimpsed myself with new eyes while looking at the photographer's pictures, daily I still couldn't see myself as anything other than inextricably flawed, so I lusted after the customers' approval. Once I wowed them with my body and moves, I impressed them with my past scientific accomplishments. The regard I received was positive. My self-esteem was based solely on their favorable reception, and how much money I earned was the principal gauge of this acceptance. In the two years I'd been working as a dancer, money had become a huge measure of value. Unlike regular jobs where you get paid biweekly or once a month and it's easy to distance your inherent value from what you do, money handed directly to me at the end of a dance undeniably tangled my personal worth with what I did to earn it.

After I quit doing bachelor parties, I was intent on making as much money as I could. In the San Francisco Gold Club we had to leave our bikini tops and bottoms on when doing dances, but I'd gotten comfortable with going topless and reasoned that if I could shed my top during dances, I wouldn't have to talk, wheedle, and cajole as much. Money would be easier and quicker. I'd heard that Las Vegas clubs were topless and open all night, so Stacy, a friend from the club, and I flew down to work.

The manager at Olympic Gardens hired us based on our appearance and experience, so we didn't have to audition. Each night we'd show up at the club early so our stage fee was minimal (if we arrived between 5 and 6 p.m., it might be fifteen dollars, between 6 and 7 p.m., twenty-five dollars, 7 and 8 p.m., thirty-five dollars, and so on) and stay as long as we could hold up, usually five or six in the morning. Often we'd arrive when the sun was still out and leave when the sun was up again—evening never existed. I'd mix an energy drink of Choline Cocktail, a powder supplement that contains choline combined with DMAE, Ginkgo Biloba, vitamins, and minerals, and we'd drink it throughout the evening. Our goal was to each make over a thousand dollars every time we worked, and we checked in with each other periodically throughout the shift to see how close we were getting to reaching it so we could go back to the hotel. After a twelve-hour shift on stilettos, we'd gorge ourselves on burgers and fries in the hotel restaurant, then fall into bed to sleep the day away.

The next night we'd do it all over again.

Stacey was about ten years younger than I and had an exotic look that attracted big spenders, but I'd typically make as much or more than her because my energy was unstoppable; I approached a lot more men. During the last song of my two-song stage dance one Las Vegas evening, standing topless in front of two men holding one-dollar bills, I saw Stacey, whom I hadn't seen in a few hours, approaching. She handed me a hundred-dollar bill and said, "It's from the man I'm sitting with," and pointed in the direction of their table. "Come over when you're done."

I nodded. A hundred-dollar bill. *You betcha*, I thought as I watched where she went.

When the second song of the set ended, I put my top on quickly and held onto my dress while I walked to their table. Against the wall on a love seat positioned between Stacey and another girl sat a man who appeared to be middle-eastern—short dark hair, olive skin and a large nose—with a protruding belly that strained against his pants and shirt. I thanked him for the tip, smiled broadly, pulled up a chair and became my vivacious character. I didn't notice at first, it was dark in their corner, but when my eyes adjusted I saw Stacey's black gloved hand on his crotch.

"That's all I had to do all night," she told me later. "He just kept feeding me hundreds." While I was seated with their group, not long—he wasn't feeding me hundreds—the manager walked up and said how delighted she was to see him again and that if he needed anything, just to ask. Though it was against club rules to touch the customers in such a way, it was obvious that he'd been there before by the way he was greeted and by the cordial way Stacey was treated by the manager the next few nights. I deduced he could have gotten away with plenty. (No business is going to turn away big spenders when their goal is to make money.)

Stacey wrestled with what to do the next night because the middle-eastern man wanted to meet and take her shopping. They'd arranged a place and time and she'd agreed although now she wasn't sure. But what woman wouldn't want to be taken on a shopping spree in high-end stores in Las Vegas? Although her sole motivation was money, she figured she could take some of the clothes back for refunds after he purchased them for her. She decided to skip work. She fixed herself up then took a cab to their meeting place.

He never showed.

I felt badly for her hurt feelings. No woman, or man for that matter, likes to be stood up. I listened to her lament, yet secretly gloated. Sure, I'd made my thousand-dollar goal each night, but she'd made two thousand the night before. If our money remained somewhat equal, I wouldn't feel less valuable than her.

Working in Las Vegas was profitable, but I couldn't rest well unless I slept in my own bed and just like the parties, it became too draining. Besides, it was expensive to travel there, stay, and eat. I only made three trips.

A pendulum stretched to one side will swing all the way to the other side when released and will continue to swing from side-to-side passing through center but not resting until the momentum has decreased with natural gravity. Likewise, my behavior also swung from one extreme to the other. Like an unrestrained child turned loose in a candy store running from one delicacy to another, gorging on new sights, tastes, and smells, feasting, I, too, was overindulging on music, lights, costumes, attention, money, and physical freedom I had within the club. Audaciously, I ran from man to man, displaying my body, sparkling with rhinestones, gathering money, and laughing without restraint every night until I became too full. Then, like the exhausted child satisfied and subdued for a short period of time willing to be passive and obedient, this new me slept during daylight while the sedate conservative me remained awake.

My rigid, dogmatic self refused to acknowledge this other, untethered self. During daylight, I hid from society and from myself the me that was revealed at night by dressing in large, comfortable, non-revealing clothes: a man's large black baggy sweat pants, a man's extra large faded black long sleeve shirt, and a black ball cap. I only went to the grocery stores or take-out restaurants for food, the drug stores for necessities, and the gym where I wore earphones isolating myself from others while pumping hard-rock music to energize me. During the day, I was still ashamed of my body and most certainly ashamed of what I was doing—teasing men for money and enjoying it. This was part of the forbidden feminine.

My new affair with this uninhibited self was in its beginning stages, and like any burgeoning relationship where I wanted to get to know someone better before I introduced them to family or friends, I unwittingly tried to keep my unrestrained self separate from myself until I knew it better. Since work was my social life, periodically I'd date men I met there, but the club magic and facade was eroded in the less-than-perfect light of day, and all wrinkles were exposed: in their shirts, in our faces, in my psyche. Within the club, the men met an unbridled woman prancing around almost completely naked, but outside the club, I refused to see myself as a sexual being. I most certainly didn't want them to see me *only* as a sexual being. The woman I portrayed in the club was just that, a woman I portrayed, like an actress; my voice was high, soprano-like as a young girl's, and I was more readily sweet and submissive. Outside work my voice was at least two octaves lower and while not being domineering, I was obviously in charge of my own life. I wouldn't be overtly sexual or have sex with these men.

The sedate, serious good girl didn't want to have anything to do with the sensually scintillating, extroverted bad girl. I was isolated not only in part from myself, but also from others. I had no friendships outside the strip club at this time, and only family on a long distance phone wire. I was lonely. But loneliness was another one of those feelings that I effectively disconnected from at an early age, and although I caught a glimpse of it at the bachelor party, it was only while talking with some of the men in the clubs that my pain was fleetingly mirrored back.

They'd become my mirrors—and I'd become theirs. I listened to and admired them, and they listened to and rewarded me. Searching their eyes for my okayness and wanting desperately to validate their existence, I always looked deeply into the men's eyes when I danced for them. On occasion, it made me squirm and anxious to be rid of them. In their blue, green, hazel, and brown eyes I'd see hope that maybe there would be something more. I'd see hope that just maybe we'd go out on a date, just maybe it could go beyond dinner. I'd see hope that just maybe their lives wouldn't be so empty, that just maybe I'd feel the same way. It was this hope that I couldn't bear to see. I didn't like regulars because they all hoped when they kept coming back. I was the magical nymphet their female perfection fantasies consisted of, and they were the attentive generous caretakers I desired.

An outspoken doctor from Dallas came into the club one evening, and as we talked he noted, "You can keep men at a safe distance in here."

He was right.

No one could get close to my heart in ten or twenty or even sixty minutes. The cheery facade I wore to play the part of seduction was rarely broken by the superficial conversation. One slow night however, I struck up a conversation with someone who didn't want to be in the club (he'd been coerced by his friend), hoping that if I started him talking, he'd change his mind about dances, and I could make some money any-way. The conversation turned to loneliness and dating, and he wanted to know why I was afraid of meeting people, why I was afraid of becoming intimate. He'd broken through my stoic hardwood veneer for a brief moment. This break could have repaired itself fairly easily with a quick glance around the room seeing other half-naked women, but when I learned he'd recently put his long-time companion, a dog, to sleep, tears welled in my eyes. My cats were my best friends.

I had to walk away.

Just as a helium-filled balloon hugging the ceiling will slowly descend as it loses air over time, these occasional phrases spoken to me, along with my momentary flashes of desire for myself to be with an other, released some of the hot air I'd been using to buffer and insulate myself from my own feelings. Like the head that had hovered above my body in that hotel room but then connected to feel fear for my safety, my head now descended to my body and connected to feel incredible abandonment and seclusion. It wasn't the men's hope I'd been seeing and squirming to get away from—it'd been my own.

A few months after returning from Las Vegas to San Francisco where we couldn't dance topless, but instead had to be creative with our conversation to entice men to give us twenty dollars to dance for three minutes in a bikini, the job again felt too difficult. After only a couple years, I was tired of having to initiate dialogue and be exuberant. The rote rhetoric I used to amuse and coax was emotionally and psychologically debilitat-ing. An actor on stage for eight hours breaking from my role only for a few minutes to pee or freshen makeup in the dress-ing room when absolutely necessary (if I was sitting with a good customer I didn't want to leave because I didn't want some other girl to entice him away), I grew weary enacting the same scene continually. Like syndicated *MASH* reruns that have aired for over twenty-five years, I knew all the lines and all the moves. I'd use my daily allotment of energy to stand in heels, pretend I was interested in conversation I really wasn't, and stretch, bend, and contort my body in ways that weren't usual.

I wanted quick cash.

Stan came into the Gold Club on a slow Sunday night. We met. We talked. I danced. He paid. When he came in the second time, it was a welcome surprise. I sat with him, and he again paid me generously to intersperse dancing with conversation. When he returned for the third time I knew it was more than coincidence.

We fell into a routine.

I'd welcome him, sit and catch up for a few songs, then ask him if I could dance, which he'd let me do. This worked well when it wasn't busy in the club, but when it was I'd get anxious and agitated watching other women making more money than me. I only worked three nights a week, and the few hundred dollars he was giving me in a night wasn't sufficient to monopolize all my time for the entire evening, yet a part of me enjoyed the steady, albeit intermittent, supply of money without having to work so hard. Impatience, irritation, and gratefulness battled each other within myself until I explained to Stan that when there were other men sitting alone, it was my job to approach them.

He was patient. He'd sit and wait for me to return.

He was loyal. He'd turn down attention from other dancers.

I wasn't looking for a relationship—with him. He was overweight, had a glass eye, and had been dominated by his mother, so he was socially inept. When you're seeing someone once or twice a week though, a natural progression is to learn about them. He began to share his life with me and I felt obligated to share my own. This behavior wasn't new. I'd felt pressured by men my entire life, usually for sex, and just like I'd given in to, or given myself up to, men in the past, I now gave away too much emotional energy to Stan.

Other dancers used regulars for money, regardless of what they felt or didn't feel for the men, and I tried to follow their example. I called him a few times where he worked to say, "Hi," but it felt insincere to pretend I was interested in him when I really only wanted to see when he'd be back so I could get his money. I certainly didn't want to spend time with him out-side the club, as others did occasionally to keep their regulars happy. He was a sensitive man who unabashedly shared him-self with me, and I genuinely cared about his feelings as if he were a lost puppy. Still, I didn't have the courage to explain all there would *ever* be between us was a club relationship because I didn't want to cut off his supply line of money. I was a greedy girl who was fearful she wouldn't make enough. However, he was one of the ones who hoped, and I didn't like using that hope against him. It was a game I felt very uncomfortable with.

The club had been slow for months, and I was tired of talk-ing. I thought it would be easier to make money dancing nude, but I'd heard stories about the nude clubs in San Francisco where girls were rumored to perform sex acts. I didn't want to do that.

I searched out and found an upscale club in Sacramento where no alcohol was served and no touching was allowed. Unlike Las Vegas, where I had prearranged flights and felt I had to stay even if I was tired and missed my own bed, I liked the thought of having control of when I could leave by simply getting into my car and driving a couple hours home. After an exploratory day trip, where I was hired by sight and experience again, I planned my stay, made reservations at a Motel 6, and packed my bags.

Although I wasn't privy to this insight at the time, in retrospect, the pattern is clear. I was still running away from difficult people and situations.

Standing naked on the runway that first day at Centerfolds in Sacramento, my arms in the air exposing myself in the large venue for bouncers, managers, and other girls, as well as customers, not just for a few private citizens in a house, I felt as free as a butterfly that finally gets to stretch its wings after spending months in a cocoon. The Who's Roger Daltry carefully crooning, "See Me, Feel Me," in their rock hit with the same title, comes to mind when I reflect on how the people, witnessing and applauding me that first day, helped my awareness expand. I was no longer ashamed of my body, no longer felt guilt. My body, every single inch of it, in whatever way I wanted to expose it, within this safe venue, was applauded. I could no longer deny it. I felt like the unabashed child who continues to throw its clothes off just because it feels good.

Still, I felt incredibly fatigued, isolated, and lonely in a Sacramento hotel where no other soul on the earth knew where I was. Unlike the years when as a laser service technician I'd call my mother from hotels throughout North America and we'd talk and laugh and I'd feel that at least *someone* knew where I was, there was no one to call. I knew my mother, and especially my father, didn't want to hear I was a nude stripper in Sacramento, California. Even within the club I had no one to talk to because many of the girls were as young as eighteen, since no alcohol was served, and they were cliquish and standoffish.

During one of the nights of my second excursion to Sacramento, Stan showed up unexpectedly at the club. I was delighted to see a friendly familiar face and quite flattered that he would drive all the way from the San Francisco Bay Area to see me. I danced topless for him at his table but when he suggested the chair dance, I hesitated. I'd only done one previously, and had been happy to, but now the fifty dollars for three minutes for what I had to do felt unsettling. It was an extremely fast way to make money though, so I couldn't not do it.

In none of the clubs I'd ever worked in before or after this one in Sacramento (about ten total), had I ever seen anything like this chair. The man sat in a luxurious recliner, then a wood platform slid into place and isolated his body; only his head was left sticking out. He couldn't move his hands up. It was on this wooden platform that I was to stand, dance, wiggle and sit—right at eye level. There was a pole to the side and I'd watched other girls and determined the sole purpose of that pole was to hang onto it as I slid my butt onto the floor, then lean against it for support. The basic allure of this mini stage was that it protected the dancer so thoroughly she could peel herself apart and expose her pink center. Why else would a man in a nude strip club pay fifty dollars for three minutes if it weren't to view some real woman's vagina up close and personal?

I did it.

Initially, a part of me felt defiantly wicked, like a sinful little child saying *I've got a secret and let me share it with you—just you and me*—but that quickly evaporated and gave way to feelings of shame and over-exposure. This was too intimate. No one else, not even myself, had ever seen me so close.

When he bought a second dance, though, the businesswoman within me thrilled, overriding my apprehension. Besides, I'd already done one song.

In Sacramento, I'd hoped my body would say it all, and there'd be no need for quick wit, snappy comebacks and the manipulative maneuvering I needed at the Gold Club, but because there was no alcohol served, I still needed to finesse and arm twist to make money. After a few trips, I quit traveling to Sacramento.

I saw Stan at the Gold Club a few months later, but I didn't even pretend to want to stick around. And he didn't want more than two dances after chatting. I moved on. He found a new girl.

Initially, the ultimate exposure in the dance clubs helped remove the chains that had bound me in a prison of self-castigation. I was showing off the only true possession I'd ever had but had denied, berated, punished, loathed, harmed, and neglected, and the people (mostly men but also women on occasion) were more accepting of me than I was of myself. Conversely, after only a few short years, this close examination and intense focus was draining instead of invigorating. Although I was gaining acceptance of my body through spending time with others' praise, it also magnified my insecurity. I grew weary applying instant tan and worrying about whether my butt had pimples on it. The crunch and sting of the botox needles I thought I needed to conceal my age, hurt. Physically it became torturous.

Also, the exaggerated socialization I exposed myself to every time I worked was like speed dating speeded up. Instead of twenty meet and greet dates in a few hours, on a good night, I not only had twenty to forty meet and greet dates, but I took these introductions and parlayed them into sensually intense exchanges. I'd plop into a chair at a table with men who had just seen me dancing at the table adjacent to theirs and say, "Next," warming them with a gregarious smile. Although this was a game I could play, it became emotionally depleting.

The job was now just that—a job.

And it perpetuated my isolation.

I *needed* silence. My work was exhausting, so during the days I spent time alone not talking to anyone but my therapist once a week, reading self-help books and thinking. Just as in order to nurture a friendship, an idea, or a philosophy we need to spend time educating ourselves about the subject of our interest, in order to befriend ourselves, our bodies, our thoughts, the totality of who we really are, we have to spend time with ourselves. Within the strip club, parts of myself were being mirrored that were long ago rejected: my body, my sexuality, my desire and need to be seen, my desire and need to be admired, my incredible loneliness. I began the education about myself by myself. I held the answers inside, but never one to trust that I could do anything correctly on my own, I decided to return to college.

EMBRACE

Morality does not consist of simply following other people's orders about how we should behave. . . . Choice lies at the heart of morality.

Ira L. Reiss
Solving America's Sexual Crises

To say I thought of returning to college on my own would be a lie. The truth is that like most things in my life, the decision was influenced by something outside myself—a man—more than likely my father, though he and I never discussed it.

Psychologists posit that we women search for our fathers in the men we yearn for and love as adults. It's uncanny how, upon reflection, an Englishman, Geoff, whom I fell hopelessly in love with, reminded me of my father in so many ways. Occasionally an aromatic mixture of male sweat and cigarettes wafted over me when I was in his company, and the recognizable smell transported me to my childhood and the comforting presence of my father. Also, looking back to that time in pictures, he resembled my father's mannerisms and dress. But the most obvious similarity was in his absence. He lived in

England so our meetings resurrected the excitement of happy homecomings just like those that occurred when my father returned from far away places. Unfortunately, this relationship also reconstructed the agonizing disconnect I felt every time he left for one of those foreign countries.

Sometimes Geoff and I would say goodbye and I'd wave to him then be left alone in the airport gate, wishing the gaping hole he'd walked through to get to his plane would spew him back out—legs, arms, and torso flying into my embrace. Other times, I'd wind my way through lengthy airport customs lines, my face wet with tears, distress pulled mercilessly from me on display for not only him, watching me through glass, but everyone else as well, as if I was an experiment in enduring human separation. This was *familiar*—the root of this word identical to *family*. And just as I'd had no choice as a child, I felt I had no choice in this love as an adult.

During my angry rebellious adolescence, sneaking out at night, skipping school, and disobeying him, my father, an army First Sergeant at the time, bellowed at me the same sentiment, I'm sure, that he directed at his young troops in training, "You don't have the brains of a crippled piss ant." I don't hold any malice towards him. I'm certain that, besides getting plenty of practice with his young GI's, he was also repeating, if not the exact same words, then the same sentiment he received from his parents when he was a child. We humans do that—repeat the ingrained messages we learn within our family of origin. But in order to counteract this criticism and prove to my father I was smart, I'd enrolled in, then excelled in technical school— even though I had no interest in science, optics, or electronics. Similarly, this Englishman who resurrected images of my father impelled me to return to college after he spoke the words, "You're not stupid; you're just uneducated."

I met Geoff on a fun, busy night at work, a night where my positive exuberance had warmed many hearts and loosened just as many wallets. They were often like that—the work nights. They were either filled with one uplifting happy encounter after another, or else they were filled with repeated rejection and struggle to pull a few measly twenties from a few men. This night had been pleasantly easy from the start, and the adrenaline kept my mind off my aching feet, hungry stomach, and sore throat. Although the crowd had thinned out significantly as it usually did at 1 a.m., one hour before closing, immediately after I put my cocktail dress on and left one table, I'd stand in front of someone new asking if I could dance. Since it was late I wasn't concerned about making small talk.

He speaks first, "Are you finally going to dance for *me* now?"

Every woman wants to be admired and sought after. This man's obvious attraction melts my strip club armor a bit and peps up my tired body. "Why yes I am," I say rather decidedly.

He takes charge again. "Not here, let's go over by the wall."

"Fine with me." The song booming from the loudspeaker has already started. It's easier to keep track of how much to charge if I start dancing at the beginning of songs.

He's interested in talking rather than just staring or trying to touch, so I turn and twist and smile, and we exchange words while I dance in front of him, his back against the wall. We chat easily. We're both writers. His English accent is exotic to my American ears. "You're not from here, are you?" I pry.

"No I'm not."

On the radio that day, I'd heard of a rock concert happening in San Francisco. "Are you here with a show?" I hopefully inquire as I move my body yet hold his attention with my eyes. For the brief time I lived in Wisconsin with my parents before I went to technical school, I'd been gloriously irresponsibly innocent as only the young can be, going to local bars every weekend, listening to live bands, dancing, drinking excessively, and making love. I'd forever associate the carefree feeling of those days with rock-n-roll. Perhaps I can feel it again.

"Yes, I am. How did you know?" he queries.

He isn't with the rock show I learn, but yes, he's here from England for a corporate show and he is indeed a sound engineer. His admission that at one time he worked for and traveled with Todd Rungren, living the rock-n-roll lifestyle, raises his allure.

I make a couple hundred dollars from him before we begin shooing everyone out the club doors for the night, but before he leaves he asks me if I can meet him the next day at Café Trieste, a coffee shop off Columbus in North Beach.

I hesitate. Men ask often, but I usually don't go.

"It's just coffee," he pleads. "You drink coffee right?"

I do, large quantities of it. Taken aback, pushed to make a decision quickly, I agree.

The next morning, I regret my decision but have no way to contact him and cancel.

When I walk in late (I thought I knew where the coffee shop was, but I really didn't), I see him sitting with his laptop, pounding away on the keys, a dozen thirsty red roses lying in a neat bouquet on the table.

"I didn't think you were going to show," he blurts, obvious pleasure in his voice.

He buys me a coffee, which I need badly, and we talk for a while. He's funny, engaging, attractive and has the cutest wire rim glasses; he reminds me of John Lennon. I'm pleasantly surprised that our conversation is easy. My experience has been that relationships started at night usually don't transfer well to daylight. I've been living in San Francisco almost a year and life has already become usual with my work routine and lack of social activities. This man is unusual.

"Let's enjoy the sunshine," he suggests, so we pack up our belongings and walk the few blocks to Washington Square Park. He lays his coat down on the ground for me to sit on, in a manner reminiscent of genteel chivalry I'd only ever read about in Harlequin romances or seen in medieval English movies. We talk about nothing and everything. He's married, but separated, has one daughter, and is working in a company and job he no longer enjoys but doesn't know how to transition away from. I've made a hard transition, from technician to dancer, so I relate my own joys and troubling experiences. He's silly and serious, intertwining facts with humor. In the bright June afternoon, it's refreshing to laugh and be with a man without having to take off my clothes and entertain him.

I relax.

Everyone, it seems, is like us, escaping for a few moments the confines of their tiny rooms and apartments in the crowded Italian North Beach area. We're surrounded by people walking, jogging and reading, and dogs barking and playing Frisbee, yet for that moment, we're separate. I forget my loneliness, and he forgets his responsibilities.

I have to leave. I have a commitment to attend a women's group in Oakland but agree to meet him later at an Irish bar close to my apartment.

Later, not even a full twenty-four hours after we've met, we rendezvous for the second time. I walk into the boisterous bar, find his welcoming face, and sidle up next to him. He orders himself a second pint and me a Seven-up. The crowded nightspot forces us close together. I'm not drinking, but I feel high.

After our drinks, we leave the noisy bar and take a walk along Aquatic Park. I'd like to say with certainty that the moon is full, but all I know for sure is that I'm full of deep interest and lust for this foreigner who is becoming more handsome as the minutes tick by. He pulls laughter from me again by hopping around on one foot in the sand while making light of his brain as having been fed meat from tainted cows; Mad Cow Disease was then constantly in the news having just been discovered in England.

I'm cold, it's after midnight, and though I'm not sure what I want to do with this man, I'm enjoying his company. I invite him to my apartment.

We sit side by side in my eight-hundred-dollar apartment that provides a million-dollar view of San Francisco Bay. When his hands finally reach for me and his lips kiss mine, his tongue probing slowly, we both feel the heat from the afternoon sun return. I'll let him lead me anywhere.

He stops.

He moves me to sit in front of him, and as I lean against him for support, we both stare into the black night and twinkling lights of Marin. He wraps me in his arms, and I feel his warm breath in my ear as he speaks to me from behind. The last bit of hesitation I have drains through my body and out my toes. My dream man has always been someone who, although he knows he can have sex with me, doesn't, so in his holding back, he becomes my dream man, my knight in shining armor, my savior.

When the sun slithers slowly over the Berkeley Hills, glides across the bay and spills in through the picture window that spans an entire wall of my tiny one-bedroom apartment on Northpoint, it's time for him to go. He has a scheduled flight to New York to put on another corporate show and then he'll be flying back to England, with no plans to return to San Francisco ever again.

I kiss him gently at the front door and watch him disappear down the stairs to his undisturbed room at the Holiday Inn where he'll grab his bags quickly and make his way to the shuttle for the ride to SFO. I watch his back move farther and farther away, getting smaller and smaller until he vanishes altogether. I sit, alone in my single person's apartment on my single person's futon couch, and watch the single rotating beacon from Alcatraz going round and round illuminating the tiny tear in my heart. I gather Dinky, my trusted feline companion, into my arms.

He's left a phone number, but why?

I sleep the day away, waking only in time to get my shower and gather my bags and costumes for work. Sometimes I walk through North Beach, China Town and the Financial District to get to the club on Howard, but tonight my body and soul are weary, so I ride the bus. Acutely aware of smothering strangers sitting to my right and standing on my left, every time a new person squeezes onto the already packed transport, I become smaller. I grit my teeth as I watch the grimy city streets filled with blowing trash roll by through the greasy windows. I crave the club chaos of pulsing lights, beating music, men who smell of alcohol, men who will tell me I'm beautiful, men coming through and going out the front door. Their coming and going I can handle.

In the dressing room, I lament about finding, then losing the man who I'm sure is the love of my life. Another dancer, Mandy, speaks up, "You can go to New York."

She's right! I have money and free time whenever I want.

Unable to wait until I return home that night, I pile my quarters up and place them on the pay phone shelf at work so I can call his mobile phone. I leave a message asking if I can come visit him at his hotel in New York. When I get home there's a blinking light on my answering machine. "Yes!"

A last minute flight to New York from San Francisco isn't cheap, but for the first time in my life I don't care about money. I fly all night and arrive at LaGuardia at 6 a.m., energized even after the sleepless red-eye. I grab my bags, jump into a cab and sit in the back while large brown tenement buildings, freeways, and graffiti I've never seen before whiz past me on my way to Manhattan.

He's told the front-desk concierge I'm to be let into his room, but the men behind the check-in desk haven't gotten the message and they can't get him on his phone. Exasperated, dealing with an irate woman in their lobby, they put me into another room until Mr. Eaton returns and can verify that yes, I'm his guest.

I vigorously shower away the more than eight hours worth of grime from airports and recirculated plane air, think about putting makeup on but dismiss it, then fill my hungry stomach and empty heart with waffles and cartoons. Too excited to fall asleep I nonetheless lay comatose from lack of it.

Knock, knock, I hear faintly.

I bolt out of bed to open the door.

He's standing on the other side ready to rescue me from the loneliness of a New York hotel room and a city I know not a soul in.

I move into his room and sleep soundly all afternoon.

Looking out over Central Park, directly across the street from our room, the sight of black buggies and aroma of horse droppings shift me to another world. During the next few days, we walk among crowds of people on busy streets, holding hands tightly so as not to be disconnected. We ride to the top of the Empire State Building and hoot together during a simulated roller coaster ride, ecstatic at how much we both love roller coasters. We look down from the World Trade Center Observation Deck and exclaim over streets filled with endless lines of yellow cabs, so many in fact, they resemble tiny erasers in a row. We eat hot dogs from street vendors.

One evening during our full three days together, we come upon a crowded sidewalk and learn that the Olympic committee has planned to pass the 1996 torch right in front of us as a celebration of our union. I climb on top his shoulders and watch from my perch, just as I climbed on boyfriends' shoulders as a younger woman to clap, dance, and soak up midday Georgia sun during outdoor rock concerts. The sounds of cars honking become background music to our seductive dance. The humidity of New York summer sheathes me in glistening desire. The Hollywood movie version will show coming attractions with impassioned kisses and hesitant fingers unbuttoning his dress shirt. There will be a quick camera cut away returning to the heroine glowing between luxurious sheets in a bed she doesn't have to make, waiting for her man to return to take her out to expensive dinners.

Reality steals into my fantasy though when we meet a friend of his he hasn't seen since his rock-n-roll days. While they drink and reminisce, their conversation gets louder even though we're the only patrons in the small street-corner bar.

I'm bored. What am I doing in a bar wasting time? Why am I with a person who sits in bars? I'm in a strange city with a strange man and there's nowhere else to go. *He's cute, and I want him desperately.*

I maintain a contact high and shrug my discomfort off. I can't see past the fix. I'm addicted to the high I feel with him. Through the usual two to three drinks he has with each meal, I get to vicariously relive the effervescent slushy haze that has always helped me master my feelings.

The night before we're to separate, I lash out at him. "Why?! Why have you been so damn charming and complicit," I rage. He's going to leave me again just as they all have.

He soothes. We talk. We coo. After we make tender, hopeful love we watch *Babe* on pay per view. I let myself succumb to the childhood fantasy that I can do anything—even make a relationship happen with a man who lives half a world away.

On the cab ride back to LaGuardia, there's none of the excitement and enthusiasm I felt days earlier, but we snuggle close and devise loose plans, trying to figure out how we can see each other again. After hugging and kissing me at my airport gate, he scurries to his. I stand holding onto my memories and souvenir umbrella that we purchased from a street vendor one afternoon when we were caught in the rain. I lean on the sturdy pole that holds a black canvass large enough to cover two people but that is oversized for one. I watch his back get smaller until it vanishes altogether as he weaves in and out of the crowd, moving away from me.

Our destinations lay twenty-five hundred miles in opposite directions and for each mile we're to be separated, I shed a tear. Unwittingly, I've recreated my familiar pattern of love then loss.

Throughout the next nine years, Geoff and I whisper heartfelt loyalty to each other, unleash vehement criticisms, break up, fall silent for years at a time, then reunite. In phone calls, I express ever-lasting love and longing that can't come back to hurt me because I'm already alone and wanting. In e-mails, I express anger and distress, distancing myself from the guilt and discomfort of even expressing my anger, and shielding myself from rejection if he comes back in writing to say that he, too, is angry. Whereas some people use the anonymity of e-mail to hide, I use it to express my deep feelings in ways I've never done before. Nothing I say or write can hurt me or make me more alone.

It was early in our relationship, one month after we fell in love in New York, when he returns to San Francisco to spend ten days with me, that he remarked, "You're not stupid; you're just uneducated." It didn't hurt me at the time. He'd meant it as an explanation of my ignorance around art and history, but it got me thinking about school again.

In school, I knew the rules.

I enrolled in Vermont College in Montpelier in 1997, at the age of thirty-seven. I was used to setting my own work schedule, and in this college I could design my own program of study, work independently, and still keep my preferred schedule. However, I realize now that by attending a school on the opposite side of the United States from where I lived, I continued my pattern of creating distance from others. For the six-day residencies, I flew into town, met and quickly became friends with other students, then left just as quickly, before they really knew me or I had an opportunity to know them. This was a safe way for me to begin testing my okayness as a stripper in the world without having to "come out" on my own home turf. I read, studied, and wrote extensively my opinions and analyses of books by authors like Nancy Mairs and Susie Bright, who wrote about bodies and sexuality. In Gerda Lerner's *Creation of Patriarchy,* I learned about matriarchal lineage before women were placed into categories as either good or bad. Through reading Merlin Stone's *When God Was a Woman,* I learned about goddess worship before the world evolved into the popular modern-day religious view of one male god. I read books about women and current culture's influence on our way of thinking, such as *The Beauty Myth* by Naomi Wolf, *Where the Girls Are* by Susan Douglas and *Between Women* by Luise Eichenbaum and Susie Orbach. I wrote about what I was studying and learning and mailed this, along with my own writing, to an advisor who remained invisible to me, and whom, if I repulsed, offended, or disagreed with, I didn't have to see. My words returned to me with red marks in a manila envelope.

In the same manner I'd kept myself distant from Geoff and my college constituents, I kept myself distant from my female coworkers at the club. Throughout my life I'd heard sweeping generalizations made by women about other women: women are catty, gossipy, petty: they're backbiters. Perhaps I adopted a twist on the familiar old cliché, "if you can't beat 'em, join 'em," to *if you can't join 'em, beat 'em*, when I struggled in eighth grade as the new girl trying to make friends with Maureen and Kristy. For much of my adult life, I've felt in competition with women to be more beautiful, thinner, richer, or younger. I've felt either jealous of other women (and lower on some imagined scale of worth), or I felt superior to them. I've rarely felt equal to them.

Today, I see that I could have subconsciously been competing for the man, something women in prehistoric times needed for physical survival, and in later centuries, were conditioned to do for financial survival. Modern-day media has historically fed into this mindset with such rivalry-splashed headlines as Elizabeth Taylor "stealing" Eddie Fisher from Debbie Reynolds, to that of the late princess Diana and Camilla Parker Bowles competing for Prince Charles and the more recent, tabloid celebrity melodrama that chronicled Angelina Jolie beating out Jennifer Aniston for Brad Pitt's affection.

I, too, once had a rival.

Ten years before I'd met Geoff, when George wasn't speaking to me after I'd slept with his roommate in a jealous drunken haze, I started spending more time at the gym. Casual acknowledgement of a short thin woman with a pinched yet friendly face and high hair reminding me of my grandmother's, quickly turned into casual hellos spoken in passing, then longer conversation. One afternoon, while taking a break from my own exercise set, I stood talking to her as she did ab crunches on a machine. She nonchalantly asked, "Are you the same Susan who dated George?"

"Yeah," I blurted, anxious to talk about him, yet ashamed. Did she know about my bed hopping with his roommate?

"I'm Noreen," she went on. "I dated him off and on for two years."

I searched my memory. Was Noreen one of the names on the Christmas list I stole a peek at when I snooped in his dresser?

Neither of us were dating him or anyone else at the time, and our shared resentment of his playboy lifestyle and jealousy towards any woman he was sleeping with bonded us as instant companions. We compared notes of his habits—in bed and out. George had brought out the animal passion within me, and I can only assume in her as well (we didn't delve deeply into each other's sexual activities), and like two wounded animals we jabbed at the source of our injuries. We made him our focus, plotted against him, and even joked about egging his house. The old cliché, *hell hath no fury like a woman scorned*, doesn't compare to two women scorned united in a single purpose. For a spring holiday we sent an anonymous card stating he was evil and despised.

We confided in each other we were happy to be rid of him.

When I went to her home to have dinner and watch a movie, I scoped her place out knowing he'd spent time there. I was relieved that, although she owned a home and I didn't, it was merely a mobile home—small. I pictured him there, smiling, using his seductive moves. Did she fulfill his sexual fantasies like I had? Similar to a late-night TV wrestling personality masked and garbed in a flashy outfit with a name something like "Avenger," I smiled into her face hoping to conceal my identity and real purpose—to spy. I tried to imagine what he saw in her smaller frame, wrinkled face, and sarcastic tone and inwardly felt superior because she was ten years older than me. My lust for him, though never *really* diminished although I confessed to her it had, was temporarily quieted with the knowledge that at least she wasn't sleeping with him either.

Months after meeting and becoming fast friends with Noreen, when George surprised me and came back saying he'd date only me, I'd won the competition. With his drugs, go-fast Harley, and our late-night sessions, I had no more energy to feel guilt for being disloyal to our previous mutual hatred of him. I dodged her phone calls until I couldn't avoid her any longer.

We ceased talking. I was sleeping with the enemy—and enjoying every minute of it. I'm sure she'd have done the same.

With this history and mindset, it's no wonder that for the first two years I worked in the dance club I didn't talk much or socialize with the other women. It wasn't merely affection I was competing for; like women of the early twentieth century, my survival literally depended on how much money I could get from the men. I put on my makeup and fixed my hair at home and spent as little time in the dressing room or talking with women on the club floor as possible. Every night I worked I was required to parade with the rest of the women in evening gowns, and this nightly occurrence, three times a night in fact, reinforced this competition between us. It became second nature to not only gauge my feelings about myself by how much the men paid me, but also by how well I did or didn't do compared to other dancers. Unlike the bachelor parties where there was only one other woman to measure myself against, within the club there were hundreds.

The first year I worked, while I also had my Lab job, I thought of this new job as play and every night I went, I had a good time. The law of the universe works on attraction, and since like energies attract and money is a positive exchange of energy, this carefree, unencumbered, pleasant me attracted men and their money. There'd be the occasional rejection, but I'd be able to brush it off and keep going. I didn't take it personally. My identity was still based in being a brainy girl—a scientist.

Once I quit the Lab, my identity was based in being a dancer. It's chic to say "It's what I do, it's not who I am," but realistically we're a culture of people whose identities are based in what we do and how much we have. Not so successful nights would start like any other. I'd plaster a smile on and use the cheery seductive words I always used, but I'd get turned down. Now, one rejection doesn't a bad night make, so I'd brush that one off and go on to the next man. Then the next. Then the next. While this was happening I'd look around and see other women getting dances and begin to fear that I was washed up, done as a dancer, unable to make any more money. I'd begin to feel dejected, inferior, ugly, old. These thoughts would, in turn, send my esteem and confidence spiraling even lower. I'd become dispassionate and sullen. Now, if positive attracts positive, likewise, negative attracts negative. I'd slink from one man to the next trying to hide my desperation. At this point, I wouldn't have the confidence to approach anyone new, so I'd keep returning to the polite men who told me "maybe later." I'd return to them over and over hoping they'd change their mind, hoping for some crumb of affection as measured in their acceptance and money, similar to the very way I'd hoped as a young girl someone would love me. But they didn't. Occasionally some honest man would let me know he'd just said "later" because he hadn't been able to say "no." At some point, miserable and low, I'd give up and go home. Eventually I learned, after many years, to give up early, go home and get a good night's rest. The next time would be better.

In order to keep returning to such a competitive environment, I developed what from the outside might have looked like confidence, but wasn't. Confidence comes from the inside, and I had no substance inside. Instead, I developed arrogance.

Whereas confidence elicits an internal dialogue something along the lines of, "I know who I am, and if you can accept me great; if you can't, that's okay too," arrogance generates internal dialogue along the lines of, "you must see me as great because that's the only way I'll feel okay." This arrogance grew into an attitude and internal mantra similar to, "Do you know who I am?" in order to insulate myself. This arrogance I had developed to mask my feelings of inferiority and return to a workplace that occasionally felt hostile, proved to be an effective armor against rejection. Unfortunately, it also kept me isolated and distanced from other dancers.

The most difficult admission for my separation from the other women I worked with for so long is that I feared what they were doing. I'd been indoctrinated to think that being overtly sexy was wrong, so it stood to reason that getting money for being sexy was abhorrently wrong. I couldn't think of myself as indecent, I wanted so desperately to be a good girl, so I imagined myself to be superior. *I'm not like they are*, I thought. *I've had highly skilled jobs. I have a brain. I don't need this job. I'm not desperate for money or men,* was some of my internal chatter so I could feel better than the women with whom I worked. Also, while the me I saw reflected in the men's eyes was beautiful and revered, the women reflected qualities of myself I didn't want to acknowledge and had rejected: my sensual body, my love of money, my need to be admired, my need for men's attention. Everything I'd banished into my shadow bag, all the undesirable characteristics of myself my ego wasn't able to consciously accept, I projected onto those other women. If I stayed away from them, I stayed away from me. My conscious thoughts couldn't be, *I'm a lascivious girl who enjoys teasing men sexually*. Instead, I could live with, *These other women are overtly sexual, but I'm different*.

Ironically, at the same time, they appeared to be okay with their lives. And my life too was proceeding well. My decision to be a stripper didn't feel like it was impacting me negatively.

Despite the fact that dancing was now a job, I approached it with enthusiasm and enjoyed the nightly challenge and competition much like I'd competed with men in technical school. I reasoned that the nonstop dialogue and physical exhaustion of standing on stilettos for seven hours every night while twisting and contorting my body were trade offs for the freedom my dancing career allowed. I worked only when I wanted and had free time like I'd never experienced as an adult before. By day I was contemplative, serious, and earnest, while by night I was submissive, attentive, and coquettishly cute. The wall my ego had erected to keep my dichotomous selves separate from each other still remained intact although it was becoming more difficult to live one way by day and another by night.

In college I was exploring critical thinking and analysis, and as I turned these new skills inward and began questioning my preconceived judgments about my supposed wickedness and lack of morality, my curiosity about the other women increased. Under the guise of interviewing them solely for a book for a school project, my subconscious mind allowed me to remove more of the heavy solid bricks I'd used to erect the wall against these women, and ultimately, myself. As they opened their homes and their lives to me, I opened my heart to them. What had once been prejudice against them because of ignorance and fear now became understanding and affection as a direct result of spending time with them and being educated about their lives and circumstances. I listened attentively and found our commonalities. I found them to be likeable. It was through the graciousness of these women in their twenties and thirties, students, single moms, artists, and entrepreneurs, that I relaxed within the strip club venue and found myself to be normal and likeable as well. I even started to have fun with the women during work, joking on a good night, lamenting on a slow evening, and learning female tips I'd never known, like how to apply makeup. The formal education I was getting through my studies at Vermont College along with the experiences and insights I was receiving in the club helped me stop fearing my coworkers in direct proportion to how I was becoming less fearful of my sensually-expressive self.

In addition to the academic and historical writings mentioned earlier, I read personal essays by other great writers like E.B. White and Joan Didion then found my way to Toni Morrison's first book, *The Bluest Eye*, where I received the greatest gift of all. The Nobel-prize winning novel written in 1970 illuminated the concept of choice. Morrison's tragic story of a little girl's innocence and horrific abuse eloquently weaves characters who are unconsciously driven and influenced by learned behaviors. The main character's father, Cholly, had been a victim of parental rejection and abuse, and in his need for love and recognition, he married and attempted a "normal" life. But he didn't have the tools for a normal life. All he'd known was abuse and that's what he perpetuated. Not that I perpetuated physical abuse as this character did, but I did identify with his confusion of not knowing how to be in relationships.

And I identified with Pecola, the central character. Pecola did not choose to be born black, poor, and what the narrator calls, ugly. She did not choose to be born into a family full of abuse and dysfunction. She is envious of those who seem to have "perfect" lives and believes that if she looks the part, she will have love and admiration. She obsesses about having Caucasian blue eyes, an external attribute she perceives society honors that would solidify wealth, happiness, and love for her. As a child, Pecola's only choice for a better, more equitable world was to dream. I also had no choice as a child about when and how often my father left our family and went to war—or even if he'd return. I had no choice but to be continually uprooted and moved from one Army base to another. I had no choice but to leave friends. I too dreamt about being someone else.

As children, our brains are growing as our bodies are, but unlike our bodies, our brains do not grow according to one specific map. Every healthy adult will have 206 bones and a right heart chamber pumping blood to the lungs and a left heart chamber pumping blood to the rest of the body, but our brains do not develop neurotransmitters that travel predetermined paths. The brain's development is completely influenced by our external environment and our ego-stage development, and it is so complex that there are entire psychologies and numerous theories devoted to the study of these influences and results. As adults we have the mental capacity to reason and change our way of thinking and impact our own lives, but we may not have the ability. Unless we're conscious of our motivations and actions, we may unknowingly perpetuate or relive childhood hurt or trauma in an attempt to heal it or we may simply unconsciously act and react in the present based on what we learned, experienced, and reasoned as children.

In order to say that we really choose something as adults, we must distinguish between conscious and unconscious choice. The disquieting aspect of unconsciousness though, is that if you don't realize you're functioning unconsciously, you can't begin to be conscious. In other words, before you can ask for something and get it, you have to realize you don't have it—and that you want it. What I consider to be "real choice" is unavailable to adults without recognition and education. As evidenced in the first story about Geoff in this chapter, I continued to live my life unconsciously; I had no real choice. Today I see the futility in a long-distance relationship. Back then, I wasn't able to. Today I'm aware that was the only way I *could* carry on a relationship.

My awakening to myself and my consciousness occurred slowly and in stages. As a young woman, I didn't understand why I behaved in ways that caused me pain. I just knew I felt indecision, confusion, turmoil, fear, and anger. I hurt. Before I got sober, I knew I hurt from traveling too much, not having any friends, engaging in acts that I regretted and caused me humiliation the next day, and eating so much my stomach ached. Next, I knew I hurt because I wanted love but was tired of being with men who didn't really like me and where the only times we were harmonious was when we were having sex. Once I sobered up and became a dancer, I continued to perpetuate my learned way of being in relationship with myself, superficially and externally viewed through others' eyes. It wasn't until I was in pain, looked closely at my behavior and took responsibility for it that I was able to make conscious choices and examine the overgrowth that made my internal forest. And the only way out of a forest is through it.

After my second visit to Vermont College to choose my studies and advisor for the next semester, a banker-turned-contractor bought the twelve-unit apartment building I was living in and started remodeling it. Whereas the noise from San Francisco's Wharf tourist area and Hyde Street's cable car lines had always been loud, the construction noise and physical invasion into my surroundings were now unbearable. Workmen dropped tools, erected ladders, and spit outside my windows in the morning hours when I should have been deep in slumber. I was unable to sleep, unable to concentrate on my schoolwork, and consumed with anxious fear. If I wasn't rested, I couldn't work. If I couldn't work, I couldn't pay my rent. I teetered on the edge of insanity, crying during the days and trying to get rest in futile attempts.

Fortunately, in my recent residency in Vermont, I'd met a man I fell in lust with who lived in Nevada City, California, only a three-hour drive from me. I started spending more time than I naturally would have in the Sierra foothills with my new boyfriend in a desperate attempt to escape the chaotic building. It was while retreating to his home that I began to accept my nature in the solace of nature. One day I took a solitary walk in the woods. As I cautiously entered into the wilderness that surrounded his home, I nervously made mental notes of landmarks so I could find my way back out, fully conscious of my isolation and in fear of what lay within. I listened closely for the odd sound that might alert me to bears, lions or coyotes, wild animals I'd been told did exist in these woods. The forest had always been a dark scary place to me, reinforced or perhaps manufactured in movies like *Deliverance*, and *The Blair Witch Project*. I was frightened as to what wild creature I might find there. But it was daylight—I only found myself.

The small streambed that I followed to avoid getting lost, waited in anticipation of winter snow as my tentative steps crackled the fallen gold and rust leaves. I selected a redwood so large I couldn't get my arms around its girth. I hugged it, my cheek pressed close. My tears fell onto its bark as I listened to and received its wisdom. I looked up, but I couldn't find the tops of these giants that stood silent and patient. I marveled at how they were grounded into the earth, standing solid, sturdy, and stoic. I noted the thickness, length, and intricacy of the exposed roots. I cried for the girl who didn't have any roots. I cried for the girl who hadn't stayed in one place long enough to shed her leaves only to have them return to the earth and compost to nourish her growth again. And I cried for the girl who hadn't known any different about life, love, sex, dreams, her body, her spirit. I watched the ants that built entire communities on the weathered bark and felt their comfort and safety living on a steadfast object that was rooted. I was in awe that although the trees were rock-like and fixed, they were free; their branches moved. They'd stood their ground, had existed through all the seasons of their lives and continued to breathe, grow, and support other life. In their rootedness lay their strength. Each one had its place and was unique.

Then I realized the trees encased in squares of dirt surrounded by cement in the city were caged. The people living above the asphalt were caged in inflexible mortar and brick. I realized I was caged. No wonder some of my favorite music to dance to on the stage were rock songs about breaking free: Soundgarden's "Rusty Cage," with hard-driving lyrics about running, Creed's "My Own Prison," Smashing Pumpkins' "Bullet with Butterfly Wings" with a repeating chorus, "just a rat in a cage." My eternal struggle was to break free from the confining bars I'd erected in my mind.

In the filtered sunlight of the Northern California forest and the spring and fall in Vermont, I began to sprout roots that crept into the shadowed crevices of who I really was. But like a frightened child asking a grown-up to check the dark places under the bed and in the closet to make sure there are no monsters, I had to check with others. I still lived by external validation, so I now took the wild scary parts of myself I kept hidden in the darkness of the club and exposed them three thousand miles away from my home. When the fact that I worked in a strip club didn't scare my advisors or fellow students, I brought what I considered to be my monsters out of the closet in the presence of two people I loved and whose approval I'd sought but whose rules I'd rebelled against—my parents.

In my last semester, I'd been writing essays about my strip club life and planned to present pieces of these honest portrayals in an hour-long presentation to students and faculty as part of my graduation requirement. Bouncing ideas off my classmates, I'd come up with the title, "Getting Naked with Susan Bremer," and the buzz created on campus over my presentation nourished my ego yet frightened my sense of propriety. To symbolize my transformation, I planned to start out fully covered in a Japanese silk kimono that had embroidered butterflies on it. Next, I'd do some clever costume changes behind a screen while reciting essay pieces and a monologue. I'd end with myself dressed exactly as a Barbie I'd place on the podium next to me while I read, "A Real Live Doll," a treatise on being anatomically perfect but superficially motivated.

As I artfully peeled away layers of clothing to highlight the essays I was reading that November day in 1998, I exposed myself through words, something far more terrifying to me than exposing my body. I was buffered from the fear of rejection by my parents, who'd driven from Wisconsin to Vermont to be present, by the applause and rapt attention of the packed conference room. They'd known what I was doing for years, but we'd never discussed it. Their faces, when I dared to look in their direction, were also attentive, but in brief glances I couldn't decipher what they were thinking. My mother's lips were neither smiling nor drooping in shameful retreat. My father's face wasn't smiling either, yet his forehead wasn't set in authoritative disgust. I wished they'd had large numbered cards held high above their heads to indicate how they thought. No. Not *how* but *what* they thought. But they didn't. I continued through my rehearsed delivery. In the congratulatory rush afterward, we hugged, and though nothing I read that day was ever talked about in detail, I knew they were proud. At the graduation party the school threw the next night, they drank champagne, danced, and mingled with the other people.

I'd successfully passed through another stage in my internal liberation. I'd made the conscious choice to present an entertaining play on words and rhetoric, and though I'd been extremely nervous, creativity that had been freed and grown within choreographed strip-club routines resulted in the changes of clothing and maneuvering behind a screen that distracted me from the real unveiling—my thoughts and my truth. I exposed myself first in academia to strangers. When they accepted me, I exposed myself to my parents, people closer to my home and my heart, and they acknowledged and accepted me also.

But for the first six years I danced, *I* never acknowledged and accepted a crucial part of me—sexuality. The upscale gentlemen's clubs perpetuated this denial by advertising for and calling the dancers "entertainers." In everybody's mind, it's more acceptable than "stripper" and more sophisticated than "exotic dancer."

When an editor for *Men's Health* questioned me in an e-mail, "Don't you think your job is about sex?" during a time when I was journaling my club experiences and sending them to him, I was stunned. I honestly never thought about it. Tempting men and getting their money was so unconscionable that I, up to that time, could only acknowledge that I was an entertainer, I put on a show. That's all I allowed myself to be aware of even though I'd heard the rumors of sexual explicitness and misbehavior from other dancers and customers.

Similar to waking up from an exquisite dream, reality lumbered in slowly. I realized that although I wasn't having sex with myself or anyone else in the club, I was using my body and implied sexuality to make money.

"Yes!" I could finally admit my job was about sex.

I was aware.

I understood.

And once my mind acknowledged this, my body could too.

Still, I became conscious of my innate physical responses in much the same way as my safety in the hotel room—by accident.

I'd danced three songs in a row, it was late, and I was tired. The man seated in front of me was kind and respectful and had kept his hands to himself, so I detached from what I was doing, and instead, while staring at the lighted water tubes with floating bubbles that illuminated our area, thought what new dance moves to make. Madonna oozed about being "your lover," in "Justify My Love," from the loud speakers attached to the two-story ceiling. Trying to give my tired feet a break I did something I'd seen the other girls doing but had never tried before. I rested my left knee on the couch between his legs, kept my right foot on the floor and lowered myself.

I stood back up immediately.

My heart pounded and my eyes quickly scanned the room to see if anyone else noticed my involuntary jerk upright. No. All the men seated on couches and the women dancing for them were involved in their own fantasies. The man seated in front of me continued to stare at my unseen nipples through the skimpy bikini top.

I expected thundering judgment from the heavens, but there was none. I expected accusatory fingers pointed my way and the entire club floor to come to a complete stop in recognition of what just happened, but it didn't. I continued to smile and move my body in a provocative way. I turned my back to him and with a slight arch, rounded out my bottom, lifted my long blonde hair, and let it fall to sweep my lower back.

When I'd sat down to straddle his leg, I'd planned to lean in close, stretch my arms around his neck and bring my cleavage close to his nose. But when I settled my weight, I was startled and unnerved. My clitoris felt pressure. My brain was shocked. My body was sexually charged. I didn't sit down like that again for the remaining two hours of the night.

After the club closed, I dressed and drove the ten miles home in silence. Though aroused earlier, I felt only exhaustion as I pondered my reaction. What did it mean? Did it mean anything at all? What did this new occurrence say about me? Did it say anything at all? Had I crossed that line of impropriety only to fall deeper into a lascivious abyss never to return as a person who could walk amongst the day people with her head held high? Was I an awful woman destined to be shunned by good girls and nice men? Or was it simply a natural physical response, not indicative of my character and morality at all?

Even with consciousness and awareness of one's self, the journey to further enlightenment isn't linear but instead resembles a spiral. As we grow toward greater understanding, we continue to be confronted with new opportunities that resemble experiences we had in our past, and they challenge us to choose new behavior or regress to old, outdated, past behavior. The journey to recover my body completely would still take many years, and today I see it may never be entirely finished, but my consciousness surrounding my body had been raised that night. The fact that I'd conducted my life solely for others' approval had been a barrier to myself. The strip club had provided a safe haven for me to awaken slowly and spend time learning about and accepting myself as mirrored and reflected through other's eyes, but it was time to experience myself. No more would I automatically wonder, "How do *you* feel? Am I making *you* happy? What do *you* think of me?" Instead I would begin to ask, "What does my body say to *me*? How does this feel to *me*?" The aspect of myself I'd been so fearful of, the part of me I'd denied and tried to shut away in a bag not visible even to me, my sexuality, was now out in the open. *My* open. And I was a scientist. I was curious. I needed to test my own theories about physical response. It took me a few days of dancing before I was brave enough to try it again, but finally I did.

While talking and dancing for the same customer for quite some time, I silently explored the morality questions in my mind and overrode any negative feelings I still had. I was ready. I sat down to straddle his leg with all my weight. There it was again. I could feel my center swell and ache. I noted the sensation, noted the desire, then stood back up. I was conscious about the circumstances, two strangers in a strip club, and felt no desire to act on my response. I hadn't been carried away by an unbridled urge to be one with this man. But it had felt pleasurable. For the first time in my life, I allowed myself to experience sexual yearnings and not act on them or feel shame for them. I wasn't compelled to share this awareness with my customer, yet I didn't feel guilt or the need to banish my sexual feelings back into my shadow bag either. I left the club that night feeling good about myself.

Like a threatening rumor, I'd heard about groups where women sat around exploring themselves with mirrors, something my conservative Midwest façade was salaciously intrigued by but would never do. On late night television, I'd seen Annie Sprinkle invite paid workshop participants to see inside her vagina when she used a speculum to open herself up. *How bizarre*, I thought. My vagina hadn't ever warranted investigation or even consideration just like my body never had. Now I was curious enough to rent Betty Dodson's video *Self Loving*, a workshop produced in 1991, and went home for my clandestine date with myself and the women in the film.

I put the video in the VCR, then furtively searched to see if anyone was watching although I knew they weren't. I lived alone. I imagined my cats with accusatory green eyes boring into me, but they were both sleeping on the bed and didn't seem to notice. I felt indecent and lewd. I'd never had the inclination to look at my own sexual organs before. Conversely, if you had told me I should, I'd have argued against it.

I instantly liked Betty, a stylish fifty-something motherly type who radiated acceptance. She spoke with empowerment and authority. My curiosity mixed with embarrassment watching other women in a video, yet I was in awe of their bravery. Betty described the wondrous vulva and as the first woman pried her flesh apart so the camera could get a good view, my stomach fidgeted. Vulva? I'd heard the word before but had never looked it up. Now I did. Webster's 1995 New College Dictionary defined it as, "the external female genitalia, including the labia majora, labia minora, clitoris and vestibule of the vagina."

When Betty instructed us at home to get a mirror and place it between our legs, I did. I felt a slight twinge of shame and briefly thought, *if people could see me now*, but that quickly developed into wonderment and fascination. The permission to examine myself was enlivening. When I started to look at the folds of flesh, the openings, the differences in genital construction as seen in Betty's video, I was affected. I'd seen Laura's genitals during bachelor parties, hers were quite different than mine, but I didn't know they all came in such an array of styles and colors! I felt like a wave that had struggled and crashed against a breaker wall, valiantly trying to flow over until eventually it did wash over the top and playfully splashed and bounced on the other side, feeling accomplished.

Then I discovered, to my own chagrin, that even though I was close to forty years old, that even though I had attended business school, technical school, and college, I knew so little about my own body that I hadn't even known where my urine flowed from. As I looked within the opening of my vagina and found the tiny black dot that was my urethra, I felt like a great explorer. How could it be that I didn't know these basic facts about myself? In all my traveling in and out of schools, did I miss that part of biology class just like I'd missed having to dissect frogs in the tenth grade because it occurred after I left one school but before I entered another? Had I been educated about the female body but been a distracted adolescent and not paid any attention? Or had I been so ashamed and guilty of my body and sexuality that it was a taboo subject and didn't even register in my consciousness? Why had I never been curious enough to even try to figure it out? It could have been one or all of those reasons, but it didn't matter. The glorious fact was that I was learning now, and I was conscious and paying attention. Nonplussed by the discovery of my ignorance, I called my best friend and felt vindicated when she confessed she hadn't known either.

Initially, during the video's erotic recess as Betty called it, it was awkward to watch a group of women masturbating with a vibrator, but inquisitiveness soon overtook my apprehension. As they touched themselves and experienced orgasms their faces and voices exhibited a rainbow of expressions. It was a testament to the power each woman possesses in her ability to pleasure herself. I no longer felt immoral and voyeuristic; there was no staging, and these women weren't on display to excite a viewer's response. It was intended purely as instruction for those learning to be open to their bodies. This was intended for women like me.

Now that I was over the wall I'd bravely scaled, I returned the video to Good Vibrations and rented *Behind the Green Door*, a 1972 classic porn movie starring Marilyn Chambers, a once fresh young model for Procter & Gamble and Ivory Snow detergent. Though it was the first hardcore pornographic movie widely released in mainstream theaters in the United States, the monumental novelty for me was the final orgy scene. Once again, as I'd been with *Self Loving*, I surprised myself. Instead of feeling distaste and repugnance for the fleshy, corpulent people, I felt admiration. This astounded me further.

My hunger for food, sex, men, anything that filled me up, was condemned and rejected if it expanded my physical person in any way. Excess weight gain, I feared, was like a ferocious piranha devouring and disintegrating every worthwhile thing about me. These people, seemingly in a state of bliss, allowed their large bodies to be filmed, not only naked in a porn movie for sexual stimulation, but also while being fat. Was the body to be celebrated—in any size?

The next time I went to the gynecologist and she inserted the speculum I asked if I could look. Nonchalantly I told her about the recent discovery of my body and my ignorance surrounding it as she handed me the mirror and encouraged me. She explained how to view my cervix. No longer in fear of my outsides, or my insides, I left the office a little closer to myself, a little more aware of who I really was.

UNDERSTANDING:

CREATING INTIMACY
WITH THE SELF

I do not perceive even one other thing that leads to such great harm as an undeveloped mind.

Buddha
The Buddha's Words

OBSERVATION

Only when the mind is free has the body a chance to be free.

Ernest J. Gaines
A Lesson Before Dying

I'd never been so close in spirit, action, or presence with other women's bodies before. I didn't attend gym class in high school, and in health club dressing/shower areas as an adult, I'd seen other women's bodies but had carefully averted my eyes and willed them to do the same towards me. Now, here I was, surrounded by women of various shapes and sizes who walked around naked in the dressing room, applied makeup without tops on, and squeezed each other's breasts to check out the new boob job. Like the big little kid I became while ooh-ing and aahing at Fourth of July fireworks, I secretly marveled at and applauded their lack of inhibition and casual display of their bodies. I rejoiced in their bold immodesty and through osmosis felt uninhibited enough to begin engaging in unencumbered nudity myself.

One evening the crowd thins out sooner than usual, and I walk downstairs to the dressing room at 12:30. On previous nights like this, I would pack up and go home before the 2 a.m. closing time, but management has recently mandated that we aren't allowed to leave early.

Allanah, a loud, big boned though well proportioned brunette in her early thirties, walks in, "I'm not going back up there—I refuse." She plops into the chair next to me that's situated against the tabletop in front of the wall-length mirror.

Heather, Peaches, and Doreen walk in, "It's awful up there," they moan in unison.

"Stay down here," I say while unstrapping my platform shoes to shed my confining stripper costume, put on regular clothes, and get comfortable. "This is the best part of the night," I chuckle while smiling at Peaches, a twenty-seven-year-old blonde who carries her baby fat quite provocatively.

Heather is counting her money. "I only made one-fifty," she laments.

"That's all I made," Allanah announces.

"Last Wednesday I only made forty-six dollars," Angel sighs as she walks through the doorway. Angel, an inexperienced dancer, has a tendency to sit and talk longer than she should when someone buys her a drink.

Because the night is slow, it's been a struggle to make money. Our spirits are jovial but only as an antidote to our frustration and fear that the trend towards lack of customers will continue.

Daisy, a petite twenty-two year old who's new to the club, has been sitting in the corner quietly observing us veterans. She pipes up, "I'm having more fun down here and learning so much. How do I get a job as a housemom?"

"You should have been here when we were comparing pussy lips," I laugh.

"It's true, I do have the biggest lips," Allanah boasts.

Daisy stares.

"Show us," Peaches yells.

"I will," Allanah exclaims, "but I have to have someone to compare to. Vixen, show us yours too."

"Okay," I add, amused. I'm awestruck at the ease with which I accept the challenge to drop my drawers, but I'm also reticent about sharing such a highly private part of myself. I have at times walked and stood nude in the dressing rooms, we all have, but I'm always acutely aware of my nakedness and feel self-conscious until I, at the very least, cover the area that I now say I'll so freely display. At the same time though, there is a hidden, stifled part of myself that wants to participate; the thrill of it, the absurdity, the oddity of it, the once in a lifetime chance to be a part of something human yet, by some standards, forbidden.

I undo my buttons, pull the jeans over my derriere, and lift my green turtleneck. "I still think mine are just as big as yours," I direct to Allanah.

Both Allanah's and my female genitalia consist of fleshy labia. Hers do look longer, but I suspect she's just pulling them more.

Heather squeaks, "Mine don't look anything like that."

We all turn our attention to Heather, whose child-like voice betrays her age of thirty-two. She's standing with her jeans around her ankles also. She's right. She has two folds of skin that meet perfectly in the center of her body and create a slit.

"Porno pussy!" Allanah shouts.

"Porno pussy?" I repeat, questioning.

"Yeah—you only see those kinds of pussies in porn movies."

"Are you sure?"

"Yeah, I've never seen big lips like ours. If you find one let me know. I want to watch it."

"I did bachelor parties with a woman who looks like you," I direct to Heather. "Before then I never knew women were made differently."

"Where's your minora?" Allanah asks Heather.

"What's that?" Heather questions.

"The skin on the inside," Allanah informs and shows by pulling on hers again.

"Oh those. They're here," Heather says as her fingers pry her skin apart to reveal two minute pieces of skin on the inside of her personal center.

I can't even see them.

"Is it hard for you to come?" Daisy meekly inquires of Heather.

"Yeah, it takes a lot of work. You two must have it easier," she says, pointing to Allanah and me, "because your clitoris isn't covered up by skin."

My loud guffaws followed by an involuntary snort fill the room. I'm having a blast. Not that I've always wanted to be surrounded by exposed women, but I'm mystified, rejuvenated, and liberated by our openness and frankness. I suddenly see a myriad of women I used to work with in offices: the staid stern expression of a conservative Michigan bookkeeper, the naïve innocence of a Filipina secretary, and the highly intellectual yet austere physicists at Livermore. I even imagine the members of my former women's psychotherapy group who'd been bold enough to come to the club: the overweight administrative assistant, the fifty-plus systems analyst I thought of as motherly, and the seventy-something widow who'd amused us all with tales of her younger, forty-five-year-old boyfriend. Nowhere else can I picture exposing my femaleness in such a clinical, nonchalant manner.

"Isn't this like what guys do when they're young?" I say to the crowd. "Don't they have peeing contests or something?"

More women begin piling into the dressing room because the club is about to close.

Stormy, a statuesque curvy brunette with a full back

butterfly tattoo and a vacant stare rumored to be because of a past heroine addiction, enters. "What's up down here?" she asks as she looks around with a sly smile.

"We're checking out each others' pussies," Peaches declares as she starts to lift her dress.

"Cute underwear," a voice from the crowd of ten women says.

"I need to do laundry," Peaches informs as we all laugh at her pink, bleached-thin, fullback undies.

"Yeah, me too," I chime, "That's why I'm not wearing any."

"You look like us, Peaches," Allanah says, walking up and getting a closer look at Peaches' flower. "Where'd you get that clean shave job?"

"I had it lasered off. I'll never have to shave again," she remarks as we all stand checking out her perfectly symmetrical quarter-inch line of brown hair.

"I want to get in on this," Stormy voices as she removes her night costume of patent red vinyl skirt and halter. She's the only one completely naked but she's surrounded by six women with their underwear around their ankles.

Within minutes there are at least twenty women in the small ten-by-fifteen foot dressing room and almost all have their pants down or their dresses up.

"You should see Bunny's clit," someone suggests.

"I heard my name," Bunny answers as her thin, 5'9" frame enters the room. Bunny is anything but soft and cuddly. She's bony, crass, vulgar even in her attempt at sensuality with the way her face and mouth contort to simulate ecstasy. The music she chooses to dance to on stage is usually rap-filled with derogatory slang directed at women.

"They say you have a huge clit," Allanah bellows.

"Boy, do I ever," Bunny responds. "It's like a small penis," and she pulls her bikini bottoms down and lays back across the dressing room table.

We all gather close. I can't see that well. The genitalia-gawking-girl-group has grown to a large number, but Bunny is laying it all out for everyone to see. I suddenly feel like I'm one of the green three-eyed aliens in *Toy Story*. I imagine our mouths opening in unison as we exclaim, "ohhhh," and clump close as many pairs of feet stamp trying to surround Bunny like they did as they moved toward Buzz Light Year.

It's late, 2:10 a.m., a time when customers are usually gone and most of us are already in cars or taxis on our way home, but we've lingered as a group longer than normal. For a brief amount of time in our microcosm of the competitive world at large where women are made to think they must compete for male attention, we've thrown aside our battle weapons of seduction and have removed our masks of purpose and bravado. Allanah isn't bullying, and we're not strutting to defend ourselves against rejection, men's or each other's. We aren't performing and manipulating customers, competing for the cash prize, while inwardly fearing one another's skill and success.

Our physical commonality has bridged our age and psyche gaps, and it feels to me as natural as if we've been comparing outfits in a dress shop. It doesn't matter that sometimes I feel superior because of my age and experience in the world; some of them are almost twenty years younger than I. It doesn't matter that sometimes I feel inferior because of their youth and their time to have more experiences in the world than I. We are women. We are naked. We are equal. Stripped to our bare essence, our bodies, although uniquely different from each other's, are exactly the same. There is no shame, only honest curiosity. Stripped of our clothing and external embellishments of managed hair and precision makeup, there are no winners or losers. These women are mothers, sisters, and friends, and I finally understand that *all* women's insecurities, mistakes, regrets, and fears, while looking different at times, are in reality, identical. With this understanding, I drop the, "better than," and "less than," psychic weights that have kept me separated from and fearful of other women.

Before I became a stripper this tendency toward rivalry was covert. Like a nose tickle that irritates intermittently, it subtly caught my attention when I'd see a happy woman smartly dressed or enjoying the company of a man. My overt competitive nature didn't emerge until my physical body craved release. When the desire for connection became so strong I couldn't deny it any longer, I'd paint my face, wiggle into tight jeans, and go out. I'd dance to rock and roll and flirt the night away while comparing myself to other female gazelles in the adult jungle. As the heavy drums beat time to the mating ritual, I'd focus on an unclaimed man. I needed to attract, to conquer, to win. I also had an impulse to be conquered, yet I was afraid of it. Being a single woman and having no way, or what I considered to be no acceptable way for sexual release (even masturbation felt taboo), I would drown my inhibitions along with my misguided sense of propriety (nice girl's don't). Alcohol let me feel in control and engage in the mating hunt without restraint until the next morning when my sober mind repulsed and castigated my body. Some of the men from those encounters were what the current culture now describes as "friends with benefits," and I could more easily resign my actions. Others were one-night stands that I sorely regretted. Wearing a thick layer of remorse in the fuzzy afterglow of inebriated sex, I'd hide from my roommates, and later, as a single woman living alone, from myself. I would shut myself away in my home for as long as possible until I could forget my humiliation and face myself in the mirror again, or until I had to return to work, whichever came first.

But here, within this safe club reserve zoned for feral behavior, I now embraced the untamed unrestrained wildness within and became like a lioness on the prowl, head thrown back, throat exposed. I'd been trained by example and now mimicked some of the behaviors I'd seen others doing for years. Mandy, the club bully whom I'd been afraid of when I was a new dancer, bounced on men's legs, ran around the club without her cocktail dress on, and brazenly hid men's faces in her breasts. Two and sometimes three girls surrounded one man while giggling and hiding their actions in close embrace. Fiona, a very dark Russian, owned porn sites, passed out business cards and invited men to the club to see her. It was rumored she fingered herself to hold the men's attention while dancing in the dark corners. She was even suspended from working for a week because of it. Sexually-charged rumors seemed to grow and thrive within the club walls. Once a housemom said a condom had been found on the floor upstairs. *How?* I wondered.

So now that I'd opened myself to physicality and realized it was natural to be a sexual being, the strip club atmosphere became an aphrodisiac. It was no longer merely about performing for the paying customer and gaining acceptance but was now about my ability to feel pleasure and enjoy what I was doing. Once I realized my urges and actions weren't harmful to myself or others, I could be objective about my behavior. What I once feared, I now wanted to disassemble, scrutinize. and explore from all angles. It was like the broken alarm clock my friend and I had excitedly dismantled when we were kids in order to see all the mechanisms and learn how it worked. We thought we would take it apart, figure it out, and put it back together working as good as new. The novelty and mystery was soon gone however, and within an hour we quit trying to make it function. That would have taken time and knowledge we didn't possess or have the patience to learn, so instead we finally placed the parts inside and secured the back. After that, it remained broken and forever clanked and rattled when you shook it. I was older now, and though this dismantling occurred within me, I allowed myself the time to examine my inner structure and finally possessed the tools to see how it would all fit together again.

I began straddling more patrons' legs. It was easy to become aroused and stimulated when flirting with attractive investment bankers, youthful dot.com executives and long-haired musicians. These were the men who populated my fantasies. I entertained thoughts of being with them, sexually and otherwise. Perhaps I could be their girlfriend. I even allowed my deep-seated fantasies to emerge that I'd ride off with one to live happily ever after in their expensive city condominium or tranquil country estate. The power I felt by keeping them captive with my body coupled with the hard-driving music, colored lights, and mirror-reflected images, all swirled within me and excited my libido. I sat on their legs, squirmed around and felt my clitoris feeling pressure and my body wanting more. I had the urge to ride their legs and bring myself to climax. But I couldn't. Instead, I observed myself without judgment and criticism and began to understand my powerful body longing.

One evening, I sat down next to an attorney who was conducting business away from his home in Los Angeles. We briefly exchanged pleasantries, and since the club was bustling with customers and I'd been able to secure dances easily all night, I asked him quickly if I could dance for him. He agreed, so when the next song started I stood and began my seduction routine. Eventually, after I'd preened and removed my cocktail dress slowly, I sat down to straddle his leg at the end of the song, which I'd learned usually ensured a second dance. This man was nice. I genuinely enjoyed our conversation and liked him. He talked to me about his garden in southern California and though he wielded power and control in his daily life, I deduced he was gentle. I expected that he'd be respectful and obey the no-touching rules, but what I didn't expect was that

I'd become sexually aroused while dancing for him. I hadn't expected this because he was overweight, soft to the touch, and not particularly sexually appealing. I was sexually stimulated, didn't understand it, and felt uncomfortable. This realization contradicted what I thought I knew to be truth. Could it mean my ability to be physically excited went beyond appearance? Or was it that my body had a wisdom and "mind" independent of my intellectual prejudices? Like the dismantled alarm clock, my sexual reality was exposed. And I shook. I wanted to put the pieces back together in a prescribed way with a logical blueprint I could rely on, but I didn't have one. My old blueprint of sexual shame, guilt, and attempted goodness through abstinence hadn't worked. And this new sexually and sensually freewheeling blueprint within the club darkness didn't feel acceptable either. Was my club sexuality the right way? Or was my restrictive home sexuality my right way?

While I didn't realize it until years later, I'd interviewed women I'd worked with at the club in order to mirror myself and gain acceptance. Initially my motivation to interview them was based in defiance and self-serving justification to negate what I'd read, that women who stripped had been sexually abused. I didn't have a history of molestation, and at that time I couldn't admit there had been *anything* wrong with my past. I didn't have the safety of self yet to discover that I'd put myself into less-than-desirable encounters as a young person, and I didn't have the courage or fortitude to look at myself honestly. Instead I focused on what angered me about others' perceptions of women in my industry and became indignant when reading or hearing there could be any motivation behind stripping other than being free and fully accepting of one's self. And just as I had no idea that I was trying to justify my experience when I initially interviewed women, I also had no idea I was trying to accept myself when I set out looking for a blueprint to counter what my conservative mind thought was my sexual wantonness within the strip club. I tried to align myself with who I considered to be society's fringe groups because I felt like I was living outside "normal."

First I attended COYOTE, Call Off Your Old Tired Ethics, meetings in San Francisco and met Margot St. James, a former prostitute who was making headlines at the time for running for city office. Sitting at the quiet bar before the meeting started, I unintentionally overheard the conversation between Margot and another member. I thought they sounded high. The meeting was unorganized. I decided not to vote for Margot and never went back to their group.

I next attended an EDA, Exotic Dancer's Alliance, meeting in a small room in a building on Market Street. There were only a handful of women, and they worked at either the Mitchell Brothers O'Farrell Theatre or the New Century Theater. The main topic was the ongoing class-action lawsuit against the Mitchell Brothers wherein dancers wanted to be classified as employees and given health benefits and compensation for past wages. Other issues centered on management's abusive treatment of the dancers and turning a blind eye on threatening customer behavior. I couldn't identify with their concerns or complaints. I was happy where I worked and thought the working conditions were fine. The clubs these women worked in were rumored to be sex emporiums, and I couldn't help but think that if the working conditions were that bad, why didn't they just go to a different club? Also, their callous weathered demeanor and speech put me off. One of their organizers, a petite blonde woman, was angry, shrill, and hardened. I never went back to that meeting either.

Around this same time, after reading *The Beauty Myth*, I attended a Naomi Wolf seminar. Sitting in a circle that Saturday afternoon, while introducing ourselves and discussing concepts, an outspoken woman caught my attention. During the bathroom break, I introduced myself. The attraction I felt for this woman, whose name was Peggy, grew when I learned she was sober and worked in the sex industry as a prostitute. Perhaps she held the answers to my evolving questions around my own sexuality. She seemed to have it all. Not only was she attractive, fit, confident, and living on the fringe of normal society yet seemingly okay with her choices, she was also married. I was intrigued. I'd never known a prostitute—or at least anyone who admitted to being one. We exchanged numbers.

After meeting a couple times for coffee and lunch, we attended a women's seminar held in Berkeley. We met that day at the auditorium, and she was as perfectly made-up as she always was; black eyeliner and thick mascara framed large eyes, medium-length blonde curls gelled into place, and she wore a stylish skirt and top with matching heels. Seated next to her, I felt underdressed in my jeans, Doc Martin's that resembled my father's military boots, and scant foundation to cover my bare face. As I sat there slouched in my seat, comfortable and casual, my right foot resting on my left knee in what is a typical masculine position, she remarked flippantly, "I feel like I'm sitting next to a man."

During Susan Griffin's lecture about courtesans, Peggy raised her hand and challenged the author's view that there weren't courtesans working today. She admitted she was one, a "call girl" by another name, and while in awe of her courage to expose herself, I also loathed the attention. If I could have slid right off that seat and under the one in front of me like a slinky cartoon character, I would have.

As soon as the seminar was over, fifteen women surrounded her, a couple admitting they used to work in the profession or knew someone who still did. They were drawn to her honesty.

My previous disconcertion changed to admiration for her courage. Next I learned that she lectured about prostitution and did advocacy work with public education for sex worker rights.

I also noticed that every time we had a break that day at the seminar, the first thing she did was run in the bathroom to make sure her hair and makeup were perfect. This became unnerving. I'd abandoned the need to impress people constantly and took a more relaxed approach to my appearance. I reveled in the fact that I didn't have to be 'on' all the time.

She took me to Cyprian Guild Meetings, private meetings of San Francisco prostitutes, where I met some of her friends. There were fantastic women doing noble work advocating for prostitute safety and discussing issues, but after the honeymoon phase of our relationship ended, I saw other qualities in this group that I wasn't enamored with. I saw pervasive singleness. Most of the women were alone, and I yearned for a partner. I saw some who emphatically defended their work by talking about the healing social work they were doing. I could understand this defense because through stripping I'd learned that many men were lonely, but I wondered why they had to defend it so strongly. I wondered what their lives would be like after their bodies were used up.

A few of us piled into a car one weekend day to drive to Marin and support Peggy during a lecture. As we were talking, a prostitute in her early fifties with a lively spark in her wrinkled eyes made the comment that I'd be joining them someday. This statement scared me. Did she know something I didn't? Was there a "look" one had before entering the profession? We'd gone to pick this woman up and I'd been surprised to see her small chaotic home. My home was also small with furnishings and knick knacks strewn everywhere, yet I hoped for more in my future. I didn't want my life to stay this way. I'd thought about their work, this was true, but I also knew how hard it was at times to keep up my cheery stripper facade and how at the end of a night, I was tired of men. In the club, I could walk away from the ones I didn't really want to dance for, just like we women have the opportunity to walk away from a bad date or not go on one in the first place, but I also knew that because money was involved, I'd tolerate some customer's inane conversation or excessive use of hands past the point of acceptability. There'd be an internal wrestling match where my sense of personal space and boundaries were pitted against my lust for more money. I couldn't imagine the mind game I'd have to play with myself to have sex with strangers when I didn't really like them just because I needed the money. And I didn't want to imagine it. Although the bad girl within mused over the control and power a prostitute might feel at times, I didn't really want to be one.

When I looked beyond their politically-correct rhetoric, I saw defensiveness, anger, and hurt. I was beginning to understand myself without judgment and knew that if I was okay with my choices, then I didn't need to defend myself against anyone else's opinion. These women weren't being honest about their self-acceptance. And I saw disrespect and abuse. The way Peggy talked about her husband not contributing to their household income and the fights she told me they had made their relationship sound unhealthy and dysfunctional. Also, I'd met the former husband of Janine, another sober prostitute. We'd become friends and he'd confided some of their problems. He told me that during their brief marriage, after having sex, she'd once said, "It was just like work." I drifted away from this group also.

Not one to give up before exhausting all avenues though, I found out about *Spectator Magazine's* monthly meetings and attended one in the back room of Jezebel's Joint, a bar on Polk Street. I thought that a group of people writing and advertising adult services ranging from strip clubs to bondage, dominance, and sadomasochism might have the qualities and live life by examples I was trying to grasp onto, but once again I felt like I didn't fit in. It was scintillating to be meeting in a dark bar with people who weren't keeping their sexuality locked up in their minds and homes, but then again, the darkness made it feel seedy. Also, some of the concerns were outside my realm of experience. A transvestite phone-sex operator spoke about an advertising concern and then broke into a rant about lifestyle choices and decisions. I met Carol Queen, a local PhD sexologist and author, but her openness about sexual practices unnerved me. I didn't want to talk about specifics. I felt dirty in this small shadowy room and judged these people as I judged myself.

After an article I'd written appeared in *Gauntlet* magazine, I invited the porn star Nina Hartley to lunch; she had also written for *Gauntlet*. Her wife—for many years she lived in the Berkeley Hills with a man and his wife as a threesome—joined us, and we discussed Nina's work as a sex educator. I had a good feeling walking away from that meeting but never did meet with her again. Perhaps her role as a porn star put me off more than I could admit to at the time. Perhaps an unreturned phone call on her part, coupled with my busy schedule with my Art of Sensual Dance video and classes, broke our connection. My memory fails me in this regard, but I do know that while enjoying watching porn on occasion, I'm uncomfortable with the idea of taking off my clothes for total public access.

People all over the world band together with similar interest and purpose. So too I, in an effort to understand myself, had continued my education by exploring within groups for answers to questions about myself. I was no longer fearful of my body and sexuality *within* the club but was searching for external acceptance and community, hoping it would lead to internal acceptance *outside* the club. However, the anger, defensiveness, and obsession with attention that I found reminded me too much of my past (and sometimes present) self, and I quickly moved away. Even though the circumstances and people were interesting to my scientific mind, they also made me feel squeamish and uncomfortable. Perhaps there were people who were comfortable with their sexuality, but since I wasn't, I didn't resonate with them, although through their ability to stand up for their beliefs, I gained courage for my own self-expression.

One answer I did find, though, concerned my opinion about my moral character. I looked to one last group trying to understand my behavior, Sex and Love Addicts Anonymous. It's true that I wanted to be in love and had placed total dependence on another when I imagined I was in love, but when I attended those meetings I wasn't in a relationship that was causing me distress. And yes, I enjoyed sex. But this behavior wasn't consuming my life or causing myself or others harm. In time, I came to the conclusion that while I'd had one-night stands in my past, sexual promiscuity, a label that had always seemed negative, didn't really belong to me until I became conscious. My indiscriminate sexual behavior had been misdirected action I thought would secure love and was born out of an ignorance of not knowing what love really was. Once I understood this, I took this information, stored it away in my psyche and moved on with a clear conscience about my sexually-permissive attitude. The label didn't bother me anymore because I truly had a choice.

After seven years of dancing, at the age of forty-two, I owned my body, took control of my libido, and became the empowered 21st Century woman I'd been hearing it was my right to be. The fire within me was fueled by my skimpy outfit, the strip club's atmosphere of expectation, and my control over who I danced for. I craved connection like in the inebriated nights of my youth, only now I was sober and knew it wasn't about love.

I walked upstairs to the VIP floor one night and our eyes met. He motioned for me to sit on his lap since there were no extra chairs. While his buddies and my colleagues made small talk and waited for their first round of drinks, Luke and I settled into comfortable adoration. The nervous tension I usually felt because time was money, evaporated. I instinctually knew I'd be dancing for him. Like the old gray cotton shirt with a happy aerobics bear on it and the faded words, "I love exercise," my mother bought me twenty years ago to cover myself after working out, I wore his embrace with familiarity. It wasn't long, fifteen minutes at most, and he asked, "Are you going to dance for me?"

I took his warm hand and walked him to the back room, the VIP "red room," and we took one of the only available chairs which was close to the entrance. Although advertised as a private area, the room was really only a twenty-foot long narrow corridor, not even five feet wide, opening to the deejay booth. Comfortable armchairs had been placed along the walls and the lights turned low to create romantic atmosphere. In reality it was a well-traveled path by dancers on their way to the deejay booth to select music, managers wandering around keeping an eye on things, and the housemom collecting fees from dancers who hadn't paid for their shift yet.

When I walked through on my way to see the deejay I always kept my eyes straight ahead, careful not to infringe on a couple's privacy. I expected others to give me the same courtesy. One of the VIP Room allures was that it had a reputation of being an area where "more" could happen, an idea perpetuated by men who'd either had more happen or who'd lied about having more happen and by dancers who'd used "more" as a temptation to get men back there to make still more money. Men had to buy a block of dances to be able to be in the VIP area. One evening I even had a man in the red room remove himself from his pants when I turned around to show him my backside. When I turned back and saw him holding his hard spear, I politely told him we couldn't do that here, and he politely put himself away and zipped up. He let me finish the dance. I collected the money. Then he left the club, perhaps in search of friendlier places.

Tonight was different. My moves were the same, yet not. I was nervous, something I never experienced after dancing for so long.

As I flipped my hair over his head to create a private tent and shield our faces from onlookers, our eyes met, then closed, as our lips brushed each other's and sent electric jolts through my body. He gently tugged the thong bikini I was wearing, pulling taut the fabric and inflaming my nerve endings. My temperature skyrocketed and fireworks sizzled and popped amongst us. Our furtive kisses and passionate yet restrained pulls on each other's clothing ignited my fire, and my body ached for the twenty-seven-year-old surfer who was visiting San Francisco from San Luis Obispo.

I drew him into the dance and instead of being simply the object of the voyeur's attention, I became the voyeur as well, fantasizing his touch beyond what our obvious surroundings allowed. The erotic perception I usually tried to arouse in each customer using slow calculated moves was now magnified by our public display. Like heavy teenage petting embarked on for the first time yet forbidden by our parents, our lust too was forbidden to be consummated. We were a naughty couple trying not to get caught. Our mutual heat felt like a blaze so forceful I imagined uniformed firefighters from the station down the block to come smashing through the front doors spraying their water hoses at any minute. I'd felt an uncontrollable lust to couple before, usually with an elusive man at the end of a date, but this surpassed the hunger for mere connection. There was power, control, the ability to take, and to have.

His money ran out.

I needed to make more.

I tore myself away with the same amount of force needed to tear apart two halves of a zipper when material is caught between them, but not before I suggested meeting after closing. He voluntarily divulged where he was staying for the night.

I showed up at his less-than-four-star hotel room wearing white thong underwear, which he playfully chastised me for, and the flames leapt high. I was cognizant and aware, needy and physical. I was impassioned and horny and assertive. I wasn't afraid to be alone in a hotel room with this stranger, like I'd been while dancing for the stranger who solicited me early in my stripping career, because I'd initiated this encounter. After, I returned home drunk with conquest and as physically satiated as if I'd done a grueling triathlon then gorged on buttery pasta. I'd boldly used him for my own pleasure, just like I'd been used by men in the past. I'd had sex at will, because I wanted it; older generations might say, like a man. In this respect, he was my first.

Once I took a club-induced longing outside the club, it was easy to do it again. It was as if all my years of denying and repressing my body were compressed into flint that when sparked, quickly ignited and threatened to burn everything in sight. A select few men, usually younger than I, aroused my interest and passion within the club and led to my assertiveness outside the club. I wanted their touch. I wanted their lips on mine, and I was confident enough to direct them as to everywhere those lips should be. I craved their attention and their cocks, and I wasn't ashamed or embarrassed to let them know. This bold use of my sexual power was new and exhilarating.

For years I'd been telling Adam, a slim middle-aged Asian who frequented the club, that I was looking for something more when he repeatedly tried to get me into bed by asking, "Don't you just want to have sex?"

"I've already had plenty of sex," I'd laugh. "I want more." The *more* I'd spoken about then was love, not merely sex, but before that would materialize in my life, acceptance of myself as a sexual being, it seemed, needed to happen. The *more* I found first was a burgeoning understanding and enjoyment of my instinctual sexual nature. I was hungry for the pleasure I'd denied in all those guilt-ridden encounters of my past, all those sexual escapades and relationships where I hadn't owned my feelings, pleasures, and sensations. I'd been ignorant around my right to have pleasure, and that had led me to ignorance around the vast amount of pain I'd inflicted upon myself by being with boys, then men, who had no respect or regard for who I was. They'd cared not for my feelings, only about how I felt to their touch. In every single encounter to this point, I'd either been stoned, drunk, unwilling yet resigned, concerned about how I looked, concerned about the other's pleasure, concerned about what the act meant or didn't mean or where it would or wouldn't lead. I'd never had sex sober, confident, and willing to revel in the act for the act's sake only.

Now I did.

I filled myself with young lovers who were more educated and prepared than I to carry and use condoms. I filled myself with their youth, and they replaced the men of my youth I'd been unable to connect with. I took from them their nonchalance and compliance to please in a sexual way, and I held them close to my hungry heart. I witnessed their youth and their folly and remained friends with them because I didn't expect them to fulfill anything other than my physical itch. Like the huntress on the prowl I'd been fearful to be, I now roamed the club selecting other beasts like myself who had long wild hair and slim muscled bodies. In their twenties they had decades longer to live than I, and I swallowed their callow perceptions. If I didn't bed them, and there were only a handful I did, when I danced for them, I held them close to my breasts and exalted in the fact that I was old enough to be their mother when they said I was the hottest woman they ever saw. This Mrs. Robinson fantasy precipitated my nurturing instincts, and I held them even closer knowing full well their youthful insecurities because I'd lived mine. I hid my age in the darkness of the club, and for a few nights each week, I was again the insecure girl, only this time I could get the guys and get the attention. I relived the uncomfortable newness of myself as a transient teenager, but on my turf, with my newfound confidence, and I soothed that rejected awkward adolescent within who, no matter what I looked like, would always feel like she had stringy hair, acne, and the wrong outfit.

For seven years I'd been immersed in a world where, like mischievous children, everyone tried to circumvent authority's rules. It was no surprise to me, then, that late one night, about 1 a.m. when my feet were tired, the club was sparse, and I was having fun doing multiple dances for an attractive New York bank executive, I pushed past another personal boundary.

I wouldn't call it peer pressure, more like normalcy through immersion and association, but for some time, my dances had incorporated moves I'd seen other women doing. I still performed my slow sensual routine I'd done so often I could have mimed sexy standing in cow manure, but now I also allowed myself more sit time, to be more specific, straddle time on patron's legs, as a way to rest. We weren't supposed to take both legs off the floor but enforcement of the rules had relaxed over the years, so I'd overridden my self-imposed virtue and would sit on a man's lap facing him with both knees on the couch. I'd alternate this move with some standing moves as well as single-leg straddles. Just like women have done for millennia when they lay there, compliant when fatigued or bored, I'd let the friction of our bodies do the work. The heat felt through my bikini bottom would arouse them and my facing-straddle gyration would affect the center point of their trousers. This insured I'd keep dancing and making money, but in a basic relaxing way. If this strategy was working, I didn't have to troll the floor looking for new men. I'd gotten lazy in my job, just as I'd gotten lazy in my personal life, not attending events that interested me like book signings and lectures, where I could meet men I could have meaningful relationships with.

David was tipsy, but he'd been a gentleman our entire hour together. We'd dance a few songs, then sit out a few songs, then dance a few more. Some of the men liked this pattern. It saved them money and usually kept me around, especially when it was late and there weren't many customers. If it'd been earlier and there was a larger crowd, I might have gone looking for quicker money. Unless I liked the man, it was excruciating to sit and pretend to enjoy conversation for a couple songs while watching other women dance every song. But David was polite and funny in a late-night goofy kind of way, and I was grateful for his generosity. I didn't pester him for more than he could pay, and he didn't try to feel me all over as if I were a soft angora sweater. We had plenty of time, and there was no pressure.

We were fairly secluded on the main club floor in the back, and as I danced for him, I'd become aroused, but after the two-song combination, I'd sit and the feeling would diminish. Then, during our conversation about working out at the gym, he blurted, "Have you ever had an orgasm in here?"

Astonished, I retorted, "No."

Men love to please women. More specifically, they like to view and to know they've brought their lovers to orgasmic pleasure. David, who entertained the same fantasy, perhaps embellished by exotic stripper daydreams, next asked, "Do you think you could have one with me?"

"I don't know," I said honestly as I settled into quiet contemplation. I didn't consider myself an orgasm faker. I'd never put on a show like Meg Ryan's character in *When Harry Met Sally*, but a few times in my relationships over the years I had escalated my voice in order to hurry my partner's release.

I thought about this in between counting the number of songs I'd been idle and offering a few, "uh huhs," and, "me toos," as David talked about weights and exercise machines.

As I got up to start dancing at the start of a Britney Spears tune, I placed my hands on his shoulders and leaned in close. He looked up at me with hopeful eyes and whispered, "Do you think you could come for me now?"

Sometimes in relationships I'd felt pressure to perform. When a lover would look down at me while his hands worked eagerly to please, I'd feel obligated as if he was going for a prize, and I had to give it to him. I'd strain and force and will myself to sublime surrender, sometimes because I wanted to but usually because I was expected to until *Bingo!*, over the crest and everyone felt like a winner. I'd been asked this question before by other hopeful men in the club, but had laughed it off and hadn't even considered it. Now I simply replied again, "I don't know."

And I didn't.

I'd gotten aroused while dancing, this was true, but I'd never carried it through to climax. This *had been* outside my realm of decent behavior. Also, with expectation came pressure, which usually wasn't conducive for desired results. Besides, I wasn't quick. I don't know of many women who are.

But why not?, I now thought. As if there was the devil on

one shoulder counteracting the angel on the other, I mulled over questions like, *Who would know? What's it going to hurt? Who's it going to hurt?*

I continued dancing and sitting and straddling and after two songs I just straddled and squirmed. When the Red Hot Chili Peppers' "Under the Bridge" ended and Wheezer's, "Keep Fishin'" came on, I said huskily into his ear, "I'm going for a third song."

He didn't say stop.

I pressed my breasts into his chest while my left white stiletto remained on the floor and my right knee rested on the couch, his left leg between my two. Like two accomplished ballet performers, he kept his hands steady on my waist and supported me to complete my move. Then the next song started. While Incubus crooned "I Wish you Were Here," I continued pressing myself harder into his leg.

My breath next to his ear quickened.

Then a sound escaped.

I laughed—with relief—and embarrassment.

"I've never done that before," I said.

"Thank you," was all he said.

He paid me the full amount of money he owed and after sitting, for the most part in silence, for two more songs, perhaps an obligatory amount of time he felt needed to be spent as if he were a lover determining how soon he can jump out of the post-coital bed, stated he had an 8 a.m. flight the next day and needed to leave. I walked him to the front door and said goodbye after we hugged.

On my way to the dressing room downstairs, I laughed out loud to no one in particular. *I just got paid to feel good*, I thought. "What a fantastic job," I voiced.

I no longer saw my sexuality as taboo. I'd hung out with it—understood it—valued it. Brief affairs in my personal life allowed me a more vocal release but within the club over the next few years, when I allowed myself to experience discreet orgasm on rare occasion, I never let a customer know again. After thinking about this first episode in depth, I realized that while I felt okay having an orgasm, after all they do feel great, what I didn't feel okay with was selling or giving away to strangers this highly personal part of me. I wasn't going to fake it either. I was as real as my evolution and maturation allowed, never one to pretend I was something or someone I wasn't. To have let strangers imagine they'd experienced a special moment within my person simply for money would have devalued and demeaned it—and me. Matter of fact, if I'd have acted that scenario out complete with ritualized panting and pretend heavy breathing at some customer's request, *then* I would have felt indecent.

I was no longer the young girl, then woman, who'd denied her body's powerful force, given it away to secure love and acceptance, and rejected its value. But I couldn't be angry with my former self. Rejecting my body had been a lifelong habit starting before puberty. It had escalated through drug use, specifically stimulants, at fourteen when a friend with prescription black beauties for weight loss gave me a couple. I'd enjoyed the feeling they induced so much I learned to crave any type of stimulant that increased my energy and decreased my appetite. They'd kept me energetic and thin.

Once I gave those up I continued to reject my body's fatigue, working both as a laser technician and exotic dancer, pushing myself through exhaustion while existing on caffeine and sugar. After I quit the Lab and worked only one job, I'd continued my frenetic pace through compulsive exercise and doing bachelor parties and going out-of-town to work in other cities. When I abandoned those maniacal unbalanced ways of working, I still had a perfectionist need for physical excellence that was exacerbated by prancing around in almost non-existent outfits so I returned to the gym alternating squats, leg presses, lunges, the butt blaster, and the inner and outer thigh machine with bench presses, crunches, pushups, stretching, and Stairmaster marathons. I'd first joined the gym after leaving my husband in my mid twenties and had enjoyed the gym community and liked having a place to go, but it soon became another way to escape my thoughts through obsessing about my body. After a decade and a half, I no longer exercised to feel strong and healthy, only to assuage my excruciating feelings of inadequacy.

Fortunately, my body, as it was awakening to its sexual urges, was also becoming aware of the physical straight jacket I'd placed it into. As I walked around the club, I realized I'd been holding my stomach in my entire life in order to have that flat abdomen so idolized in ultra-thin models today. I held my stomach firm and rock-like, never fully breathing in, my body taking as little space as possible. I pondered those times in my twenties and thirties, when I'd exclaimed that I couldn't breathe, as to whether it was anxiety or simply a matter of mechanics. I literally hadn't relaxed enough to allow air to pass my throat and extend my abdomen. I didn't know how. Holding my stomach in was automatic. I even justified it by repeating what I'd heard fitness experts say, "Holding in your stomach muscles helps your back muscles." But that's not why I did it.

I was afraid of my stomach. If I let it relax and fill, my sin of overeating might be revealed. Just like my appetite for sex at times seemed untamable, so, too, my appetite for food seemed unable to be restrained. I either under-ate or in the pendulum-swing affect, over-ate. I felt superior when I was hungry and my stomach flat. I felt in control, likable, and loveable. When I was hungry, I was unable to feel anything else.

The years taken to question my sexual views, ponder my body's responses, and really determine what my adult brain and body could *both* agree on, provided me a blueprint for personal transformation. I'd traveled my own road and written my own map! As long as I wasn't being physically harmed or causing harm to others, I could safely stay with myself. I'd learned to stand outside myself, not in a detached can't-bear-to-look-at-what-I'm-doing manner, but in an inquisitive patient way. I'd learned to negate and detach from my restrictive superego and was no longer a scientist of classified targets and optic theories, but instead a Scientist of the Self. I was curious about my actions and patterns and intent on finding their origin, relevance, and meaning to my adult life. Like the Buddhist practice during meditation of labeling thoughts as "thinking" then moving on without judgment and criticism, so, too, I now observed my restrictive patterns and educated myself by viewing others.

I watched with my trained analytical eye as partners and families languidly strolled past my table at the local coffee shop one Sunday morning, casually dressed, sloppy even, seemingly unaware that their stomachs were protruding. I pondered all the different female shapes I saw, and, in an effort to categorize myself, learned that while once all people were classified as ectomorph, mesomorph, or endomorph, there were new terms used to describe the female shape: the A frame (pear shape or spoon shape), H frame (ruler), V frame (cone shape), oval frame (apple) and the 8 frame (hourglass). I'd been so rigorously trying to fit into one particularly perfect mold that I never realized ordinary humans were enjoying life and having fun no matter what their size and shape. I thought that if I perfected myself I'd grab that ever-elusive love relationship and spectacular life that models and actors chosen by advertisers to sell their products told me I was missing. That day, and for many weeks and months, I watched people with round bellies, saggy butts, and wrinkled faces laugh and eat while I sat caged in my rigid, taut, hard body—alone and lonely.

My observations didn't stop at bellies and body proportions. I also noticed breasts—women's breasts. It didn't seem to matter what their size and shape were, some women openly flaunted them with low-cut necklines, tight sweaters, and clingy camisoles, daring, just like women in magazines. Only they weren't in magazines, and they weren't perfect, and it was daylight! They had stomach pooches and big thighs and sometimes their breasts were smaller than their midsection and sometimes they were larger. They were life-filled and three-dimensional instead of being flat on a glossy piece of paper.

Within the club, I was still trying to keep myself two-dimensional, height and width, no girth. I wanted to learn how to take in all the air my body required to fully live and flourish, but if I did that I'd have to expand and become bigger—and so would my thinking. The map I'd been making for years connected me to pleasure. If I was to follow it now, these same introspective landmarks would lead me through feelings I didn't want to have anything to do with. Like the joke about the stereotypical stubborn male who won't ask directions when lost, I didn't want to consult this new map. The overabundance of meaningless encounters at night fatigued me so greatly that after working, I didn't want to talk to anyone else, man or woman. It had been easy to blame my isolation on my job, but was that the real reason I was alone?

Universal Wisdom, far greater than my own, drew me close to Mother Nature's bosom. She held me tight while I was forced to explore this question as well as many others I'd so judiciously avoided and had no intentions of ever learning the answers to.

TRUST

*I've been absolutely terrified every moment of my life—and
I've never let it keep me from doing a single thing I wanted to do.*

Georgia O'Keefe

I enjoyed my apartment in San Francisco and knew the ren-
ovation work would eventually be finished, but the new owner's
inexperience (he used toxic chemicals to seal earthquake support beams in the basement), his dismissive attitude about safety
(he rudely suggested the only reason I was complaining was because I was a woman), his blatant disregard for tenants' rights
(he illegally invaded apartments without permission and was
discovered one day when the school teacher living on the bottom floor was home sick, sleeping; he walked into her place and
used her bathroom before she woke up and confronted him)—
all these incidents accumulated to push me to look for a new
home. I'd tried to stay, however, alone in my apartment, sobbing
regularly from lack of sleep and the inability to concentrate, I
finally admitted I didn't want to continue living that way, fighting in pursuit of my renter's rights. Remaining a victim in my
home was jeopardizing my sanity. Not even the frequent trips to

the Sierra foothills to visit my boyfriend diminished the distress I felt as soon as I returned to my chaotic apartment building. I moved into a converted recreation room behind someone's home in the Berkeley hills surrounded by forest and visited by field mice, raccoons and an occasional deer.

The 360-square-foot one-room studio became my escape from cable car bells, city buses, obtrusive work crews, and club noise, and I filled it with only the items necessary for a reason to return: my two cats, my clothes, a few special knickknacks, and my bed. I didn't even own a television at the time.

My San Francisco apartment had included a bay window that provided the epitome of reality TV: sailboats, cruise ships, and tanker barges on the bay, yearly Blue Angel flying team exhibitions, fireworks at Aquatic Park, and a neighboring rooftop where I watched a pigeon die while trying to shield himself from other scavengers. Now, instead of watching life through a window, I could participate. I talked to and tried to shoo away the large raccoon family that peered in the sliding glass door looking for food. While trying not to get too close, I smiled at and spoke to the neighborhood skunk after he scratched on the door one evening, surprising both him and me when I opened it. And I was an attentive mom when I had to learn how to take swollen ticks off Skimo (pronounced Skeemo), who thoroughly reveled in the wild feline hunt after being cooped up for years in the apartment in the city. The giant five-foot diameter redwood that stood sentinel next to my front door greeted me when I returned to my hideout. This new home was exactly that—a home. Even though small and funky (my front door opened to the bathroom), it provided an antidote to the extreme extroversion that was my job. I had no idea it would become the nest that would hold me safely while I battled the fears of my past and present.

Even though I'd grown up with two parents and was fed and cared for regularly, I lacked the consistency that Erick Erickson in his developmental stages theory, postulates is needed from birth through age one-and-a-half for the child's development of trust. What I experienced instead was a consistency of uprootedness and a consistency of separation from my father. By the age of two I'd been separated from him twice for a total of seven months.

I don't have a clear recollection of my feelings about my father leaving at that time, but I do remember when I was five, as clear as if it were a snapshot in front of me, the day he returned from receiving downhill ski instruction in China. "Daddy's home, daddy's home," my sister and I yelled excitedly as we slid off our chairs and away from the dinner table. Wearing a starched Special Forces uniform and Green Beret he stood majestic; safety and love enveloped me as he scooped me into his arms. He carried presents—carved wooden bears. The realization that love and comfort was wrapped up in that small bear comes to my awareness today, but somewhere in my past the symbolism and meaning of that token of affection was lost to me in my attempt at sophistication. I decided it wasn't important, just an extra thing to pack and carry around in my travels. I don't have that carved wooden bear anymore, and I wish I did. I'd discarded it along with other objects, memories, even people whom I felt had abandoned me, including myself.

Well-meaning phrases such as, "We'll start fresh," "Be a big girl," and, "There'll be new people to play with," offered to help soothe my anguish at yet another move, I had interpreted as messages telling me to bury my feelings. At the age of twelve, after arriving in my sixth new school and trying to fit in with Maureen and Kristy, my mom was told during a parent-teacher conference, Susan will follow anyone. Of course I would. I wanted to be liked, and I needed to be liked quickly.

Time was limited. By the time I was in my sophomore year of high school, I started sentences but didn't finish them so often that friends used to tease me about having a brain disease. I lacked the courage to express my thoughts because if they were deemed stupid, foolish, or incoherent, someone might not like me. Eventually, I didn't even acknowledge my thoughts or opinions to myself anymore.

Adolescence, a time when most are learning how to navigate feelings, for me had become a repetitious series of escapes: through the bedroom window at night to meet a boy, with vodka and orange juice in the morning before school, marijuana at lunchtime, school studies, excessive masturbation, and rock music that contained macabre defiant lyrics such as Black Sabbath's "Sabbath Bloody Sabbath," where Ozzy Osbourne sings about the realities of life killing you.

When I was thirty-two I visited a friend in another state who asked questions about my life. Instead of realizing she was making conversation and just wanted more information, I took it as a personal affront. My stomach constricted, and I felt conspicuously grilled as if I were an enemy being tortured for answers under a bright single bulb. I didn't know why I felt scrutinized and irritated. I just squirmed and changed the subject. I know now that it was my defense against having to peer too closely at my own motivations and behaviors. I'd never questioned myself. I'd never experienced my feelings—I just ignored them. I could show you how happy I was—that was an acceptable feeling—but the ones I thought were bad, the ones like anger, that, along with my sexuality, I'd banished to my shadow bag, those I denied and never learned I could live through in order to release them. Just as I'd had no relationship with my physical body, I had no relationship with my body of emotions. I didn't even know how to identify them. As an adult, I'd disappear from the relationship, quit the job, or move to another location whenever something arose that was difficult.

Initially, I exposed my body at the club as a way to dress up my insecurities; I'd always focused on my body as a way to circumvent vacillating self-confidence, vague self-esteem, and volatile emotion. Like two boxers in a ring, I'd won hard-fought rounds where I'd duked it out with my shadow side while learning to embrace my sentient body, and a new pattern evolved. Trying to out-maneuver my shadow had tired me greatly, though. Weary, I wanted to take the boxing gloves off, but how does a trained fighter learn to let her guard down and stop protecting herself from feeling? I had no one to help me. Fear had not only driven me away from myself, but also from the people I loved. I was afraid they would get too close and perhaps attack, or worse yet, leave. I'd moved twenty-five hundred miles away from Wisconsin and my family for just this reason.

I didn't know the brave capable Susan my grandfather saw when he'd expressed to my mom, "Susie, she can do anything," while I was a traveling service technician working on laser systems. I only knew the quivering mess of insecurities and anxiety. Even though I'd traveled the North American continent on my own and stood seemingly fearless on a stage without clothes, I was terrified. My grandfather and others didn't see that fear because I wore a tight cloak of bravery to camouflage the vulnerable, less-than-perfect me. In spite of my subconscious vigilance to keep my demons, repressed feelings and unexamined emotions, sedated, they began to stir with all the sparring and jockeying I was having with my shadow. Just like the Emperor in the Hans Christian Anderson fable, *The Emperor's New Clothes*, who, naked, continues to walk proudly even after being exposed by a young child uttering the words, "But he isn't wearing anything at all," I, too, kept my proud strut, counting on my naked body to deflect attention away from my insecurities. And it did—for a while—until I was alone.

At the end of each shift, I retreated to and concealed myself in the small studio apartment you couldn't see from the street that was as quiet as the forest that surrounded it. The hypnotic rhythm of the fog as it dropped from the trees onto the wooden roof lulled my protected psyche, and with each pat, pat, pat of the falling condensation, I was lured into a trance of safety. The feelings I'd suppressed by keeping frantically busy and distracted bubbled up to antagonize and harass me, but the sturdy serene redwoods and patient docile deer, who regularly greeted my awakening as they ate foliage from the patio, calmed me. I hibernated there, as a large grizzly will do for winter, only my hibernation lasted six years and became, without any conscious forethought, the longest time I ever stayed in one place. I often thought of moving throughout those six years, but the safe anchor of nature held me steadfast. Surrounded by nature's silent acceptance and comforted by the unconditional love of my cats, I began to change. With the passing seasons, I slowly evolved, in increments even I could manage. I released pent up anguish, rage, and sorrow. I felt. I learned that I hadn't been taught, just as my parents—and most people—aren't taught, that I need to feel myself in order to heal myself.

One day I woke up around 11 a.m., felt like my usual energetic self, and then, after being up one hour, found my energy so low all I wanted to do was lie on the couch. I called into work, claimed sickness and watched movies all day on my recently purchased twelve-inch portable TV with VCR attached. I didn't think much about the fatigue. I just allowed myself to do nothing, realizing I was tired from working and going to the gym. The next day I woke up in late morning, felt good and assumed I'd have energy for the day. But an hour or so later, before I was even dressed, I was again exhausted. My arms ached, my legs were heavy, and all I could do was muster stamina for the ride to the grocery store and to Blockbuster for more movies. *Tomorrow I'm sure I'll be fine*, I thought.

But I wasn't. I didn't want to be bothered. I didn't want to think. I didn't want to talk. I took my phone off the hook and didn't call anyone.

The empty take-out food cartons from Whole Foods, the Thai restaurant down the street, and Barney's hamburger place piled up around me. The cats lay with me. I rented four movies at a time and watched them each three times so I wouldn't have to go to the video store every day. I was afraid. The last time I'd been fatigued, I'd been able to at least gather enough energy for work. Now I couldn't even do that. Every day I wondered if I'd ever feel normal again. Would I ever get the energy to go back to work? Would I ever feel like doing anything other than lying on the couch? Would I ever shower regularly again? Would I turn the phone on again?

I didn't know.

I'd lived through one similar experience of exhaustion in my early dancing days and through acupuncture, rest, and healthy food and vitamins, I'd been restored to health after a few months. While I never imagined it would take as long as it had at that time, the tiredness of body, mind, and spirit had eventually passed, and I'd felt rejuvenated. Living through that experience had taught me that my body knew best what it needed, and so now I hoped it would tell me again when it was ready to return to work.

I relaxed.

For two weeks I wondered, watched TV, and tried to muster energy, only to find that after I drove the few miles to the video rental place and the specialty food shop, I was exhausted once again.

I waited.

I listened to myself.

I journaled.

I cried with sad movies, laughed with happy ones.

I stayed with me and didn't leave. For the first time in my entire life, I listened to my body and gave it what it wanted without anyone else's opinion or authority to base my decision on. I gave myself permission to do nothing—absolutely nothing.

I trusted.

Two weeks later I returned to work, fully rested and energetic.

Maybe it was depression. I had been pushing myself for years, draining emotional and physical energy. Years later, I've come to believe that my inner child, long ignored, had taken charge for those two weeks. Like a stubborn three-year old throwing a tantrum in order to protest something she didn't want to do, she wasn't budging from the couch. She was tired of moving—everything; body, mind, homes. And she'd found a safe place and an adult—me—who was finally ready to listen to her. I realized this when I started recalling the foods I'd eaten during that time. I usually ate healthily; tuna, salads, vegetables, and seafood, but for those two weeks I indulged in all the foods small children love to eat; spaghetti-o's—for the first and only time in twenty-five years—burgers, pizza, cheese, potato chips, popcorn, ice cream, Oreo cookies, and chocolate cup cakes. I gave her the safety, consistency, and time she needed and eventually she was ready to be an integrated part of the "whole" me again. I won her trust. She no longer needed to fear I'd ignore her. She no longer needed to fear I'd leave her alone.

As children, we learn to be afraid of many things like stove burners and fire, stepping into a road that has speeding traffic, and catching a bumblebee with our bare hands. These are rational. They keep us safe. They're black and white.

But some fears are in a shade of gray somewhere along the color spectrum between black and white. Fear of missing something important has pushed me out of my comfort zone and out my front door to attend worthwhile events when it would have been easier to stay home. This same fear, though, has prevented me from being still and listening to myself, instead distracting myself through chasing an elusive "happy." Fear of criticism and rejection has motivated me to follow through with commitments like giving talks when I'd rather not because of nervousness. However, this fear has also inhibited me from voicing my opinion and prevented me from saying "no" when I needed to. It has also kept me unconsciously rejecting love before the object of my desire could reject me. Fear of being older and alone has pushed me to continue searching for love and to become the best person I can be so I will attract the best person, but it has also kept me in relationships that were destructive to my emotional and physical health. Fear that I'd developed as a confused teenager—the fear of becoming as dependent on someone as I thought my mother was on my father—kept me striving for personal excellence, seeking fulfilling work, and being independent, but it also kept me emotionally hard. Alone in the Berkeley Hills, I found myself uncomfortably aware of and beginning to understand some of my happiness-limiting fears that under the microscope of stillness were being magnified.

I had to face them.

Like any smart person who is comfortable and safe, I didn't plan on it and didn't want to. I liked my secure reliable world, coming and going as I pleased, working when I wanted to, and being unencumbered by responsibility and commitment. At the same time, however, I'd grown tired of the dazzling mask I wore in order to pretend I loved multitudes of men at my job. In the silence of my home and with clarity of mind, I saw on a continual basis—not just the occasional glimpses I'd seen previously—that I was excruciatingly lonely for someone to share my thoughts, dreams, and fears with. Through my sobriety and awakened consciousness, a sliver of my reality had managed to emerge.

I began to understand how my history of pursuing long-distance love relationships held together by phone and e-mail, of obsessing about men who were addicted themselves, of lusting after those who could only provide material baubles of diamonds and money as signs of affection, and of trying to manipulate and change men who only had *some* of the characteristics I found attractive, kept me isolated and unable to attain the love and bonding I'd always dreamt about. I was attracted to these types of men only because they reinforced and maintained distance; they, too, didn't know how to develop intimacy. Now, with each minute, hour, day, I spent listening to, sitting beside, and staying with myself, I was creating a relationship with—and learning to love—me. There was no one else. Unbeknownst to me then, I was paving my road to self-love. All my self-help books had told me the importance of this, but I'd never understood how.

One evening as I was journaling in my private hideaway, my hand began writing bigger and bigger words until they were so large only a few could appear on the page. Next, my right hand began striking the notebook violently. For fifteen minutes I relentlessly brought my arm up and down in fury at an unseen opponent. I repeatedly stabbed, stabbed, stabbed, while crying, stabbed, stabbed, stabbed until I was completely drained. Alone in my safe room, acting crazy like an old cat woman I once feared becoming, I didn't hold back or censure myself but railed against abuses and injustices that to this day I cannot clearly identify.

Even in the midst of this cataclysmic expression I was aware enough to look for a single person or incident my attack was directed at. *Who? What?* I thought, but I couldn't find one. I just continued to stab, stab, stab. It was as if forty years of unlimited derision, unparalleled shame, and toxic rage that I'd held inside for so many reasons, were all beginning to be expelled through my right arm. I had churned within for decades over my inability to express and defend myself. Men's hands, unwanted, touching me. The unkind remarks, the cruel dismissals, feeling always the outsider, feeling life's joys and pleasures weren't available for me. It was four decades of fury released in a moment's eruption. Like a mythical dragon who creates fire by boiling fluids inside its belly until they're hot enough to be released, I'd churned within and was discharging a firestorm that had been bubbling to an extreme temperature. Even the bottom sheet in the sixty-page notebook had penetration marks.

Afterwards, I realized that just as my fear of being an old woman living alone with cats was unfounded (I was already living alone with cats and life was okay), most of my fears were unrealistic. I'd just lived through something that had grown so large it was indistinguishable and nameless. It felt good to be on the other side. I now knew I could live through any feeling experience.

~

"You really look mad. Smile.," a friend wrote in my 1976 high school yearbook on top of a picture of me sitting in the common area with a cigarette in my hand.

I didn't look mad. I looked downright hostile. I was in my second school of my sophomore year and it wasn't even Christmas yet, faced once again with the need to make new friends. I wore glasses, had acne and was probably contemplating an abortion. I wore anger.

In my official class picture for that year I was smiling, but I wore a marijuana toke stone held in place by a piece of leather tied around my neck symbolically choking the feelings back into my body. By my third high school in the same nine-month period, I didn't feel the anger anymore. I floated a few feet from the ground on booze, grass, and speed to present the illusion of participating in life. I'd quit wearing fury for others to see, but it survived within my body unabated. I had enough unit credits to skip my junior year, so I graduated the next year. My senior high school picture presented an externally tailored sixteen-year old: eyeliner, shiny long blonde hair, flattering glasses.

While growing up, I minimized my anger and swallowed it back into myself in order to be accepted. As an adult, in an effort to be "nice," I rationalized people's injustices against me and excused their behavior when I thought I'd been wronged— if I thought about it at all. My anger wasn't a part of me I wanted to know. Most of my encounters with it ended horribly. It seemed unmanageable, fierce, and violent. It was as uncontrollable as my fear of dogs. Similar to the behavior of Gypsy, the black cocker spaniel we had when I was four who attacked and bit people even after we'd muzzled her, my anger would continue even after apologies were exchanged. I'd feel vindicated only by covertly maligning the perceived transgressor.

Like the dog who came running and barking at me from out of nowhere when I was ten, my anger would sneak up on me then tear around the corners of my psyche coloring the reality of the situation. Or like the dogs that so terrified me at seventeen that I took a ride with a male stranger instead of walking home past them, my anger was sidestepped and avoided. Just as my desire for sex had emerged covertly, so, too, my anger was only unleashed in drunken or drugged episodes. I'd yell, scream, and cry when my inhibitions were low or when I was at a safe distance. Using e-mail helped. I didn't have to face anyone.

Underneath anger usually lies fear and hurt. Perhaps this explains why I cried when I was angry; this response, too, seemed uncontrollable. And theory has it that anger turned inward is depression. Was it the fatigue of holding all that anger in that pushed me to check out of the world for those two weeks? Was my inner child simply so angry she decided to stubbornly stand her ground? Regardless of why this was happening, there was chaos within me that was manifesting itself on the outside.

～

One evening around six, I park my car on Hawthorne Lane, a side street perpendicular to the club entrance, throw my purse and costume bag over my shoulder, grab my clothes on hangers, wait for the traffic light, then walk across Howard Street to the Gold Club entrance. My hands are laden with the man's suit tailored to fit, a button-down white shirt and brown fedora. Typically there's an employee in a tuxedo standing outside, greeting the night-shift girls with a smile and an open door. I don't know the front doorman this evening, but although he's talking with a young woman, he sees me walk past, and we nod to each other. I stand in the fading afternoon light with San Francisco rush-hour traffic whizzing behind me and anticipate his opening the door. While I would normally open the door myself, I can't because my hands are full.

I wait. My arms strain with the load. I look behind me, but his back is turned to me. I sigh. My belongings grow heavier. I look back again. The more my shoulders and arms throb, the more agitated I become.

Unable to hold everything much longer, I step back from the door, stand to the side of them and interject with irritation, "Can you open the door for me?"

The bouncer's eyes, red from what I don't know—lack of sleep, car fumes, a drunken night beforehand perhaps—are menacing as he glares at me before he finally moves to open the door.

Having grown incensed at his disrespect and lack of professionalism with each passing second, I walk into the club and downstairs to the office. "Isn't it the bouncer's job to open the door for us?" I ask one of the managers sitting at his desk.

"Yes," he replies, and I proceed to explain how the one outside right now isn't doing his job. Feeling self-righteous and justified, I leave the office, take the few steps to the dressing room, deposit my heavy load of costumes for my feature show, then walk into the hall between the two adjacent changing areas to talk to another dancer.

It can't be more than a minute when the door to our dressing area swings open, hits the wall close by, SLAM, and the enormous 6'3", 250-pound man the club has hired to keep drunken men surrounded by near naked ladies in line, storms in. Growling like a big black bear in his black tuxedo and overcoat, he quickly erases the distance between us and rains threats upon me as I look up into his dark face. Towering over me he yells, "Don't you ever dis me again. I'll throw your ass out in the street. I'll kick your ass all over Howard! Don't you ever dis me again!!"

"I DIDN'T dis you," I fight back. "You ignored me. I'd like to see you try!" I too am angry. I stand as tall as my 5'4" frame allows. I'm not backing down.

And I'm not crying.

"You just wait till you get outside," he counters.

"I'm not afraid of you," I scream back.

He must be twice my size, but I don't care.

The encounter booms from the beginning, so it doesn't take long for managers to come and break up the heated confrontation. As I shake the adrenaline out of my system and reassure everyone I'm all right, it registers that I'm not intimidated or frightened. His venom released in spittle and warnings hasn't shaken my roots.

Fighting is nothing new in the club. Though it isn't a nightly occurrence, occasionally there'll be fights between girls in the dressing room, sometimes an incident between a girl and a customer. On a few occasions bouncers have to throw a customer out, but there has never been a fight between a dancer and bouncer.

Surrounded by well-meaning and nosy coworkers, I relate the entire experience beginning at the entrance door, and as I do, my mind grasps some coherence. This misunderstanding has erupted between two people battling their own demons. I live in my reality—fatigued, forced to paste a smile on and placate men I'd rather not spend time with, demanding respect from everyone else because I don't always have it for myself. He lives in his reality that I can only guess is something along the lines of catering to mostly white women who are capable of making large sums of cash in a single night who oftentimes don't even acknowledge his existence. I consider this awareness and calm down.

Ten minutes later I'm called into the managers' office and offered a seat. Both the day and night managers are present as well as the bouncer, his head lowered. "If you don't feel comfortable with him working, we'll let him go," they tell me.

I hold the power within me to affect this man's livelihood, and I can finally get back at all those who've ignored, rejected, or denied me. But …

… I'm still 'nice.'

… I'm striving to act instead of react to life.

… I'm no longer angry.

… I'm truly not scared.

"No, he doesn't frighten me," I voice with conviction.

We regard each other in passing for the rest of the time he works there but never speak to each other again.

＝～

Nine months later I'm tired and it's been a difficult night for me, so I decide to leave the club at midnight when the party is in full swing. I'd parked my car close to the front door, a perk of getting to work early, but am now blocked in by a limousine in front of me that has parked in the red zone. There's contact between our vehicles. I ask the outside bouncer whose limo it is. He tells me it belongs to a driver that regularly comes to the club dropping and picking up people. He radios the inside bouncer to get the driver.

I don't want to stand outside in my worn makeup and old clothes under the Club's neon lights, so I move inside the front door to wait for him. A few minutes later he saunters up, a drink in one hand, a girl on each arm.

"You hit my car," I accuse.

"I didn't hit your car," he retaliates.

"Yes, you did and you need to come outside and move it," I retort with a dismissive matter-of-fact tone.

He waves me off with his hand and turns to walk away.

The girls giggle.

I move directly in front of him and block his way. "You NEED to come outside," I declare loudly.

Begrudgingly he sets his drink on the hostess's counter and follows me outside.

He looks at the two vehicles and then rants, "You fucking bitch. There's nothing wrong with your bumper. You stupid white cunt. Leave me alone."

I listen incredulously to his vulgar epitaphs.

He turns to walk back into the club.

I'm livid. Even if there isn't much done to my car I'm not

about to back down now. "There is indeed something wrong with my bumper," I roar.

He turns towards me. "You stupid white whore," he screams.

Enraged, I unleash, "You stupid ass nigger!"

Wham. I'm painfully aware of what I've said—the words sting the inside of my mouth—but I'm unable to roll back time. Instead, I defend myself the only way I know how. I write down his license plate number. "You're drinking and driving. I'm going to call the cops!"

He quickly quiets, jumps in his limo, and speeds away. For days I think about reporting him to authorities but never do.

⸺

I felt powerful and right when I challenged the limo driver and he obeyed and came outside, but using the "n" word was worse to me than cursing. It negated that strength. My behavior was deplorable, something beneath the person I thought I was. But he'd angered me so fully with "whore" that I lost control. The word had dogged me since my uncle had used it when I was ten. Deep within, I believed I was conducting myself like one. Others' words can only affect us when they touch something already within us, and his use of this word triggered the self-doubt that still existed within me because of my choice to be a stripper and have sex at will. I'd lashed out at myself as much as him.

Just as customers in the club had mirrored my loneliness back to me and my coworkers had mirrored the need and greed I'd tried to run from, these two men mirrored what I'd always thought of as a black forbidden emotion—anger. Just as the limo driver had triggered and caused me to react against my own self-doubt when he'd called me a whore, these men's in-the-moment disregard for me not only triggered my anger with them but also triggered the anger I had within myself for my own disregard and rejection of myself. I'd been giving my power away to men for what seemed my entire life. Like I'd done in the safety of my home, staying with my anger as it emerged in isolation while journaling, now, while in the safety of my club family, I spewed and invited witnesses to my anger at a concrete decibel level that they, and I, could hear. In voicing my anger at these men, I, at the same time, vehemently exchanged words with my internal anger and didn't back away from or cower in the face of it.

As I noted earlier, fear and hurt are underlying sources of anger. I'd been hurt by men and still was each night they'd reject a dance with me. I feared this rejection; I literally needed them for financial survival. In my imagination, I needed them for emotional survival as well. And I feared their strength. As a woman, I've been inundated with messages that I should be wary and cautious of men. They're usually bigger, stronger, and can exert power over women in too many ways.

Michael Moore creatively illustrates how media reporting perpetuates this fear, even promotes a culture of fear, especially a fear of the black male, in his documentary, *Bowling for Columbine*. Although I didn't walk around consciously fearful, it was still there as an underlying current that ran through my body and psyche, like the electrical wires that supply your home with light when you flip a switch but otherwise remain obscured. However, in both these heated exchanges I described previously, I stood tall and courageous against the anger I'd often denied and against people I normally feared. And I'd survived.

Webster's defines courage as "the quality or state of mind or spirit enabling one to face danger or hardship with confidence and resolution." I've also heard it in layman's terms; "it's not the absence of fear, but the ability to act in spite of fear."

Drugs and alcohol at one time had given me false courage but at great expense to my mental and physical well-being. The adoration and accolades I received from men had also given me artificial courage. But the courage to listen to myself, all alone, within and in spite of myself, honestly, without judgment, and live through my experiences, this *real* courage, came only when I began learning I could trust myself. Trust, which is a sense of security, is the first prerequisite to positive self-esteem. Individuals need this sense of security before they can look at themselves realistically or risk the possibility of failure. Trust can't exist in an environment of fear.

When I ran a half marathon at age twenty-nine, I willed myself to work through the pain of shin splints until the endorphins kicked in and dismissed the pain. Working through my psychic defenses like denial, dissociation, intellectualization, repression, idealization and projection wasn't so easy. With consistent persistence, however, I broke down these defenses.

Now I was building my understanding and consciousness up. I was beginning to trust that I'd be okay no matter what I thought or experienced. Just like I'd pushed through the physical exhaustion of running the half marathon, over thirteen miles, then stretched and recovered with rest and hot tub soaks while the lactic acid within my muscles subsided, I had withstood the release of pent-up feelings and emotions and emerged on the other side unscathed and furthermore, healed by the experience. I was now more grounded in myself than ever before and learning to be flexible in my opinions and thoughts about my actions. I felt like the tall redwoods in the Nevada forest that I'd hugged, firm and rooted, with their tops free, swaying in the wind.

When I reflected on how my attitude could have caused some of the exchange with the bouncer, I realized I'd been impatient and demanding in my approach to him. Perhaps there was nothing wrong with my bumper. On an easier work night,

I'd have dismissed the limo touching my car, approached the driver light-heartedly asking him to move it, and the verbal war wouldn't have happened. While I had displayed courage in my defense of myself standing up to the two men, I displayed even greater courage afterwards in my examination of my actions and attitudes. I was beginning to see how my mood affected those around me and reflected back.

Along these same lines, when I stopped focusing on what other people wanted from me and turned the focus to how I felt, I realized that my income for an evening had little to do with what I looked like but instead depended upon my energy and demeanor. In other words, the money I made was a direct reflection of how I felt. When I felt tired or anxious, I received a lot of rejection from customers. In our club we had women who were not the stereotypical bombshell with exacting 36-24-36 measurements, but who instead were curvy and plump, lively and happy and who did quite well financially. Outside the club I began to notice that when I felt chilly or rude, I encountered other people who mirrored these qualities back to me, but if I greeted people with congeniality they usually responded kindly.

One October the Gold Club purchased red and black patent corsets, black patent shorts, and knee-high boots, and four of us dancers rehearsed a choreographed routine to perform on the main stage at the San Francisco Exotic Erotic Halloween Ball. On that night it was exhilarating to be milling around backstage at the Cow Palace, San Francisco's civic auditorium, talking to other performers and waiting for Dennis Rodman and his girlfriend to arrive in a limousine. Nina Hartley was one of the emcees. I felt better than the mere ball attendees who actually had to pay to get in—like I was somebody—finally.

I don't remember why the woman who'd designed and taught us the routine didn't have the music with her when she arrived at the venue, but we four waited for the organizers to let us know they'd received our music CD from the Gold Club. I chattered excitedly with a woman from the club who was there performing with a collection of male and female bachelor-party strippers. She introduced me to Marty, a male stripper a few years younger and a couple inches shorter than I, who wore only black leather suspenders and shorts to offset his green spiked hair.

It was a carnival. Instead of the gigantic thin man who measured an inch thick when you turned him sideways and the large fat woman who you couldn't imagine even sitting down, there were respectable adults acting like children who'd finally gotten to remove their clothes and run naked through sprinklers on a hot summer day. The air was charged with testosterone and hormones and pheromones, and I'm sure somewhere in that large venue there were moans of ecstasy from two people, or more, who'd stolen away into a dark corner.

Although my feet hurt in the patent stilettos, I distracted myself with the people, the moment, the anticipation. A gargantuan King Kong walked by with enlarged, albeit fake, genitalia, a petite woman sporting bleached-blonde ringlets by his side. I even saw two men whom I'd taken pictures of the year I wore the black lace body stocking—they were still hard to miss. On the back of their white construction outfits were the words, "Handy Dandy Dildo Company," and on their construction worker's rawhide tool belts hung lifelike and multicolored dildos. In their hands they each held a smooth white vibrator that they buzzed up along women's faces and arms to tease. Their construction hard hats had even been modified to resemble a skin-colored stovepipe hat rounded at the top.

After a few hours, the clock ticked past nine and the leader of our group left to check with management about our place in the lineup.

We three remaining Gold Club dancers mingled and took pictures with other half-dressed performers: thin, sexy, muscled men wearing small shorts, and women like ourselves dressed in provocative bustiers and lingerie.

An hour later she returned with a grim look on her face. "They didn't get our music. We can't go on."

Boots laced up, body snapped in, face painted extensively, hair sprayed into place, I was devastated. I'd been bragging us up. Although we hadn't practiced enough to perform flawless choreography and the entire routine seemed a bit tame for the extravagant event, I'd still wanted to be recognized on that stage.

I lamented to Marty who'd been hanging around me quite a bit since we'd met.

He offered a solution. "I don't have a partner. You can go with me. We'll run on, dance as a pair, then run off. Just follow my lead."

I was in! I had slight twinges of guilt that my other three Gold Club partners wouldn't be going on, but I easily dismissed them.

I waited with Marty by the stage entrance door. Every time it opened, we heard booming music and thousands cheering.

The group that we were to go on after was called.

My stomach flopped, mind raced, nerves twitched. I held Marty's hand loosely.

Ready to spring, we waited for the loud baritone voice to call our name.

Then the announcer said something I couldn't hear and someone yelled, "Go!" Marty pulled me. We were running onto the gigantic stage standing three feet higher than a bobbing mass of heads.

The previous performers ran past heading the opposite direction.

We stopped just as suddenly as we started and Marty stood facing me. Music I didn't recognize blasted around us.

Marty ripped open my corset.

We hadn't talked about this.

The noise swelled.

Momentarily stunned, I nonetheless obeyed when he next grabbed my waist and yelled, "Wrap your legs around me." His muscled arms held me as I bumped against his chest and we simulated sex. My top flapped opened and closed. My breasts bounced up and down.

Forty-five seconds later he set me down, grabbed my hand and yanked me off the stage, running.

Exhilarated, sweaty from the exertion and bright lights, I laughed with him backstage about the spectacle we'd created. "I hope what I did was okay," he apologized.

"Sure." I was no stranger to being topless on a stage.

As our breathing slowed and hearts settled into a more sustainable rhythm, two silver bodies appeared in front of me. They wore only g-strings and single green fig leaves in their hair. It took me a moment to recognize Diana, a coworker who was getting her law degree. "We saw you projected on the big screen and wanted to come back and say hi. This is my boyfriend, Thomas."

Surprised, I hadn't realized I'd be in big-screen living color; I was proud of my stage debut. Months later, I learned that a cable news channel was airing reruns of the Ball when someone came up to me at work and said they'd seen me. I worried briefly, *What if my mother sees?*

Caught up in the spirit of the event and liberated from any stage fright, when the Miss Exotic Erotic contest was held that night for a cash prize, I entered. I needed the five-hundred-dollar prize and craved the attention. As I stood in line on stage, the debauchery of my earlier display boosted my bravado. When the announcer called my name I ran past the end of the stage onto a small two-foot by two-foot platform that jutted out, fell to my knees in a style I'd perfected as a dancer, flipped my long blonde hair, and this time ripped open my own top in order to elicit the largest response. The audience cheered and yelled. I had made it into the next round of the competition.

Next we lined up across the stage, each woman facing the crowd. When it was my turn and the emcee walked over and introduced me as Vixen Wilde, a name I'd adopted for feature shows, the audience clapped lethargically. Although I'd shown the crowd almost all I was physically, I couldn't sustain the energy created by my surprise act only minutes before.

The audience rejected me, and I was disappointed. The thought that I was one of many women rejected by the audience didn't console me. My esteem was based on a fickle throng of strangers who saw an image of boobs, blonde hair, and a blur of red and black. Backstage, I swallowed Marty's words as a consolation prize. "You were the most beautiful and the sexiest woman up there." My ego, fully deflated, plumped up slightly.

After this brief lapse into self pity, almost as quickly as I'd been eliminated by lackluster reaction, I did an about face in my thinking. Their rejection wasn't about me. The audience response had no bearing on who I was and didn't say anything about my worth. This was a large mass of people feeling outrageous and unrestrained who projected their scandalous fantasies onto others like myself who were acting out theirs. I understood that this contest was an obvious example of what I'd been doing my entire life; putting myself in others' vision, hoping they'd like me based merely on what they saw.

Not too long before I'd started go-go dancing and then moved to stripping, I stood in a high-cut body suit one evening exposing my gams in a sexy legs contest at a local bar hoping for the thunderous applause that would signal I was the best. When it didn't happen, it affected my feelings about myself for days and made me hungrier for external praise. I obsessed about the contest and speculated on the reasons I wasn't chosen, replaying in my mind how I could have changed the outcome. I wore the rejection like a big hooded sweatshirt covering my face and smile. The difference this time was that after this Miss Exotic Erotic competition, while the old familiar feelings of "less than" rushed in immediately after my dismissal—it was my conditioned unconscious response—my new powers of thought, introspection and clarity of mind, quickly dispelled the outdated no-longer-useful way of thinking. I saw the event simply for what it was: a salacious competition and risqué spectacle in the spirit of adult fun. This time I didn't have to grasp onto someone or something to help me feel better.

Contrasted to my first Exotic Erotic Ball experience when I'd stood drugged, covered, and rooted in one place feeling inhibited, and the second time when I disguised myself, this time I was completely out of the closet to others and to myself as a woman with an identity—and a body.

Marty took my phone number and called a few days later inviting me to his restaurant in San Mateo. *Hmm*, I thought, *an uninhibited male who is also a successful business owner. This has potential.*

I met him at his restaurant, which was really more like a diner, for breakfast one midmorning and thoroughly enjoyed the omelet his staff prepared.

We talked.

The second time he called expecting to arrange a more intimate date, I reflected back to our phone and in-person conversations. He seemed caught up in immature dialogue with other bachelor-party performers, and his ego was centered in his physique and stage persona. I recognized this because mine had once been like that too. Sure, he had an excellent, muscled body that I could have devoured with delight, but that type of physical satisfaction was no longer enough. Sex, simply for the act, didn't fulfill me any longer. In fact it prevented me from the real intimacy I wanted with someone. I saw the irony in the title of Jenna Jameson's autobiography, *How to Make Love like a Porn Star*. Porn stars don't make love. They act. They pretend. And I'd been acting my entire life. I no longer wanted to pretend. By getting to know the real me, I'd been creating intimacy with myself, and I no longer wanted meaningless connections to others. I was beginning to expect the same treatment from whomever I would choose to bring into my life—and into my body. I couldn't settle for less than what I was learning to give to myself. I'd even written a poem after one previous sexually stimulating but emotionally vacuous encounter with someone else.

Technical Ecstasy

The generic term denoting ecstasy emits
from your cavernous mouth
Oh baby, oh baby, oh baby

Steel cold arms hold me tight and
prod my flesh with hollow fingers
My erogenous zones feel the heat of your circuitry

Deprogramming my brain with interference
Your computerized data center forces
electrical impulses through my body

Lips of supple leather caress my skin and
kiss as instructed in the training video
You have practiced before on other mechanical dummies

I see through your vacant eyes into the bowels of your logic
Your flashing red and green lights
Must arouse, must arouse, must arouse

You have been programmed to excite
Press pressure point #2, pinch pressure points #3 and #4

Buzzzz whirrrr, buzzzzz whirrrrr, buzzzzzz whirrrrrr
I hear your files downloading, where your heart should be

I declined Marty's offer.

At the time I was still using my job as my social outlet and didn't have the energy needed to get out and meet new people, especially men, so I turned to someone very reliable and available at my beck and call—someone who never disappointed. As boyfriends go, he was perfect. He never challenged me. He didn't demand a lot of time. I didn't have to interrupt my schedule to see him. He completely fulfilled me, and in my imagination, our union was sizzling, sensual, and slow, similar to the fantasy heroes in Harlequin romance novels and their bodice-ripping moves.

I'd met this man by accident when I rented the movie *Blow* one night. The fact that he was only a few inches high on my television screen didn't diminish his impact in my life. He was cool (he had long hair), handsome, successful (he ran his own business), sensitive, and loyal. I watched the movie over and over and over until I memorized his words, voice inflections, habits, and gestures. I bought the VHS. He and Penelope Cruz, playing his wife Mirtha, had a lifestyle I envied—rich, sexual, wild—until of course they got caught and George Jung, Johnny Depp's character, was thrown in prison. Then I had empathy and compassion for him and wanted him even more.

I rented his other movies and under the guise of studying his acting, fell in deep deep lust with the most unavailable guy to me ever.

Honestly, it wasn't physically or emotionally satisfying, yet it did occupy my time and kept me entertained in the absence of a real boyfriend. However, it also magnified my isolation and loneliness. Although I never thought it necessary to discuss my Johnny Depp fixation with my therapist, I did talk about the lack of living, breathing men in my life.

"What do you expect?" she asked. "Do you think men are going to magically appear in a line at your front door?"

I laughed and conjured an image of a long line of men snaking its way from my tiny front door.

"You've got to get out and meet them," she continued. "Enroll in a class, pursue a hobby …." Her words faded as my mind drifted.

I already knew everything she was saying, yet at times it seemed to be too much work. On more than one occasion, Johnny had visited me in my dreams. The warm glow of those midnight fantasies felt real—until I woke up, and fighting for the last tendril of dreamy vapor before it disintegrated, realized I was still alone.

The poisonous effects of my denied sexuality and repressed feelings didn't just go away. They needed to pass through my consciousness in order to be completely expelled. Not every past injury or torment that I'd buried has been released with such vengeance as my in-home rage upon the notebook, but past hurts and feelings slowly surfaced once I trusted I could be with myself. With awareness, a sense of safety and time, their intensity dissipated, and the social and psychological limitations I'd unconsciously imposed faded away and quit influencing my actions and reactions. No longer blocked from myself, I could feel more easily in the moment. I was becoming more whole. As I opened myself to feeling within myself, I also opened myself to feeling for others. This metamorphosis within was a natural and necessary progression to developing empathy for others, but all this feeling sometimes became debilitating.

In San Francisco one afternoon, I turned a corner and saw a huge traffic snarl. Traffic was at a standstill. Horns blared. Focusing more closely on the bedlam, I saw an unkempt man standing in the middle of the road, hollering. The noise, stalled chaos, and collective anger of the drivers pushed me to my own annoyance. *What the hell is this?* I thought. Seconds later, clearly able to see and decipher the situation, my irritation turned to sadness and my initial thought evaporated. Heavy hearted, *homeless veteran* flashed through my mind as I watched the handicapped man muttering to himself, struggling with his crutches on one leg.

Witnessing this spectacle I continued my walk, but I could only make it another block before I had to set myself down. His defiance and rage, which I'm sure he needed to defend himself from a world of constant pain, pierced my nonchalant day. I imagined myself homeless with only one leg and all my earthly possessions on my back. The burden was heavy. With the sun on my bent neck and the tourists chattering and pointing at famous sights all around me, I tried to hide my distress but couldn't. I too was confused and disillusioned in an uncaring world. I too was weary trying to secure the things in life that I yearned for so deeply. On the steps leading to Ghirardelli Square, I let loose tears for his futile attempts at trying to find his place in the road and my disheartening attempts to find my place in the world. There I sat weeping in the midday, more naked and exposed to the world than ever before.

ACCEPTANCE:

VALUING
THE SELF

*The only way to real balance within one's self and peace
in the world is to face the dark side with openness and
courage—and come to terms with the truth of reality as it is.*

Mathew Bortolin
The Dharma of Star Wars

RESPECT

So many folks thinking and wanting you to be somebody else will confuse you if you are not very careful.

Kaye Gibbons
Ellen Foster

A weak "no," escaped my lips.

It certainly didn't sound sincere.

"Again, try it again," the woman urged.

Encouraged by the group leader and the women who spoke before me, I bellowed "NO!" surprised and embarrassed at my own vehemence. Emotion, loosened by the explosive command, snuck out as a few small tears. It had been over twenty years since, unable to speak the NO that crashed against the back of my lips, I let Kyle have sex with me in the front seat of his car. Since then, there were countless No's that I'd needed to say but which had never come out.

With every woman in the circle who yelled "No" and stood her ground effectively, my "No," more entrenched, became part of a collective group of "Nos" that we shouted in unison for the women who had yet to learn to say No: polite women, demure women, restrained women, befuddled women, placating women, domestic women, belittled women, battered women, responsible women, scared women, nervous women, shy women—in essence all women. Our "Nos" grew even louder as they ricocheted off the concrete walls in the enormous converted warehouse in the Mission District of San Francisco.

Although I didn't usually feel threatened, defensive moves seemed like good skills to have so I'd enrolled in self-defense training for women, BAMM, Bay Area Model Mugging. In our first lesson we introduced ourselves around the circle and learned about each other; a few were going to be living on their own for the first time in their lives, a few had gotten out of abusive relationships, some attended to support friends who'd enrolled, one mom and her daughter attended together.

We were shown how powerful a weapon our voice could be if only we used it. Our first assignment was to yell "No" with all our might. Easy you may think, but not so for a group of women spanning a range of ethnicities and ages who, for one reason or another, never used the full spectrum of their voices. After that, we were shown simple moves to use along with our voice to fight off an attacker, then stood in line waiting our turn to defend ourselves against a man dressed in a large padded suit and helmet. "You can't hurt me," he assured us. "I'm fully protected, so be as strong and forceful as you can. I'm not going to baby you. A real attacker certainly wouldn't."

I talked nervously with the women in line around me as we watched those before us in their simulated attacks. When it came to my turn, I tried to think in real time, but then instinct just took over; my body summoned every bit of strength it had never before used but should have. When he grabbed me from behind, I stomped my foot on his and jabbed my elbow upwards into his face wanting to connect with his eye. I missed my target. He lunged again and this time I dropped to the ground like we'd been taught and braced myself against the floor with my legs in a position to kick at him from whatever angle he'd come at me from. This first round, over in thirty seconds, awoke my determination and mobilized the fighter within me. It enlivened me to punch, jab, and kick. I felt strong.

We practiced new moves throughout the day and each woman left class standing an imperceptible amount taller than she'd been when she arrived.

The next Saturday we returned for our final day of instruction and our most fierce and final encounter. When it was my time to be in the center, self-preservation coupled with anger summoned adrenaline. The man in the protected suit lunged at me and yanked my arms behind my back in an unnatural way. It energized me. I brought my foot up and back and slammed it into his leg aiming for his knee. His strength so much more than mine, he pulled me to the ground and laid on top. Inside I raged, but I lay very still like we'd been shown to do. When I sensed he'd let his guard down, thinking I was going to easily submit to his desires, I used the move that flipped him overhead and off my body. I stood up and yelled with my full voice as I surveyed the area. The attacker lay still. The crowd broke into applause.

The entire episode happened so fast I didn't remember my arms being pulled behind me until I felt stiff later that night. I looked for a bruise over the next few days, hoping one would emerge as a badge of bravery, but it never did. As if I'd washed away past indignation and abuse, I felt squeaky clean and refreshed. And powerful! I joked about taking a walk into a less-than-safe area, but I never would have intentionally put myself in harm's way. Whenever I spotted someone suspicious, my mind went over the moves I would use to defend myself. My voice—unnaturally high, girlish, submissive at the club— was now deep, determined and direct. I could always use my voice to draw men in, to seduce them, to direct them as to what gave me pleasure. Now I could use it to defend myself against them. No longer would I remain mute. In the spirit of the old Helen Reddy tune, I saw myself; long blond hair teased high and long like a lion's mane, my mouth opened as wide as it could be, yelling wild guttural sounds. I was a woman who was finally roaring.

I'd been experimenting with my voice and gathering my courage since I'd attended Vermont College. In Sue Walden's improv classes and Lee Glickstein's Speaking Circle groups, I'd overcome my fear of rejection and had let my profession be known. Each week I was welcomed back.

Not only was I learning how to use my voice with men in an attack situation, I was also testing women's reactions to my profession by occasionally throwing out that I worked as a stripper. At a Lilith Faire concert, I mentioned to two women next to me that I worked as an exotic dancer. They didn't pick up their blanket and move to another grassy spot on the lawn. In a woman's specialty shop one day, I just mentioned, (it was relevant to the conversation), that I was a dancer. Another patron overheard me talking to the sales clerk and gave me a thumb's up. Instead of women, at least the ones I was running into, shunning and shaming me, most were interested or nonplussed at the very least. If I, as a stripper, was going to be accepted anywhere it was here in Berkeley and San Francisco where many eclectic individuals lived on the fringe of society. This was important because I wanted to transition away from the profession. I'd been so tired of it for so long, but what could I do? Having tasted the freedom of entrepreneurship, I couldn't fathom walking back into a regular work environment that wanted me to be in one place at a certain time every morning.

After college, I'd been focused on writing and the universe responded by sending writing opportunities my way. A freelance contributor for *Men's Health* magazine came into the club looking for a dancer that could write a piece about her experiences. While I wrote a humorous essay that eventually appeared, in part, in *While You Were Sleeping* magazine, *Men's Health* rejected it because they had a vision of what they wanted to print, and it didn't involve my kind of humor. They took my biographical information from me, wrote what they wanted, and had me confirm and accept it. After the issue came out, I heard that men at the Lab were angry with me for what had been written, so I took a second look at the piece. I had to admit that for a few dollars and minutes of writing fame, I'd let men dictate their agenda to me once again, and I'd gone along. I did write a few pieces that appeared in *Gauntlet* magazine, but the pay, minimal if it existed at all, proved I was going to need to do something more than writing for money if I wanted to quit dancing.

Thumbing through the San Francisco Learning Annex Adult Education catalog, I noticed a class titled Strip for Your Lover. *This is something I can teach*, I fancied, so I enrolled to study the instructor and what she was sharing. It was a fun class with enthusiastic students, and as I participated, I observed the way the women reacted to the instructor and her directions. Most were eager and excited; even the quiet students seemed enthralled. And I enrolled in another strip class given at Good Vibrations in Berkeley by an adult toy-store owner from Boston. When I talked with her after the class she said, "All the women who come are really looking for permission."

I took their ideas, combined them with my own, and approached the Learning Annex with my version of Strip for Your Lover. The woman who'd given the class previously lived in San Diego and didn't teach in San Francisco often, so they accepted mine and scheduled it once a month for three hours. I countered my nervousness (I'd never taught a class before), by having the women introduce themselves at the start and encouraged them to relate personal thoughts about any hopes, misgivings, or fears they had. Many opened up about their insecurities and inhibitions; they all wanted to feel beautiful and sexy, yet most were intimidated because they didn't look like fashion models. I tried to impart to them the truth I learned after talking with thousands of men; it's a woman's self-confidence and comfort with her body and sexuality that draws men in and keeps them, not necessarily her size. I gave to the women what I'd given to myself—time and attention—and they gave me a distraction from my work as a dancer and helped me to continue to feel cool.

Many of us, at some point in our lives, usually when we're teenagers, want to be cool. While most seek it as a way to guarantee acceptance from peers, some will lust after it as a way to display rebelliousness. Rock-n-roll is a legitimate adult industry whose roots can be traced to adolescent rebellion. It's what Philip Seymour Hoffman's character, Lester Bangs, in *Almost Famous* refers to as "an industry of cool." If one is successful at making a living at it, even into their 60's and beyond, they get to stay up all night, sing defiant lyrics, party—if their body can handle the abuse, sleep in late, dance around on a stage, and have women (and men) idolize and lust after them. The lifestyle of a dancer can mimic the rock-n-roll lifestyle. For this very reason, being a stripper had always helped me feel cool. It had even put me in close proximity to rock stars on occasion.

In that same movie Lester Bangs also says, "The only true currency in this bankrupt world is what you share with someone else when you're uncool." The women came into the class feeling shy, hesitant, and awkward, and the classes became a safe space where we all broke through the walls of silence around the taboo subjects of sex and desire; most had internalized restrictive and punitive judgments about their bodies and sexuality. Just as I'd learned while dancing that recognizing and resurrecting my sensual nature empowered me for *me*, that it wasn't strictly for the men, I empowered my students to celebrate this aspect of themselves with the same enthusiasm they celebrated their nurturing-mother or competent-businesswoman nature.

Looking past the facade that we wore to shield ourselves from criticism, our own as well as other's, we negated those old, outdated judgments and laughed with one another. We learned that no matter what our ages were, no matter what our sizes, ethnicities, or even gender attractions were, we all had similar inhibitions and insecurities. As they learned choreographed strip routines and really felt the sensual aspect of their bodies from the inside out (the one-time three-hour class grew into twelve-week classes) they'd find new respect for their bodies and would blossom like a delicate fragile iris. Their limbs would extend gracefully, and the hues of their gentle soft nature would unfold in the slow methodical ways they'd move their bodies.

Our collective bad girls came out to play in a safe space where they could be listened to, honored, and empowered appropriately instead of being shamed and ridiculed. We learned we weren't alone in our desire to seduce and tease, to be sexy and pursued, to be the vixen or siren we sometimes felt like on the inside. Together, we found permission to welcome and embrace the feminine part of our nature we'd always thought forbidden, and we grew our awareness and acceptance of ourselves as we grew our awareness and acceptance of one another.

I'd "come out of the closet" to myself, to my peers at Vermont College, to my parents, and now to women in my own home area. While the women embraced my tips and advice on how to be sensual and sexy, I learned that my greater skill wasn't in tempting men; my greater skill was in my ability to help women feel good about themselves. Just as they'd done in the BAMM class, the women would leave standing an imperceptible amount taller than when they started. In trying to become sexy and cool, we came together and became uncool, which really was the coolest, and led to each one of us feeling cool by and for ourselves.

Marketing has spun entire industries that define cool based on material possessions that one needs money for, usually a lot of it. In my early dancing career, when I was still working at the Lab, counting my stash of hundred-dollar bills every time I added to the pile, I was focused on the money. I was respecting the money more than I was respecting myself. The universal law of attraction states that we attract what we focus on. It's no wonder then, at that time, there was a recurring pattern of multitudes of men every night I worked offering me enormous amounts of money if only I would sleep with them. Each time though, annoyed at them for even thinking I'd consider their offer (my ego needed to keep up my self-delusion of being a good girl), I considered their offer. "No" didn't come easy to me then, and I had no clue I was attracting the offers. I instead became angry at them for tempting me with the Almighty Green. There were so many offers in fact that after an especially grueling night when I had to wrestle within myself and empathically say "no" eight times, I went home and vented my anger through poetry:

Stripper's Lament

You think you're sexy, you think you're cute
But let me tell you the honest truth.
This is my business, my fair thee well
If you think otherwise you can go to hell.

If you're fat and balding and out of shape
What makes you think you look so great?
What makes you think I can be attracted
What makes you think you could get me off.

The honest truth is I want your money
That's the only reason I like you honey.
So keep this straight in your inflated little head
And forget the thought of taking me to bed.

I need to eat, I need some shelter
And I could care less if you're so wealthy.
This is a fantasy, nothing more
Excuse me sir, I'm not a whore.

After the motel room incident with the stranger, when I realized he could overpower me and nobody knew where I was, I became clear that I wouldn't engage in prostitution for *any* sum. I had a new small measure of respect for my safety and the offers quit coming. Eventually, I even let go of the anger at the men for asking. They were victims of the media stereotype that all dancers were prostitutes just like I'd been a victim of a money- and image-obsessed society. On the rare occasion when someone did ask, which was probably only five more times in eight years, if that many, I'd laugh it off and interpret it as the shallow compliment it was. It was merely a job hazard, a complication of the circumstance.

Cool, as measured from outside ourselves by someone else, is also a way, we mistakenly think, to gain respect. Initially I thought I had the respect of the men in the club, (today I know differently). The fact that I hid my dancing profession from co-workers and family exhibited a lack of respect, for it, as well as a lack of respect for myself for engaging in it. The tricky thing about respect is that if you don't have it for yourself, no one else can have it for you either. In retrospect though, I have to respect my process of perseverance. I always remained loyal to finding happiness and peace within in spite of my self-sabotage tendencies: although my mind was foggy with substances, I attempted therapy; although I wasn't able to change my behaviors overnight, I continued to devour self-help books; although jealousy of their accomplishments blocked me from hearing the entire message of workshop and lecture presenters, I participated in retreats and seminars that promised sustainable confidence and a better life. Little by little I'd been strengthening my self-respect muscles. For love to last, one needs respect.

Puttering around my Berkeley home one afternoon, I was listening to KGO, my favorite San Francisco-based radio station. Jill Eikenberry and Michael Tucker, a husband and wife who starred on the popular television series that ran from 1986 to 1994, *LA Law*, were being interviewed about their play in Mill Valley, where they were currently living. Among the questions they were asked was why they left Hollywood, a world so many were trying to get into. The words Michael Tucker spoke that day made as much of an impact on me as the words spoken almost ten years earlier by the counselor who had challenged me not to be a victim. "Once you're really seen by someone else," he said in reference to the intimacy he and his wife shared, "you don't need to be seen by the world."

Being a dancer, I'd likened myself to actors and had even placed them on pedestals. From these people I admired, I was ready to hear those few simple words—and understand them. I interpreted Michael Tucker's statement to be relevant to my growth, beyond intimacy shared with another, to include intimacy created within one's self. In other words, once you see and accept yourself when you're uncool—you don't need others to validate your "cool."

On stage, I no longer thought about what the customers wanted. Instead, I was stimulated by lyrics I resonated with, moved with moods evoked by chords, and reverberated with drums that struck my taut reserve. It was as if the musicians were plugged directly into my soul, the drummer pounded within my groin and the guitarist plucked my legs and pulled my arms to touch my own searing flesh that baked under the stage lights. Like a marionette on a string, my movements were commanded by the range and intonations of the singer, the literal and symbolic meaning of the lyrics, the deep guttural bass guitar and the wail of the electric guitar. Music had always resonated within me, and my love of it and of dance had helped lure me to work in the strip club, but now it infiltrated me. Because I'd seen myself, heard myself, and sat with and endured the pain I'd held within, in directly opposite proportion, I could now feel the pleasure of my body and sensuality of its movements. I felt the supple softness of my elongated neck, the smooth silky skin of my hip. I became one with the songs I had the deejay play for me, and the black hole within, that I'd begun to empty by dislodging and releasing emotions and feelings, I now filled with myself. My dancing felt personal—private.

Oddly enough, as the line between the music and me blurred, the act of preening and posing on the stage that had become as natural as tying my shoelaces, felt violating. The leering eyes were invasive. For the first time in over eight-and-a-half years I moved my hands over and upward, past my face and higher still through the length of my hair, then let the strands fall helter skelter around my head and in front of my eyes in a thin blonde shield. I wanted to guard against revealing my bare being to the crowd of strangers. I needed to escape the penetrating eyes of the men who wondered what it would be like to take this woman to bed, to kiss her, touch those breasts, or spread those legs.

My musically choreographed movements revealed the sole person of my present and the soul manifestation of a life held so close within that even I didn't know what it was at times. It was the stage lights that had helped illuminate my numb body, brain, and spirit and propelled me to see myself as I truly was, and it was the stage that I now needed to hide from. I stood rooted to the varnished wood floor wearing only a white thong and my stiletto heals, my outer skin unable to protect my core and stop the world from encroaching upon a fragile girl who never felt comfortable in the skin of a woman everyone else wanted her to be.

My work philosophy had always been that even if there was only one man in the club, his money could be mine. Once I arrived at the club I was anxious to get on the floor right away. I hadn't understood the women who would come into work and hang in the dressing room putting off getting on the club floor as soon as possible. I hadn't understood the women who sat around on the floor surveying the crowd, hesitant to approach. Writing this today, I imagine the energy I needed to be the vivacious Vixen, and I'm exhausted just thinking about it, but then there was no thought; I just did what I had to do. I amped myself up with caffeine and hard-driving rock music from bands like Disturbed and Alice in Chains and drove over the San Francisco Bay Bridge, my adrenaline increasing with each mile closer to the club. I could feel the energy of the city's concrete and decadence rising up to support me. But after almost nine years it had become increasingly difficult to muster that energy. The familiarity, instead of welcoming me, repelled me. I'd begun delaying my approach to the men.

I was tired of the persona that catered to others' fantasies.

I was tired of turning men on by licking my own nipples.

I was tired of letting them lick me in the dark corners just to make a few extra twenties.

I was tired of their hands on me.

I was just tired.

By this time the classes had grown into a video project that I produced and starred in and my days were spent in an editing studio making decisions about what to cut and use from the five-day, three-camera shoot. After hours of sitting and scrutinizing video, I was exhausted. I'd run to the club and throw on an old worn outfit. I no longer cared about having new or elaborate costumes and the only reason I continued to do feature shows was to waive the sixty-dollar stage fee for that night. Also, the intimacy I'd created within myself and the feelings the music evoked within my soul and body were mine, and I didn't want to share them with people who didn't know or care for me.

The patrons became too nosy.

Standing in front of them for the personal dances, without even the imaginary barrier of the stage to distance myself, their eyes were searing as if I'd been poked with a heated branding iron. I recoiled from their gaze. I felt the magical notes that emanated from the loud speakers so intimately that I tried to hide. I gathered the long hairs I had once used to tease and instead draped them across my face hoping to disappear.

I didn't know what to say. I no longer cared if they liked me.

Their hands grew large and dirty. Their expelled breath became noxious air and the thought of it getting on me was caustic. They had cooties.

We instruct children to stay away from strangers, and one particular night, my inner little girl wanted to turn and run. I couldn't ignore her.

Frightened of the men, I ran to the dressing room and sobbed. It was only 8:30.

I left work.

On the drive home, I admitted that not only was I frightened of the men, but I was also frightened of my disgust with them as well. How could I work if I was frightened?

I returned two nights later.

It was Saturday night, and as usual the few customers who arrived early were preoccupied watching the stage. I was hesitant to approach them, so I ordered dinner and sat upstairs hiding in conversation with friends. We finished our meals, consuming an hour. By this time a few more customers had come in.

"I just don't feel like I can talk to them," I lamented. My arms felt the exhaustion that had become common; they ached and were too sore to be lifted. My legs didn't want to hold me up. Even with ambiance lighting, the downstairs club floor looked as dark as my mood.

Trina and Jolene tried to boost my spirits. Within the last few years, I'd grown closer to Trina than anyone else in the club, and Jolene was a close second.

"You look fabulous," Jolene said.

Trina urged, "There's three at the table by the stage. You take the one with the smile, he looks friendly, and we'll take the other two." Trina was an awesome saleswoman. She knew all the right things to say and usually made more money than me. It didn't matter that she had a larger waist and smaller breasts. She knew how to sell. She didn't take no for an answer.

"Okay," I said lethargically, feeling like I *should* try. I'd buoyed myself up many times before when my energy was low, and often the night turned into a great one.

I walked towards the man who appeared to be a Hispanic blue-collar worker and tried to imagine where the encounter could go

It could be pleasant, I told myself.

It could be easy, I told myself.

He could have more money than I imagine he does, I told myself.

Pasting a grin on my face, bringing my cleavage close to his eye level, I asked him if he wanted a dance. There was no small talk, no engaging attitude, no witty banter.

I'm sure he saw a pathetic tired woman who didn't really want to dance, but who felt it was her obligation to do so. He said "okay" anyway.

I was surprised, though I can't say pleasantly, and tried to start the dance right away.

"Hey, the song's started already," he reproached. "Let's wait for a new one."

I agreed but sat silent waiting for a new song to start. When it did, I stood quickly and did the same move I'd done too many times to count. I began peeling my dress down slowly to reveal the skimpy bikini beneath. I got it down to my waist then turned around to peel it slowly over my buttocks.

He grabbed my legs.

I flinched.

An appropriate response when a stranger touches you, you might think, but it had never happened to me before.

Traumatized. Suddenly. I pulled my dress up.

I saw the questioning look on Trina's face.

I hurried downstairs to the safe dressing area.

I CAN'T DO THIS, I screamed inside my head.

"It's okay, you don't have to," I spoke out loud to myself through quivering lips.

I put my regular clothes on, feeling protected.

I gathered my makeup and costumes into my bag.

I left.

My mindset had been changing for a while. The last few shifts I'd worked, I'd had the deejay play "Nice to Know You" by Incubus, with a repeating phrase about the pain of an experience feeling like, "a waking limb... pins and needles." The song also repeated, "Goodbye," over and over.

I'd heard a dancer say once, "The only way to leave the profession is to get so tired of it the money doesn't matter."

Well, it didn't—anymore.

I was sick and tired of their groping and our griping; of their probing and my having to outwit them, like on the rare occasion when someone asked me specifics about being a Green Bay Packer's Cheerleader, an intro statistic that had continued after a deejay once fabricated it since I was from Wisconsin. I'd literally heard and said it all and I'd met, talked with, and danced for single men, lonely men, married men, young men, old men, short men, tall men, fat men, skinny men, rude men, men with premature ejaculation, rich men, poor men, frightened men, angry men, gay men, horny men, and cross-dressing men. I'd met and talked with sports superstars; Troy Aikman had requested five one's back after handing me a ten-dollar bill as I stood topless on a stage in Las Vegas, and I had first-hand experience of Charles Barkley's arrogance and Sebastian Janikowski's immaturity. I'd met Bill Maher and seen Sean Penn and Nicholas Cage, talked with Lars from Metallica, shook Marilyn Manson's hand and had been invited to party with Manson and his entourage. I'd unknowingly walked away from Gene Simmons from KISS (he wasn't in makeup), tried to finagle concert tickets from Tool's singer, Maynard, and had been resentful of Kid Rock who'd shown up at the club one night, and the deejay dumped my music to play one of his songs I wasn't familiar with. I'd entertained a member of Clinton's Secret Service (at least that's who he claimed to be, as he showed me his revolver tucked away by his ankle) and the CEOs and upper management of 24-hour Fitness and Yahoo when those companies were in their infancy. In none of these exchanges had I received the caliber of respect I'd hungered for except when talking and sharing dinner with Stephen Tyler from Aerosmith, whom I met in my early dancing days.

But I didn't need their respect anymore.

I'd developed my own.

I earned sixty dollars my very first day dancing nine years previous and hadn't paid a stage fee. My last day I paid my sixty-dollar stage fee, then walked away without making any money.

We were even.

When my mind confirmed what my body already decided—that I'd quit dancing—I stood in front of the mirror, looked myself in the eyes, proclaimed I'd no longer have to take my clothes off for a living, and felt overwhelming relief. I repeated this numerous times throughout the next few days in order to really believe it. It wasn't my last time dancing (I write more about this in chapter ten), but I had made a big decision, and I was on my way.

Soon though, I discovered that when I began trying to relax into my body, breathing deeply didn't come naturally. It wasn't until I stopped dancing and consciously tried to breath deeply that I really knew how much pressure I'd put on myself to maintain physical perfection, how thoroughly I'd judged and scrutinized myself in order to please others. Although I'd sucked my feelings in exquisitely trying to conform to a marketed version of svelte female perfection, I no longer felt I had to keep my stomach excruciatingly flat since I wasn't competing with women half my age. Still, I struggled to get air past the narrow opening that had become my throat. The thought of allowing my stomach to extend caused me anxiety. It was work. I labored to take breath deep into my belly. I had to talk to myself and declare that it was okay to have a belly and be soft, and then I had to trust my words. For fifteen years, I'd kept my muscles rocklike and my stomach hard.

Determined, I'd close my eyes and with my arms and hands around my waist tell myself it was okay, to breathe deeply, let my stomach out, to *have* a stomach even; to feel, heal, express. I would stop wherever I was and close my eyes to feel the liberating breaths within my gut and to block out what I falsely imagined to be stares at my huge round self. Over the many months of this conscious effort to learn to relax and breathe, so many more feelings that I had swallowed and held tightly began to emerge slowly. Feelings of pain, isolation, fear, loss, and loneliness yammered for release. I still needed to bring them to the surface and let them go.

I had no words for these feelings deep within me back then. Initially, some of them surfaced in a faint inner voice that I've come to learn is the meek little girl within me. She spoke in code. I designate this voice as my inner child's voice because as children we don't have the vocabulary to express ourselves, and neither did I have the words to recognize what I was feeling. This inner child who'd wanted to turn and run from the strangers in the club began to get my attention in the only way she knew how.

Dimly at first, like a flashing neon light seen from a distance, "Stella," "Stella," "Stella," flashed intermittently through my brain, shadowed and blackened by all the other thoughts and voices that I carried within my mind as if they were crammed together in a stuffed backpack. Eventually I'd get it. I'd settle down in front of an old VHS copy of the movie *Stella* wherein Bette Midler acts as a fiercely independent woman who doesn't feel worthy of love and who sacrifices her daughter's love in order to provide a better life for her. Watching the story, my feelings of sadness, loneliness, frustration, and fear were released in tears that began to wash away the crusty, stoic reserve I'd once had about expressing them. At the end of the film, Stella stands in the dark dressed in a nondescript long coat and scarf and tries to watch her beautiful daughter celebrate her wedding day. She is told by a policeman to quit staring through the window and to leave the happy family alone. In this final scene, as the rain pours over her, Stella stands as a spectator of her daughter's life, not as a participant in it. That's what I identified in my own thoughts; I was a spectator of others' joy, but never a participant worthy of having my own, and in camaraderie with Stella I'd release an avalanche of tears.

Stella was the first movie to help me begin to bring out my feelings, mostly of sadness, but there were others. Towards the end of *Frankie and Johnny* when Michele Pfeiffer who plays Frankie declares to Al Pacino's character, Johnny, that she's terrified of someone getting to know her intimately because of all her quirky habits, I, too, wailed about my own fears of getting close to someone; wanting it so badly, but not knowing how to go about achieving it. *Remember the Titans* and *The Hurricane* tapped into my feeling of being an outsider and helped inspire hope as I connected with strength in perseverance and purpose. *GI Jane* and *Enough* helped me identify with being a victim of men, yet again impassioned hope and power. Today, I can express emotion without movies as a crutch, but for the longest time, I needed their catalyst to unearth the buried, undeniable parts of me I wasn't familiar or comfortable with.

My own DVD, originally titled *The Art of Sensual Dance*, then renamed *Striptease for Real Women*, generated income, but I needed more money in order to pay the myriad of financial bills I'd amassed while making it. Through an acquaintance, I heard about a catering company that was hiring. I was used to working nights and weekends and liked the flexibility of choosing my own schedule and going into different venues to set up the parties, so the job appealed to me. Besides, I'd always made guest appearances in others' lives; first as a transient military child, then as a traveling service technician, third as a dancer, and lately as a teacher of individualized strip routines when women invited me into their homes and shared details of their intimate lives.

This pattern of anonymity continued in the catering profession. Mingling briefly with guests, then leaving, was attractive. Also, the party atmosphere and music appealed to the gregarious dancer within me. But unlike stripping, where I had to finagle, coerce, outwit or preen in order to get paid, now I had no responsibility other than taking direction, smiling at the guests, serving, and cleaning.

Late one afternoon, as the sun shone through bay windows that overlooked a grassy meadow, I was serving cake during a wedding reception. My mind was focused on getting the cake served quickly, and my concentration was only aware of who had or hadn't received the slabs of marbled vanilla chocolate confection with dainty yellow flowers. I was holding two plates of cake in one hand and setting down a third in front of a guest when something hit my head.

Laughter burst forth through the entire hall.

I paused, hand in midair.

"Are you alright?" someone asked.

"Yeah," I murmured, stunned and chagrinned.

"The bouquet bounced off your head."

I looked down. On the floor to my right lay the neatly gathered white and yellow roses that had sailed over the eager single women's hands.

"You're next," the woman I was serving announced too loudly for my comfort.

I good-naturedly laughed, "I don't even have a boyfriend."

"Then it's going to happen fast," another woman at the table chimed in.

I chuckled even louder.

Another guest repeated that thought later in the evening and my response was, "I don't even have any prospects, any interest in anyone."

But inside I hoped.

Were they right? Was this some strange omen from the universe? What were the odds of being hit directly on the head by a wedding bouquet? I certainly wouldn't have stood in a group to catch one. I hadn't been a guest at a wedding for over ten years.

I wasn't swept off my feet in a hasty romantic gesture within a short time after that, but I was hit over the head with a new awareness of respect for ceremony and tradition.

My initial thoughts about the weddings we catered were that they were sad. I thought that since we arrived with our truck, unloaded and set up into an empty hall, then cleared everything back out after five or six hours while the bride and groom were still there, it was a manufactured event, a man-made fabrication without meaning. Yet after six months, I was surprised by my tears at the strangers' wedding nuptials.

I was exposed to formal customs and sacred rituals of various cultures such as Jewish, Russian, Indian, Asian, and Native American. While two people declared their commitment to each other, the small voice that once told me which movies to watch was now telling me that I wanted this commitment for myself. For many years, my closely held dream consisted of being connected with a partner through marriage. These thoughts were so private though, that even I wasn't aware of them.

At the age of forty-five, with no prospects in sight, it was much easier to navigate my daily life if I didn't focus on what I didn't have, but instead focused on what I could get—and what was familiar. For me, that was using my body, using my sex. My history of substance abuse and chaotic men was in the past, but the strip club had been a way to continue to live in that kind of disheveled dysfunction. Now I didn't have that to distract myself, so I found myself lusting after inappropriate men again. I wasn't the dancer anymore, but I missed the numbing effect of it. I tried to recreate the chaos by blatantly throwing myself at one bartender I worked with regularly who I found deliciously oafish. He was an alcoholic who reminded me of an ex-boyfriend. Over and over, I made subtle and not so subtle hints, suggesting we have casual, no-strings-attached sex. He wasn't going to respect me, I knew that, but I wanted a distraction. I did know how to have sex even if I didn't know how to have love with another. In my home, I'd surrounded myself with symbols of my idealized love with a partner; miniature statues of a man and woman embracing. These hard lifeless objects were easier to control and possess than real love had been for me. I didn't know how to secure love, and that longing had been subdued in recent years in defense of my hard-won sexual liberation and prowess.

Without reciprocity on his part, the bartender obsession I'd created in my mind evaporated. Someone had mentioned once that she thought my "picker" was broken, and looking back at my history with men confirmed this odd thought even though I'd laughed when she'd said it. Later, I admitted it was a logical—and simple—explanation as to why I had so many relationship mis-steps. Those romances had always started with lust, so now I reasoned that if I felt an initial physical attraction towards someone it was probably because the man wasn't available to me in some way; I was attracted to distance and unavailability and those men had only brought me heartache. What might materialize if I tried something new? While never making a conscious pact to stay out of relationships or unhealthy, unfulfilling sexual encounters, this new way of thinking turned into what amounted to a year without sex, the longest time I'd been celibate since my mid-teens.

I didn't know how, or if, romantic love would come, but I never gave up hope. If I met a new man and he had qualities I admired, I decided to go out with him. I'd even made and honed a list of the traits, physical and emotional, that my ideal man would have. After each failed relationship or lackluster date, I added to or altered my list then put it back in my wallet. I looked at it on occasion. I saw hope in that piece of paper, and I saw hope in the ceremonies I now witnessed every weekend. My eyes were opened to the honor and sanctity of the marriage union and brightened with the community of family. I saw relatives come together from all over the world. I saw beauty in the eighty-seven-year-old grandmother from Yugoslavia who could only walk with assistance and the elderly white-haired couples that sat side by side, watching the young people dance. For the first time in my life, I saw innocence and peace that radiated from sleeping babies.

Still, after one year, I began resenting the people at the weddings even as I envied them. The need for love and family that I was beginning to feel was rare and raw, a new wound that I wanted to band-aid. Covered by denial, this yearning remained outside my everyday awareness, only emerging towards the end of an event when I felt fatigued and battered by the constant reminder of my lack of connection with others. Just as I had glimpsed my desire to be the intended bride and not the bachelor-party girl years before, I now had the momentary glance at my desire to be close with others as I lightly skipped around guests collecting dirty dishes and glasses while trying to remain unobtrusive and invisible. Afterwards, I'd return to my one room with my two cats. Though I'd kept this dream at a distance for many years by embracing the affection of my feline friends (what could be more wholesome a love than breathing in the soft pink innocence of a cherished cat's underbelly?), my appetite for a richer life was becoming enormous as I observed what else could be served on the platter of life. This deep bottomless hunger reminded me of the emptiness of my life. I was starving for love.

But these weren't my family and friends. And it wasn't my food. Still, I was surrounded by it.

I'd prepare food, pass hors d'oeuvres, and serve meat, salad, and vegetables to guests from behind the buffet table, unable to eat for hours unless I could pop a morsel into my mouth without anyone seeing. I now ate like I'd experienced my sexuality in the past—sneakily, guilt-ridden. Often, I had to endure the overpowering emptiness in my stomach.

I'd freed myself from mind-altering substances, extreme busyness, over-exercise, over-work, and bad relationships, but I was a woman who'd obsessed about food as well. Throughout my twenties and thirties, I'd tried to protect myself from food and control it just like I'd tried to protect myself from loving and needing too much. A sweet confection was similar to sweet affection. If I gave into the temptation, I'd gorge myself. The men would consume me, so I would run away. The food would fatten me, so I would exercise to exhaustion.

Just as I'd known for a long time that the men I was choosing weren't good for me and it would be beneficial to steer clear of them all for awhile, I also knew that I responded to certain foods in an unhealthy deleterious manner. I knew that binging on gallons of ice cream in the evening or eating a meal so huge that all I could do was sleep afterwards didn't make me feel good; but just like I'd known that being hit by Kyle didn't feel good and crying while having sex with George didn't feel good, I couldn't easily stop myself. Similar to how using my body and sexuality had swung like a pendulum to extremes before this time in my life, so too did my eating swing over my lifetime. I'd either undereat, feeling slim and perfect when I was hungry, or I'd overeat, feeling gargantuan and heinous.

For twenty years I'd been educating myself on nutrition and the detrimental effects refined sugar had on the human body, so I began attending Overeaters Anonymous meetings and decided to treat my inability to control my sugar binges as an addiction. I abstained from it.

I felt great. My sinuses cleared up and premenstrual cramps went away. I felt successful and certain this was the way to combat my food issues. But after eight weeks of not eating any refined sugar, the power I'd given the sweets by regimenting my approach to them, either all or nothing, and the lack of what I felt was sweetness, love and family in my life, converged.

After helping to serve a four-tiered lemon wedding cake one evening, I found myself wanting to dive right into the white creamy frosting and swim around in the luxurious lemon gel until it was absorbed into my pores. I pictured myself doing it. It was light and fluffy. It would support me. I could float, backstroke. I could nestle my face next to the rich texture and feel it massage my skin like a scrumptious peach papaya. Whenever I wanted, I could dip my hand down, bring up a sinfully rich handful and slather my face with it before licking each of my tasty fingers.

I decided to taste a small piece.

It was yummy.

I felt satisfied.

Momentarily.

I found a reason to stay in the kitchen and help clean up instead of going back out on the floor and clearing dishes from the tables. I decided on a second, bigger piece. After all, there was a lot left over and everyone had been served. After I ate this second piece of lemon nectar, I scooped up a pile of frosting that had gotten pushed to the side of the cake platter while we were cutting it. My tongue was excited by this ambrosia to my neglected palate. I wasn't a chocolate fan like so many others. Lemon was my favorite.

Then another server brought extra pieces back to the kitchen. We'd cut and plated more than the number of guests and as the plates of cake sat on the counter, they called to me.

"Susan. Suusaann. Sooossssannnnn. We're delectable ... sweet ... comfort ... filling .... Sooossssannnnn."

I tried not to look in their direction, but they chimed together in unison and their clustered collective voices masked any other voice of reason that might have been present in my mind.

Though I'd eaten a second helping of frosting, I now reached for the third, fourth, and fifth pieces of cake. It happened so fast that by the time I'd finished them all, I was stuffed. My stomach ached.

I'd had enough.

Maybe.

I went back for more frosting. It had a cream cheese base, not too sweet but sinfully special for my inner child who felt neglected and shut out of the party.

At two a.m. I awoke to a spinning room and nausea so extreme that it felt like I'd drank too much. I got to the bathroom quickly, rested my head on the commode, and willed myself to vomit. I even tried sticking my finger down my throat to relieve the feeling, but I just gagged. After a significant amount of time the feeling subsided, and I returned to bed, certain it was all over. An hour later, a violent stomach upset woke me again, and I made my way to the bathroom to hug the porcelain base, breathe in the odor of the unclean bowl, and wish the room to quit spinning. Craving sleep but feeling I would upchuck at any moment, I tore myself away from my comforting embrace with the toilet and contorted myself to fit on the tiny bathroom rug. I covered myself with a damp towel and lay there for another two hours of fitful dozing. I never did vomit, although I wanted to.

Throughout my entire adult life, I'd given food power to make me feel elated, happy, sad, then bad. I'd tried staying away from it like I'd distanced myself from others to control uncomfortable and unwanted emotions. I'd stay away—then I'd be safe. But my attempt at control left me out of control. The food didn't hurt me. I did. I'd dumped so much sugar into my small frame that I overdosed. I couldn't control others, and I couldn't control myself. My feelings just were. My appetites just were. No label—not good, not bad—just *me*. I had to learn how to nourish myself healthfully at the same time I was learning to nurture myself emotionally. I had to learn to get that sweetness for myself. I had to accept my need for a richer life.

In Berkeley, there was a Longs Drug Store I often frequented. It was in close proximity to the laundromat, grocery store, and bank. At this Longs, there was a homeless man who regularly sat outside the store property on the city sidewalk and asked for money as patrons walked in and out. Although it's not my nature to encourage long-term homelessness, when I'd first moved to Berkeley I'd given him five dollars because he told me he had kids and needed the money to get a room out of the rain. As I saw him well fed and in the same place begging all the time, for years, night and day it seemed, I resented giving him that bill because I realized I'd been duped. Week after week, month after month, he'd be there talking, cajoling, and oftentimes his persistent niceties unnerved me. "You sure is looking nice today," he'd yell as I walked away from him. Even his, "Have a nice day," began to rankle me. It wasn't what he said sometimes but what his tone implicated to me; that he was thinking about more than casual weather. Eventually, I felt so harassed, I started parking my car out of the way so I wouldn't have to walk by him.

One evening, 8 p.m., I was walking from the laundromat to the drug store, and there he sat on his little wooden box with his headphones on, soliciting the few people who were still shopping. As I walked past and made my way toward the store entrance, I heard, "You sure are looking mighty good tonight."

I was not amused.

Immediately, automatically, as if someone else was directing my actions and I was performing on cue, I whirled around, started walking back to him and demanded, "What makes you think you can talk to me that way? You have no right to talk to me that way!"

I was shaking. It was dark, and the area was deserted except for the people in the store. Standing, he was over six feet tall. Nonetheless, my BAMM self-defense training and the solid concrete sidewalk gave me stable strong support.

I demanded an answer.

He feigned ignorance and pointed to his headphones as if he couldn't hear me.

"You can hear me," I voiced loudly and substantially. "I'm going to report you."

I stood my ground a few seconds longer to punctuate my seriousness before turning around and walking into the store. I reported him to the store clerk after I grabbed my laundry detergent and bleach.

"Yeah, we don't like him here either," I was told. I hadn't asked to call the police, but I was comforted by the clerk's knowledge. Although I was anxious, I was also curious to see what would happen when I left the store. I felt like Skimo, my thirteen-year-old cat, who after two months of living with a new dog and hiding in one room to feel safe, emerged full force, hissing and chasing the dog through the living room. I, too, had felt trapped, but had finally had enough and came out of my corner ready for a fight.

I was still shaking when I rounded the store doorway and discovered, to my relieved amusement, that he'd packed up his few belongings and scrammed after the petite woman called him to task.

While I sorted clothes and added detergent to the washers I felt proud that I had finally challenged this man's invasive remarks instead of swallowing them. I gleaned strength and confidence from his cowardice. Later, someone walking by the laundromat commented that he'd seen me standing up to this homeless man, that people had complained about him for a long time, and that even the police didn't like him there. I didn't solicit or need a stranger's validation of my actions, but it was reassuring that someone had noticed and approved. A lifetime of approval seeking doesn't evaporate over a night, week, month or even year, but this approval was for a worthwhile solid cause—my liberation and respect.

This was my third run-in with a large black man, a member of the group of people whom I'd learned to fear in 1976 when our family moved to Ft. Benning, Georgia, and I, a lonely scared fifteen-year old, entered my third high school in less than six months. In the early days of desegregation, all us army high school kids were bussed into the middle of an all black neighborhood in the city of Columbus that lies southwest of Atlanta and borders Alabama. While I'd been exposed to different races before, a fear of an entire race was born from rumors of race riots on a daily basis, regular bomb threats, and the unease felt by being surrounded by an entire group of people that were different. In classes, the boys were loud and unruly, and some of the white women teachers lost control. In the run-down tile bathrooms, the girls' voices boomed. It was their school, their neighborhood, and this interloper into their community never felt safe. Inwardly, I shrunk, and outwardly, I stayed as unnoticeable as possible.

However, when voices were escalated and faces were pressed close together recently, I hadn't backed down. Even when one man told me he was going to kick my ass all over the road, I didn't retreat. I'd faced my fear of men, racial difference, and my anger. I'd defended myself and had enough conviction and respect to honor my position and value my person. Confrontational encounters such as these have never occurred in my life again. The universe had tested me until I was ready to fearlessly assert my newfound self-respect.

I'd successfully passed these life tests.

I'd successfully learned to say "No."

Now that's cool.

LOVE

We are the most alive and the closest to the meaning of our existence when we are most vulnerable, when experience has humbled us and has cured the arrogance which, like a form of deafness, prevents us from hearing the lessons that this world teaches.

Dean Koontz
Seize the Night

I cut my hair and dyed it red. Then contemplated turning it solid brown. Next I painted blonde streaks in my red hair. I bought a blonde color kit to lighten the red because I thought the darker color made me look too old. I grew it out some.

While sitting at the salon in the stylist's chair admiring another woman's long locks, I contemplated getting a permanent to have lasting curls.

I wore a long strawberry blonde wig to feel covered and comforted by the familiarity of tresses against my back.

Every couple weeks my hair was a different shade of red or blonde. I'd defined myself through my former longhaired stripper persona, but there was no more applause, and I didn't know this new woman. Though I knew who she wasn't.

She wasn't the twenty-three year old who'd competed with her sister for a man's attention on her last night in Milwaukee while celebrating her new career and her move to California the next day. She wasn't the woman who in the past accepted men solely on the basis of a lustful craving and how unattainable they were. Once, at a Fetish Ball, I began necking immediately upon meeting a passionate Russian who only told me his first name. After that incident, he only came around a couple times a year. And for ten years, I'd had the tempestuous on again, off again relationship with Geoff that nurtured my fantasy of having a boyfriend, but in reality, kept me safe from experiencing *all* the nuances of actual intimacy. I wasn't that woman anymore, the one who lived in such denial of her feelings that they remained unconscious.

Driving to Berkeley one evening, I passed Emeryville and then the Ashby exit on my right. Thoughts ricocheted around the day, the future, and the radio program I was listening to when suddenly it was as if I was transported into a modern-day science-fiction movie. A hole in the blacktop opened as I drove over it, and an extraterrestrial spirit inhabited my being. "I want a baby," poured from my lips. Then, as if the entity left me and retreated back into the concrete just as quickly, my coherence returned, and I voiced aloud for the KGO talk-show host and myself to hear, "Where did that come from?" I hadn't even been thinking about babies.

I never thought about babies. I was the person who was rankled by the yellow 'baby on board' placards that hung from others' cars as if that was supposed to make me drive more safely. *I should, people should, be driving safe all the time*, I commanded to myself or voiced to others. *What makes them— babies—so special anyway*, was my underlying thought. I was the woman who, when she heard or saw a crying child, it annoyed me so, and I'd think, *Shut that kid up*. I held no caring or comfort thoughts for small kids or infants. Instead I was jealous of their attention and resentful of their yet unrealized opportunity. Lately however, as I'd grown more tolerant and loving with my own inner child, my heart opened, and their arrows of innocence pierced my shell of anger and fear and found my soft gooey center.

After that impromptu confession on the highway, I started wondering if I wanted a baby and if that was still a possibility in my life. Although I had no good prospects for a husband, my idyllic vision had always been a cuddly family of three encircled in a heart-shaped frame as portrayed in the opening credits of the 1950's sitcom, *I Love Lucy*. I thought about this burst of words for some time then admitted it wasn't necessarily a baby I wanted, but what the baby, to me, represented; unconditional love, sweetness, forever. My cognizant fantasies didn't consist of a threesome but instead of a man, ironically enough, who would argue with me. Occasionally I'd visualize an unidentified man challenging me with his difference of opinion or burst of anger. I've pondered the meaning of this unusual vision and now comprehend that the mature woman within knew that working through challenges and disagreements was a necessary and expected part of a relationship. She knew that remaining together through these trials was indicative of a lasting bond and lifetime love. Unfortunately, the uneducated adolescent and young adult within who'd learned to protect themselves from getting hurt had been in charge most of my adult years. I'd never had a relationship that lasted more than a year or gotten to the period beyond lustful attraction where differences are worked through.

Along with this new awareness and comments from a few men I'd recently dated who showed concern about whether I could still have children if our relationship became serious, I questioned my desirability and worth as a woman. Was there something wrong with me if I didn't want children? Had I missed my chance for love and family? Had I run helter-skelter only to come to a place where I'd finally gained knowledge and glimpses of wisdom but was now too old for love? Had I successfully educated myself but become so set in my ways I was unable to compromise or tolerate others? Would anyone out there be interested in a woman who'd experimented and experienced life like I had? I didn't know. But what I did know was that while I had at one time worshipped some men and needed them to love me physically and emotionally in order to feel whole, I now felt whole all by myself.

Through twelve-step meetings, I was forming a community with people who were on a path to recovering themselves and their lives, and for the first time I was being honest about how I truly felt. I wasn't hiding. Yet I wasn't exposing myself needlessly to gain acceptance and approval either. I was real. And listening—to my heart as well as to the experience and wisdom of others who modeled integrity, morality, and a sense of peace. I became open to suggestions and no longer saw vulnerability as a weakness. A love relationship with a man, my life-long focus, became inconsequential, and I began to enjoy friendship and camaraderie with many different kinds of people. I was just me, and that became okay, even in my occasional confusion as to who "me" was.

As birds sang good morning and snails retreated to their daylight slumber under rocks and plants one spring day, I walked in the Berkeley Hills. The sight of brilliant diamonds suspended in midair stopped me abruptly. I crept closer and craned my neck as I stretched my body around bushes to admire the fine threads of a spider's web. Up close, their dazzle vanished; it was only from a distance that they appeared like jewels. Up close, however, I could see their delicate strength. The small spider, being its natural self, had not only created the netting it would use to get food but had also provided a place for dew to rest and sun rays to reflect. Stepping back, I could again witness the translucent gems that had initially taken my breath away. I stood there long enough to have the sun shift its perspective so that the jewel-encrusted apparition I'd first seen was no longer visible from my original position. I'd slowed down long enough to witness this miracle of nature and suddenly my own nature was illuminated. The hairstyles, makeup, and baubles I'd lusted after and concerned myself with my entire life only helped me appear sparkly from a distance—external decoration others could reflect their ideas and projections off of. Once the irrelevant trappings of cosmetics and materials were eliminated, I, too, revealed delicate beauty and strength. In that flash of comprehension, I also saw that my frenetic activity had spun a web of distance and distraction—from myself as well as others.

My new friends did things like host parties and potlucks and I, at forty-five, wanted to be a part, but these kinds of events had always caused me anxiety. I didn't know how to "be" with me, and I certainly didn't know how to "be" with others. That's why I'd built the web in the first place. I had the directions to one such event though and while feeling nervous and resistant, knowing it would be easier yet so so lonely to stay in my safe little room with my cats, I set out with my MapQuest directions one late winter afternoon. "It's easy to find," a few people said, so I wasn't concerned. After following the map yet unable to find the address in the darkening day, I called a friend who knew the area.

No answer.

The party had already started, so my anxiety over not finding it was exacerbated by now knowing I was late. I continued driving around the general area, but as the electric LED display showed the passing minutes and the day turned to night, I panicked even more.

I drove to my friend's house to get directions first hand. On the way there, I contemplated driving home. I lived close, but, no, that was the old me. The new me wanted desperately to be a part of a group. I arrived unannounced at my friend's home, harried and hampered by insecurities.

She wrote out a small map.

I set out again. In this hilly community roads turned and twisted and had no order to their design. I stopped often to review the directions, flick my Honda Del Sol high beams off and on to read the obscure street signs, backtrack on roads I'd passed, and curse at the drivers who came up behind me trying to push me even faster than my lost soul wanted to go.

I finally found the street.

Somewhat relieved but still frantic, I searched the darkened homes for numbers. I couldn't see them, but when I saw lots of cars, I figured I was in the right place. I parked in the dead-end circle and started walking up the hill to a house; though unlit from the street, I intuited it might be the one. I would never stroll in through someone's gate though, fearing dogs, so I stood on the pavement perplexed. Suddenly, a woman I recognized emerged between two houses, and I followed her. She entered a home through a sliding glass door, and I rushed to the pane and knocked.

She was startled but opened the door.

"Is this where the party is?" I asked.

"It's next door but I'm going back. You can follow me."

Nervous staccato sentences fell out of my mouth.

"Thank you."

"It's so good to find it."

"I was driving around for an hour."

"I recognize you."

"I didn't bring anything."

"My name is Susan."

"I know I'm late, but I was driving around for an hour."

The ordeal of finding this home, this party, these people, had ended successfully, but the overwhelming tension I'd felt while trying to get here melted into fatigued relief and overpowered my composure. As soon as I entered the party, I saw the familiar faces, found the bathroom, shut myself in, then burst into tears. All my pent-up anxieties around feeling awkward in large groups and not knowing how to mingle, not knowing what to say, unsure if I was dressed appropriately, unsure if my birthday gift was appropriate, scared of showing up late, scared of showing up at all but scared of not showing up, flooded my reserve and poise, and I cried like a frustrated baby. I was safe. I wanted to sit in that bathroom until everyone was gone, and I could come out.

The loud voices on the other side of the door and my trepidation that someone would knock ultimately pushed me to dry my eyes and reapply some makeup. With hesitation, I opened the door and went out amongst the smiles and welcomes. I was hugged and warmed by the conversation and the bodies crowded together in companionship. These people hadn't seen or known of my struggle, and while voicing empathy and concern when I dwelled on it with them in conversation, I also realized I was not the focus of their attention. I hadn't let anybody down by showing up late or not bringing something to eat.

In my early twenties, I'd worked all day on a frosted chocolate cherry cake to take to a Halloween party and upon arriving a half hour late announced, "The dessert is here." Foolishly I'd thought they couldn't really have a party without me and that my contribution to the potluck had been longingly awaited.

When I saw they could, other desserts had been brought, I'd been embarrassed and ashamed about my loud exclamation. I'd remembered a phrase spoken to me before, "It's not about you." Like a two-year old I'd been so self-centered I couldn't see past my own obsession with me.

Also like a two-year old learning to be independent, leaving a room but then returning quickly to make sure the adults are still present, I now went into my new community then left again after honestly exposing myself and witnessing others. And I returned. They, like patient parents and teachers, were still there. Without a clear textbook in the school of life, I'd unknowingly gathered love for the emerging me by honestly embracing then revealing myself, then genuinely embracing others. If I took the focus off myself and concentrated on how good it was to see and converse with them, I felt less tension and anxiety. When I opened up and talked honestly, I learned that other people had similar worries. I relaxed.

The next time a party came up, I was nervous but prepared myself with clear directions, a dish to take, and confirmation that a friend would also be there. I went the next time and the next. I took little excursions into areas of life of which I had no experience in. Instead of a stoic mask of bravery like I'd worn in the past, I now presented my bare face and walked through my anxious reality enough so that my nervousness, though never totally disappearing, diminished significantly.

While for many years, I refused to acknowledge aloud that I was anything other than how my grandfather saw me—brave—I must now admit my childish behavior and cowardice. When I made the video, *Art of Sensual Dance*, I wanted to liberate and empower women who would never work in a strip club. I did it because I'd learned the important truth that all women are beautiful and sexy—as long as they feel it. But I didn't know how this video or I would be received. I never felt confident or competent enough to stand alone in the world and proclaim my expertise, especially when it came to sensuality or sex, subjects that I, until recently, felt uncomfortable with and ashamed of. This reticence became obvious to me years later when I looked at the debut cover of that DVD and realized I was surrounded by all the women because I was reluctant to stand alone. After gaining greater confidence, the reissue cover and title change of the DVD to *Striptease for Real Women* was bolder in its proclamation to the world. I'd studied Photoshop, cut myself out of a group picture, and as if it was a puzzle piece, selected and maneuvered it front and center. The first cover had been designed and agreed upon by a web designer, photographer, and graphic artist who I thought knew better than I, just as I'd been influenced by what others wanted throughout my entire life. But this second cover, now, like my own life just emerging, was my own design. I had developed the courage to step away from the group.

My personal evolution, like the writing of this book, has come into focus like a jigsaw puzzle once the pieces are connected. Writing is a discipline, just as being open to and educated by life is a discipline. Each morning, alone with my experiences and confessions, wearing flannel pj's covered with cat hair, I put pen to page, some days writing numerous sheets and other days struggling for hours on a single paragraph. I've learned that if I sit with my indecisive and hesitant words, eventually the structure and sentences are revealed and another piece to the story is written. My brain has been trained to meticulously sort through all the parts of a life, to shuffle through the feelings, memories, and daily scenes, arranging and rearranging them until they coherently snap into a logical order I can accept and even approve. This puzzle is so enormous though, that the segments won't lie flat on a dining room table, all the bits easy to see. Instead, the pieces are layered and when one is put into place, another is bared and begs to find its order in the big picture. With a loose structure and openness to life, the words, days, pieces, take shape as a still life picture of the past and an emerging scene of the future.

I'd exposed the fear and hurt my inner child had covered with layers of anger and resentment and put these pieces loosely into place, which then uncovered my sadness. There'd been damage to my life at my own hand. It was my fault. I couldn't blame others for my loneliness and isolation. I couldn't blame others for buried pain. Though previously unconscious and, I believe, unable to make "real" choices, my pattern of refusing to take responsibility for my actions kept me in a negative cycle of mistrust, bitterness, and dissatisfaction that inhibited my growth and healing. My journey had allowed me, or forced me if you will, to live some experiences not once but twice; first unconsciously, reacting to situations based on a child's misguided interpretations, then consciously through re-experiencing the past with newfound awareness and the knowing adult's ability to understand. This was *my* reality.

I'd read somewhere that the depth and caliber of your next relationship will be determined by how you ended your last. In my romantic history, the overused but oh so true cliché, "fine line between love and hate," had been prevalent in all relationships that didn't end because of military orders. Once love mysteriously evaporated, the only feelings expressed were hostility. I'd even had one female friendship end with anger.

There'd been an instant attraction with Margaret. We met at Sue Walden's improv recess class in Oakland that advertised as a way for adults to take a break from the responsibility of life through playing games. I'd attended my first recess years earlier while living in San Francisco and during what she called *The Emotional Choir*, I'd laughed so outrageously hard, the scene is indelible because of it. While Sue stood in front of us like a regal orchestra conductor, her exuberant face and encouraging posture granting permission for advanced silliness, I stood with my group of five waiting for her to point the baton our way. When she did, we began a chorus of gasps and shrieks, any syllable we imagined that expressed fear. For the few seconds she focused on us, we wailed and moaned, raising or lowering the intensity of our voices at her wand's instruction. Sometimes she had us express our anguish in unison with another group who mimicked an emotion such as sadness or happiness, sometimes we engaged our distress alone. When she pointed her baton somewhere else, the remnants of our ensemble mixed with the fervent demonstrations of the other groups vocalizing love, pity, jealousy or anger sounded so foreign and ludicrous it unleashed involuntary roars of rambunctious hilarity from deep within my belly. After that evening, I signed up for improv classes and played at recess whenever I could.

Margaret looked like me, blonde and petite, and she laughed easily. Sue Walden commented that we seemed as close as sisters that first night. For a few years we enjoyed spontaneous dinners and movies, gossip about men, and she'd helped me make large sequined cardboard butterflies, props, for my Vermont College graduation presentation. She'd attended and offered constructive criticism for my initial sensual dance classes when I was uncertain as to how to be an effective teacher. Together we'd even tempted fate by riding BART into San Francisco at the turn of the millennium and the height of the Y2K panic. We'd stood on the Embarcadero waiting for the City's midnight firework extravaganza while we held our breath in anticipation of the world ending.

After Margaret told me she was thinking about moving, our relationship started unraveling as easily as a knitted sweater whose loose end has been pulled. She was flying out to visit the Florida town she was considering as her new home and called to ask me for a ride to the airport. I told her I was scheduled to work. When I suggested she take the Super Shuttle, she pleaded with me on the phone saying it was difficult to go to the airport alone, but I replied that I needed to work because I had bills to pay. I couldn't understand her trepidation because I'd spent so many years flying all over by myself; therefore, going to the airport seemed easy to me. She couldn't understand my financial insecurity because she rarely got caught up in the money worries that dominated my thoughts.

When she returned from her trip, we spoke, but our communication was strained. Neither of us had the conscious awareness to try and determine the other's point of view, nor did we have the communication skills to work through our misunderstanding and hurt feelings. Also, it was easier to be angry with each other than to realize the impending separation and feel the pain of missing the friendship. We never wrote.

I didn't want the relationship with my former self to end the same way. Though painful and sad at times, I'd finally cultivated a metamorphic consanguinity amongst every single minute detail of myself and was beginning to really like me. I wanted to do everything possible to maintain that respect and love I'd been developing and knew it was time to let go of my former self's defensive way, mourn her dreams unfulfilled, and ultimately, her passing. I developed empathy for her confused yet protective way of progressing through life and accepted that, while bringing me heartache and trouble, my former way of being had grown out of a basic need to feel safe. I accepted that, although I'd been isolated and alone, this former self also propelled me to gain knowledge and experience life in a way that was unique and paramount to the evolution of my future self. I embraced her achievements and life lessons. I accepted my life and what I, or it, was *and* wasn't.

We instinctively give to and get from others what we possess for ourselves. The natural progression of my journey then was that I began to accept others and be honest with them. I was meeting men differently than I had in the past; I was no longer desperate for them to fill a void, and they no longer first saw me without clothes or trying to manipulate them out of money. And I now trusted, through having the experience of taking time to get to know me, that I had the time to get to know someone else. Relationships that started as friends, I'd heard, had greater chance for success, but I'd always succumbed to the instant attraction I'd feel towards a man, and we'd jump in the sack before a real friendship could develop. Now I had more patience to take the time to get to know someone.

James' band was playing one night at a wedding where I was the catering help. He looked sharp: immaculate dark-blue pinstripe suit with light-blue pocket handkerchief, dark blue-black fedora, manicured nails. As he sang and performed choreographed moves with the other three singers, his presence was magnetic. When my eyes weren't drawn to his effervescent performance, I shook my booty and swiveled my hips as I cleared plates and glasses from abandoned dinner tables to wedding standards like "Brick House" by the Commodores and Michael Jackson's "Pretty Young Thing." It was apparent that music infused both of us with energy. He approached me after their first set, we talked, and it was no surprise at the end of the night when he asked for my phone number. His, "Nice to meet you," phone message when I got home around one a.m. was an endearing gesture. What was sudden though, was that he called again the next morning. *A little too eager*, I mused, *but I'll give him a break. Everyone gets excited.* When I returned his call, I found out he was also a substance-free person. Again, I wasn't surprised. Like energies attract.

I accepted his invitation to lunch, and we met at a restaurant in Oakland's Jack London Square known for peanut shells that litter the bar floor. He was a successful musician, supporting himself through music, and I felt a twinge of envy. I was envious of his ability to be at ease with himself and his life. He seemed genuine, happy, smart, playful, and honest. He was involved in community outreach and sang in the Glide Memorial Church choir in San Francisco. Just like I'd done all those years ago in my addicted youth, I associated him with power. Here was the Rock God of my youthful fantasies. I went to one of the band's gigs and watched and danced as he performed. I wasn't initially attracted to him in a lustful got-to-get-you-into-bed way, and figured this was good; remember, broken picker, but I did respect and admire him.

I wanted to try being friends before having sex, but there were a few roadblocks that made me wonder if a romantic relationship would ever flourish. He seemed to want to get involved too quickly; his frequent calls didn't wane. He was overweight, though I really wanted to rise above what I considered to be a superficial emphasis placed on size. And he was black. While I don't consider myself prejudiced, I must admit that there was once a very handsome, extremely fit black man I was attracted to. At that time, I could not work my mind past, *What will my parents think,* or, *How will I fit into his family?* I never acted on that attraction. It had been a few years since I knew this handsome man, but my mind hadn't evolved past skin color—or girth. Perhaps herein lies the key to attraction. We're attracted to who we're attracted to and no amount of psychological reasoning can change that.

Within a short amount of time it was obvious that my mind, and romance starts in the mind, wasn't going to change. The old me might have led him on to gain artistic contacts or delayed saying goodbye to avoid hurting his feelings, but the new me couldn't mislead him or fool myself. I knew he liked me in a way I couldn't reciprocate, and I was unable to find internal peace if I knowingly contributed to fostering the hope I saw in his eyes and heard in his voice. I'd used people before, not maliciously or even consciously, but in a misdirected, pathetic, uneducated way. I'd let others use me too, but these old behaviors weren't acceptable to the new Susan, even though she'd forgiven herself for unrealistic attempts at friendship and love. I let James know that he was an awesome man, but I didn't feel a romantic connection. I let him go so he could find someone who could match his hope, and I let him go so I didn't betray my own hope for a life filled with abundant love.

I didn't want to close myself off from discovering a friendship that might grow into more, so I accepted invitations for lunch and coffee whenever they came my way. Since I didn't get involved sexually, I didn't feel that emotional bond we women so easily feel when our bodies produce oxytocin, otherwise called the "cuddle drug," during sex. If I determined I didn't want to take the relationship to the next level (now understanding that even if I liked someone as a person it didn't mean he'd make a good romantic partner for me), I said goodbye as honestly and painlessly as I could. I continued striving to be the caliber of person I wanted to meet. I was open to seeing if love born out of a mutual friendship would evolve and grow like the love I'd cultivated and grown for myself. I finally understood that I had a finite amount of energy, as well as time, so in order for a worthy man to come into my life I had to eliminate unfulfilling and temporary men. I had physical needs still, but I'd learned to take my time with those also.

As a direct result of my sexual evolution, I'd found a pleasure-safe zone within myself where rigorous, religious indoctrination and societal double standards for men and women concerning masturbation, no longer hampered my sexual release and enjoyment. Unlike the clinical exploration I'd done with Betty Dodson and her video where I felt guilt, shame, and scrutiny from my cats, I now allowed myself the luxury of self-love: methodically, slowly, mindfully, unlike the way I'd relieve my pent-up sexual urges while in drunken stupors in the past. Instead of giving it up to others, I kept it for myself.

I was learning I could take care of my physical needs without subjecting myself to unfulfilling relationships, and at the same time, I was satisfying my need for community. I was self-sufficient and self-sustaining, and while I still desired a love relationship with a man, I admitted I could have a good life without one. In years past, I'd defiantly proclaimed I didn't need a man while unconsciously hoping one would save me, but now, instead of trying to find one and force myself into his life, I could wait to see if the right person came my way that fit like a puzzle piece into mine. Many years ago, Cher, in an interview, said she'd rather be alone than with the wrong man. That's what I now knew—really knew, not just intellectualized, but really felt deep within my cells. Although spending a lifetime single wasn't my dream, I knew that if I was solo I'd be okay.

Similar to how I was accepting myself, I was developing empathy, love and acceptance of others. By developing compassion for the little me within who hadn't wanted to move, who felt awkward and scrutinized in new situations and who learned to cope by escaping, I realized that my parents were directly influenced by their inner children, raised in a restrictive generation of *Father Knows Best*, the Great Depression and limited opportunity. Back then, the concept of self-esteem wasn't widely understood, much less discussed, and their small-town upbringing didn't equip them with tools to deal with an angry adolescent. Their reprimands and restrictions were generated from a loving concern for my wellbeing. I developed empathy because I observed that they, too, were vulnerable to self-criticism and feelings of confusion just as I was. They became real people and ceased being magical humans with all the power. My love for them nudged out the last remaining bits of anger and resentment that existed in my "me" centered life as I understood and accepted that they had done the best they could just as I had done the best I could.

I began to remember their repeated attempts to rescue me from harm, both as a child and as an adult. Just as they rushed me to the emergency room at ten when I'd stepped on a sewing needle and jammed it up inside my heel, so, too, my mother was trying to help me realize there was nothing we could do about moving and that I needed to adjust my attitude when she'd yelled that I needed to change my feelings.

During my late twenties, she'd tried to give me the medicine of reality when she angrily hollered that I was running away from myself. I conceded that my father had been trying to help me learn to respect and value my body when he told me a man wanted to marry a virgin when I was fifteen. There was the actual act of physical rescue when they dropped what they were doing, jumped into their truck at the sound of my quivering voice, drove five hours one way to pick me up in Rockford, Illinois and take me home to Wisconsin when, at nineteen, I needed to get away from Kyle. And with a smile on my face and love in my heart, I revisited their caring act of spontaneity that occurred in my early forties.

$$\smile$$

We got up early my last day visiting them so we could be at the airport in plenty of time to check in and relax before my departure. We ate breakfast in the airport restaurant then made small talk and looked around the only gift shop in the small terminal. When the airline announced my plane's boarding and imminent departure, we hugged. "I'll call you when I get home," I promised.

I passed through the security checkpoint and turned around to wave again before I had to take the lonely walk to the boarding area. My final destination was 2,500 miles away from them. I continued walking, but before disappearing completely from their view, I turned one last time. They were still standing on the other side of the glass. As I've gotten older, these visits always culminate with a lump in my throat and moist eyes. This time was no different. They were still waving goodbye. My dad's silver hair and shrinking stature as well as my mom's naturally solemn smile, filled me with reluctance to keep going. I didn't know when I'd see them again.

While waiting at the boarding gate, an announcement was made that our departure was delayed. A snowstorm had started and our plane was still in Minneapolis waiting on the tarmac to take off. Settled into my chair, exasperated but comfortable, I read for another half hour. A second announcement told us our plane had finally left Minneapolis and was on its way. I gathered all my bags and went to the bathroom, then returned to my original black vinyl seat that was still vacant. When the speaker system crackled again, I looked at the elderly couple sitting across the aisle from me and remarked, "This can't be good."

The loudspeaker voice boomed that the weather was so bad our plane had returned to Minneapolis and wouldn't be coming for us at all. We ten people waiting for the commuter plane scrambled to get downstairs to the ticket agent to see what our options were. The flustered woman behind the counter sorted through the line of people and tried to appease our waning enthusiasm for air travel. She scheduled me on the last flight of the day that left in six hours, but informed me, "There's no guarantee that flight will actually happen either."

I called my parents.

"We just got home," mom surprised me by saying. It had been a couple hours and the drive was usually only an hour. "The roads are glare ice. We saw lots of cars in ditches, but we just took our time."

I expressed my gratitude at their safe return home and told them my plight. "I won't be calling any time soon from California."

I toted my carry-on bag and computer up to the second-floor restaurant again, ordered more coffee, and started working on my laptop. Engrossed in my project, I was oblivious to happenings around me. Time passed as my eyes fixated on the screen. The waitress had long ago abandoned my table after I let her know I didn't need any more coffee and that I wasn't hungry. I'm used to sitting alone in airports. I looked up occasionally, observed others, stretched my arms and neck, and submerged myself in the electronic device all over again.

Suddenly, distracted by a movement coming close in my peripheral vision, I glanced up. Approaching rapidly were my parents looking warm in sturdy winter coats and hats, both of them wearing smiles as wide as the amount of time between my originally scheduled flight and my new flight.

Flabbergasted, I managed, "What are you doing here?"

"We didn't want you to sit here by yourself for all that time," mom beamed, her countenance a sunny break in the blizzard outside.

"We just put the Expedition in four-wheel drive and drove slow," dad added.

"And if your plane doesn't take off, we'll take you back home with us," mom chimed in.

We hugged and laughed, made more small talk, and ate a late lunch. A few hours later we went back downstairs and repeated our morning ritual, watching the clock while looking at other families. When it got closer to my new departure time,

I hugged my parents goodbye, again, and put my bags on the conveyor belt. "We'll wait to leave the airport to make sure the plane really takes off this time," my dad assured me.

For the second time that day, after my flight was announced, I repeated my ritual of turning back to wave every few feet before I disappeared from their view entirely. They repeated their waves in unison with mine. In each other's vision, we each got smaller.

My plane took off, I'm sorry to say. I'd secretly yearned for another flight cancellation.

Throughout my life, wanting their approval and love but accepting it only in ways I narrowly defined, I had selfishly expected and demanded more than they could give without recognizing what they did give. They'd repeatedly sacrificed themselves; spiritually, they loved me in spite of my committing acts that went against their moral values; financially, besides providing in my childhood and early adulthood, they'd also given me money to purchase a home and produce my DVD; and physically, my father abandoned his desire of becoming an accountant and put his life on the line when he reenlisted in the Army to support his family after already serving time in the Marines. Now I wanted to love them unconditionally and selflessly back.

Then the diagnosis—cancer.

Sounds like "cancel."

People die of cancer all the time.

My grandmother died of cancer—blood cancer—acute myelogenous leukemia—diagnosed too late to take any healing measures. She was seventy-nine and too old for treatment the doctors said when they finally figured out why her blood looked funny. My grandmother, whom I never really knew, but whose approval and love I so desperately wanted. She'd wanted her oldest child, my mother, to have a career instead of marrying young, but my mother rebelliously disobeyed and eloped at eighteen. She'd then wanted her youngest child, my aunt, born a year after myself, to get away from their small town and follow me to California, but my aunt hadn't honored her wishes either. Was I living out my grandmother's dreams of doing something with her life other than taking care of home and family? It was too late to know my grandmother's secrets and for her to know mine. Though I'd gone and sat with her as she rested in her final days, it wasn't enough time to transcend a lifetime of disconnection and short meetings in my youth. My mother had tried to bring us closer together with imposed visits to the grandparents, but I had been unable and unwilling to do more than obligatory small talk because with the ignorance and arrogance of youth, I'd hidden from myself and anyone who might have connection to me.

I didn't want this pattern to repeat itself, and now it seemed that I might lose my mother. I started researching Waldenstrom's Lymphoma on the internet.

Rare.

No cure.

Perhaps remission.

Perhaps stem cell transplantation.

In my feeble attempt to help however I could from across the country, I researched vitamins, found the best, then ordered and sent them. The chemotherapy would deplete her immune system.

She resisted in her selfless self-sacrificing fashion. "Don't spend so much. I'm already taking vitamins. Really, a person doesn't need all those."

I wanted to help, but all I could do was buy vitamins and fly back.

There she was, tired and fragile in her second week away from chemo which lasted seven days a month, still mustering hope and safety for her daughter. "When I was diagnosed with melanoma in 1981," she offered, "the plant I bought in 1978 with one yellow flower bloomed again for the second and only time. The cancer was removed successfully and hasn't returned for over twenty years. The morning after this new cancer diagnosis, the cactus that hasn't blossomed for ten years displayed one orange pink flower that was gone the next day and has never appeared again. We take that as an omen from God," she promised me.

To this woman whose religion I'd shunned in my rebelliousness, I said, "I'll keep you in my prayers." And I meant it. Although I didn't adhere to her brand of religious zealotry, I now embraced the concept of a Higher Power.

I was becoming more like this woman whose reasoning and way of being in a relationship I'd rejected, and whose way of eating, like clock work, three meals a day at specific times, I'd thought nonsensical. I'd detested and joked of looking like her when I'd sat in a stylist's chair and a new haircut illuminated my resemblance to her. I'd even rejected her body, soft and vulnerable, a female body like the one I had that I'd tried to keep hard and rock-like. I now saw her frailty and wanted to care for and protect this woman whose breast I suckled, who'd diapered, dressed, cared for, and loved me my entire life.

I helped as much as she'd let me and hoped for future opportunities to have her educate me in the art of sewing and quilting and making pickles, strawberry jelly, and homemade noodles for chicken soup. I'd been struggling to have a richer life and needed her guidance. I held and massaged her hands that ached from the cancer-killing poison and told her she was the best mom in the world.

I had to fly back to California.

I called every day.

I wanted to be nearer.

My heart was open and throbbing with distress instead of beating with life because of all the distance I'd created and all the events and holidays I'd missed. Suddenly life was uncertain. Mortality obvious. My mother's body had abandoned her, just as I'd abandoned her for foolish dreams and goals I once thought important. But she's important. He's important. When my father had open-heart surgery in the mid-1990s I was physically present for a week, but still unconscious. I'd left them alone. Now they were more alone. My grandmother was dead and my sister had moved away.

In my awakening to life's finality, I'd become sorely conscious of my single person's aloneness. I lived far away from family that held an unwavering bond that, like flexible putty, bent around years of misunderstandings, keeping me close and yearning for them while at the same time allowing me to reject them. Instead of closing down though, my heart threw off its last shadowed mask and embraced the imperfections and foibles of family who I am, at times, more like than I care to be. I no longer feared being with others just as I no longer feared being alone. I could love and care for them and not lose myself because I'd gained a self.

With that surrender to honesty came a powerful acceptance and shift of perception. Because I no longer *needed* a man, I divulged to myself that I really *wanted* one. I'd guarded myself against painful love then loss by shunning connections and creating aloneness, but as I prayed for mom, I also prayed for a love relationship. With the news of my mother's illness, I became excruciatingly vulnerable to the loneliness and isolation I'd felt even with friends and the support of a community. In my confusion and distraction over what to do—call, send vitamins, pray, move to Wisconsin—a stealthy soldier dedicated to his mission maneuvered his way through my defenses and into my open heart.

A man I'd met and talked with briefly a few times in the community just started calling. Do I want to hang out, have dinner or go to an event, he queried.

I'm too busy. "Thank you, but no thank you," I politely declined.

He called again.

I already had plans.

His enthusiasm wasn't dissuaded though, and he tried again.

After the third phone call and invitation, I accepted.

Then, claiming to be overwhelmed and fatigued, I called and left a voice message canceling. I didn't have time for some new friend who seemed too eager and too nice. I'd been open to meeting new kinds of men, but this one was *too* available, *too* close; he lived less than a mile away from me.

He called me back and thanked me for modeling self-care and the ability to know if I was too fatigued to keep a predetermined date.

That impressed me.

A few days later, he called again.

He left a message when I was visiting mom and it was nice to hear a familiar voice on the long-distance wires when I checked my voicemail from Wisconsin.

When I returned from Wisconsin, a film I had a small part in was premiering. At the last minute, I conceded to myself that I really didn't want to drive all the way to Marin alone. I called Joe. I hoped he'd be available.

He was.

I wasn't concerned with impressing him so I equipped my car with towels and plastic because it leaked and met him down the hill from my home. He showed up wearing a beret, and we set off on the hour-long drive.

After that night, he invited me on an outing to San

Francisco. I'd enjoyed his company on that first evening, so I accepted. While we were eating I made it clear, "just friends."

He agreed.

Good. I certainly didn't want him thinking we were on a date especially since I let him drive and buy me dinner.

During Christmas, I returned to Wisconsin to see my mom who was in her fifth month of chemotherapy. After my sister and her husband, who were visiting from Texas, left, feelings rushed in that I'd denied my entire life—that of competition with my sister for my parents' affection. "Do you love me as much as Stephy?" this forty-five-year-old child asked her mommy through tears.

"Of course, I do," she offered lovingly as she extended her arms to me. "You're both different, but I love you equally."

The adult within knew she loved me, but the child within who was afraid of losing her mom needed to be comforted. The child within me that never felt good enough was able to hear because she was finally able to speak.

I returned December 30 to the Montclair area of Oakland because I had to work. The next morning, New Year's Eve, I woke up desperately needing caffeine, but without electricity due to a storm I couldn't make coffee. *Perhaps there's power in the village*, I hoped, and threw a sweatshirt and coat over my pajamas, smoothed my hair down under a hat, and grabbed an umbrella.

After parking as close to the coffee shop as I could get, I hurried across the street, avoiding cars and feeling as soggy and dreary as the day. Someone whistled. I peered hard through misty glasses, and there stood Joe in his beret—smiling. Feeling lonely and abandoned, the familiar feeling I had every time I left my parents, I was relieved to see a familiar face. Despite not having brushed my teeth, I smiled right back, unexpectedly conscious of my appearance.

We each bought a cup of coffee, and I made a spontaneous

decision to sit and talk with this man I considered a friend. I told him about my mom and how afraid I was of losing her, and he impressed me anew with his caring words and compassionate demeanor. We made a plan (I kept steering clear of "date") to go out for burritos in a few nights. For four months he'd taken my rejection, listened to me and validated my decisions, remained dependable, kind, and consistent, and had impressed me just by being himself. I found myself wanting to impress him.

A couple weeks later we spent the entire day in San Francisco. Walking along Ocean Beach and Haight Street together, all his qualities fused together to form one handsome picture: his conscious way of thinking—he honestly questioned himself and strived to understand his motivations and actions; his refreshing ways of seeing the world and communicating— he told me once that as he rounded the corner on his way to meet, "I enjoyed recognizing you"; and finally, his rugged masculinity, an alluring and attractive bonus.

In North Beach, during dinner in an Italian restaurant, my recent discovery that some men were concerned about my ability to have children bubbled up in fear of getting too close then being rejected. I probed, "What about children? Do you want them? I'm forty-five you know."

He paused.

I held my fork in midair.

He put his down on the table.

"First ..."

I braced myself for words of rejection.

"First ... I'd, ... I'd just like to have a decent relationship with someone."

"That's exactly how I feel," I gushed. My heart fluttered. I made a mental note to check the 'preferred man' list in my wallet.

As we browsed City Lights Bookstore later that night and

I spied on him wearing his glasses, reading, I knew this was a man I wanted to open myself up to. He was looking for the same thing I was, and he was going about it the same way. My self-appeal journey had led me to attract into my life the kind of man who resonated with my energy. The saying, "Water seeks its own level," had been true my entire life, only now my "water" looked like deep blue pristine lakes of Western Canada. I envisioned our two "waters" merging into one beautiful lake where we could begin to grow vibrant foliage and support life.

On the daily calls I made to mom, I discussed Joe only briefly. She'd seen so many men come and go that it seemed of no importance to tell her of yet another man when all I really wanted to know was how she was feeling. After her pre-scribed seven months of chemotherapy, her IgM numbers had decreased from over five thousand to mere hundreds. (The body makes these large antibodies in response to infection or cancer. The lower the numbers, the lower the cancer cells.) Her prescription was rest to heal her immune system that had been depleted because of the treatment. Joe was the only person I called with this fantastic news.

Joe and I saw each other regularly for three months and as I confided in him my history, fears, anxieties, and dreams, he became my trusted friend. We also discussed the fact that we both wanted the relationship to have a better chance of lasting than any other we'd known and decided that starting differ-ently would be beneficial. Before we hopped into bed, as we got to know each other, we talked about the physical aspect of our relationship and went to the Berkeley Free Clinic to get AIDS tests together. We'd delayed having sex to be responsible, but there was another reason I was satisfied to delay our physical intimacy. Although I was attracted to Joe and we'd engaged in passionate petting, I didn't know how to approach him sexu-ally. My sex wasn't something I just gave away any more. I was enjoying emotional acceptance and while treasuring it, didn't really know how to act with it.

Then, one evening, Joe and I reached a moment where we couldn't contain our desire for each other any longer. We'd been at this passionate juncture before but we no longer needed to postpone our union because the test results had come back. Louder than the voice between my legs though, was the tiny voice that started in my head, "No." In my past need to have men validate me, that "no," had gotten stuck in my throat and I never said it. At thirty-one I'd even cried while having sex with George because he would roll over and ignore me if I refused. But over the seven months I'd gotten to know Joe, he mirrored back to me the trust I'd developed within myself. Although I was still terrified of rejection, that small voice, which was deafening and glass-shattering if only I would have opened my mouth at twenty in the front seat of Kyle's car, now timidly escaped.

"I think I should go home," I eked out while holding back tears that wanted to rush down my cheeks. I was afraid of losing this man I'd come to rely on and was berating myself for feeling awkward and foolish.

He heard me. Then he hugged me for a very long time. Finally he spoke, "Don't go. It's okay if that's what you want to do, but I'd like you to stay. Would you like to hear my favorite poetry?"

I didn't *really* want to go. I just didn't know how to be, and I was forty-five and thought I should. In the absence of knowing how to be intimate any other way I'd always thought relationships were based on sex, but now I was hesitant to even approach that. I wanted to escape to the safety of my single room with my cats and not feel vulnerable and clumsy and tentative and embarrassed. But the same woman who'd persevered that horrible night trying to find the house party now coexisted with the fearful inner child and defiant adolescent.

"Yes," I said as my body relaxed and my mind relieved itself of pressure to perform. Years of tension and fatigue from trying to guess what would make others love me and stay were released. In that simple statement, "Would you like me to read some poetry," Joe helped swing the door open on my self-made prison that I'd already unlocked.

I stayed.

He read from Walt Whitman.

By the time Joe and I did have sex, I'd been celibate for one year, the timeline I had set for myself for discerning my boundaries and sexual value. I felt like an inelegant teenager. All my years of experience were useless because they were unconscious physical acts void of real intimacy. We took *everything* slow. He fed my heart. One afternoon when my craving for sweets dinged incessantly like a red railroad crossing sign, a friend helped me deduce that what I really wanted was to talk with Joe. He was sweet.

A few months later my roommate went away, and we had the entire house to ourselves for the weekend. I envisioned a romantic dinner with candles in front of the fireplace and afterward a living room strewn with shirts, pants, and under garments to indicate our wild romp. I also wanted it to be a surprise. I chose a lacy red lingerie set I'd worn as a dancer layered underneath pajamas Joe had given me that were too big. I was excited putting the skimpy outfit on and remembered how I felt sexy in the club while wearing it. I had six-inch stiletto heels that helped me feel powerful and sexy, but I knew those would give my intention away. I resigned to surprise him after dinner by changing my slippers for the heels, then revealing the body-hugging teddy. As I'd done on the stage, when I wore an entire suit and hat to hide myself until I was comfortable, I planned to keep myself completely hidden until I was ready.

We ate, talked, laughed, and moved the dishes and table out of the living room when we were done.

When he disappeared into the kitchen with the last remaining dishes, I excused myself to the bathroom but instead went to get the red patent shoes.

With the heels on and the oversized pant legs held up, I walked across the hardwood floor, the stiletto heels clicking loudly, to where he lay stretched out on the leather couch. I pressed, 'play' on the CD player and pulled the pants up to reveal the pumps.

His eyes reflected the fire.

I moved my arms up and out rhythmically to Portishead's "Glorybox," a song I found extremely slow and sensual. My hip tried to find a gyration. I pulled the oversized shirt to the side and brought it up to suggestively reveal the red teddy. I attempted a provocative gaze but it felt like a sheepish smile. My mind tried to propel me into a sexy strip routine like I'd done thousands of times. I knew how it was supposed to go. I knew the mechanics of how to be alluring and sexy but it felt foreign, disjointed, sloppy, and unnatural. The woman who'd instructed others how to be erotic and called herself the sensuality expert was crumbling under the scrutiny of someone she desperately wanted to entice and be intimate with. Susan was crumbling because Vixen was gone. Vixen had been tough, arrogant, hard, determined, and certain while Susan was continuing to learn how to be soft, pliable, gentle, and flexible. There was no more façade. All that remained was the intimate center of a woman/child who wanted to give and receive unconditional love.

I panicked and stammered and with swift anxiousness blurted, "I...I...I want to be sexy and seduce you but don't know how!"

He lay there silent.

"I have sexy clothes on," and pulled up my sweatshirt to show him.

He smiled and listened.

"I feel like an amateur and stupid and weird."

I'd worn my old stripper costume, one many men had seen me in, and with that came the memories and the rote feelings and rhetoric that had made up my act. But he wasn't one of those customers. And I wasn't performing; therefore, I didn't know what to do. My sexuality had been defined first by a need to be accepted and liked, then by my need to compete and be paid, then by my desire to control. I didn't know what an authentic sexuality based on intimacy was. Until this time, I hadn't even acknowledged my sexuality as being acceptable and a facet of my body I was entitled to. I couldn't have defined something I'd rejected my entire life.

"Come here," he whispered.

With the relief that comes from heartfelt confession, I was able to walk over to him and fall into his arms.

I let him remove the clothing.

APPROVAL:
FINDING PEACE
WITH THE SELF

When you understand the nature of your own mind,
delusions will change into wisdom.

Bassui
Mud and Water

A free spirit can exist only in a freed body.

Isadora Duncan

SUPPORT

Love is not something you have or don't have. It is not a possession. It is what you are.

Ellen and Charles Birx
Waking up Together

There are no new truths, but only truths that have not been recognized by those who have perceived them without noticing.

Mary McCarthy

My body reacts. "Slam!"

The pain is immediate. Within a few days my hand will be purple.

I check the wall quickly.

No hole.

About a year ago, just like this time, I'd followed Joe into his office and demanded we continue talking. "Leave me alone. I'm done talking," he'd yelled. I smashed a hole in the closet door. A few weeks later, when Joe noticed the hole, I was ashamed.

Fine, I think now. *If he doesn't want to talk, we won't talk.*

My brain reacts.

Our marriage is over. How will we divide the cats? He'll get the dog. I can move to Wisconsin, Madison, the plan I had when mom got diagnosed with cancer, the plan I had before Joe and I got together. He'll keep the house. It's in his name. I'm entitled to money from his retirement account.

I don't even know what this particular fight is about anymore. All I know is that he shut me down. I don't feel heard. Eventually, I'll see that my anger, my hurt, comes from deep, deep within me. I didn't feel heard in my family.

In a gentler moment, a holiday, Christmas I think, when we had exchanged presents along with our love, he'd said to me, "Thank you for making home safe for me." He was terrified of home, afraid that someday he'd come home and I'd be gone. I had followed that with, "Thank you for making the world safe for me." I was comfortable in home. I wanted to make it nice and never leave. It was the rest of the world I was frightened of.

Unfortunately, I'm not able to control my mind in this fragmented noisy place where conscious reason has given way to traumatic history and unmet needs, and I'm no longer an adult with a rational mind, but instead, a child battling out something from my past. This home is suddenly unsafe. I want to escape everything, even my body.

I put my walking shoes on, throw a coat over my pajamas, grab my keys and leave the house without saying a word. The pre-dawn air is brisk, and as I start walking fast, really fast, I warm up quickly. I'm indignant, incredulous, inflexible. *How dare he. How dare he not want to talk.* My mind churns over words and phrases as if they're in a boiling pot of alphabet soup. My body becomes just as hot. My legs are strong as they pound and push the pavement. Entire blocks disappear behind me as if I have wings and fly over them; I know the streets are there, but I have no awareness of walking them.

Our fights hadn't started until after we were married. The magical symbiosis of a new relationship sustained our compliance with each other during our first year living together. Then Joe took a new job, and packing our belongings and moving to a new town kept us united in a common purpose and distracted us from conflict. During that time I was also planning our wedding, and we were buying a house. Once all these exciting yet stressful life changes disintegrated, we were left to live with each other in mundane reality.

During the first year of our marriage we'd get in an argument, and my mind would immediately react with, *This is over,* and I'd stomp off by myself. My concrete face would hold back rage, and I'd pace like a trapped animal. After a few hours my mind would have sifted through the self-justification that if only he'd be, do, or say something differently we wouldn't have arguments, the anger would have subsided, and then the threadbare loneliness I'd experienced my entire life would seep into my bones. I'd be remorseful, apologetic, and hypersensitive thinking I'd finally done or said the unspeakable, and now Joe would really leave me. This thought was intolerable.

I had an old bottle of Trazadone, a sleep aid with antidepressant properties from a four-year-old prescription, so after a troublesome argument one evening I took half a pill—enough to put me to sleep but not enough to give me foggy head in the morning. A few weeks later we had another argument, and I took another half of a pill (this argument too was around bed time).

I couldn't fool myself. Sure, I was controlling my intake, but I also knew I was using the pills to escape. If I didn't talk about my uncomfortable thoughts and feelings they could lead to relapse. It had happened before.

Long before I'd met Joe, while I was still working in the club, I started working with a husband/wife production team doing research in anticipation of producing my video. I worked closely with them, strategizing over the phone, exploring the striptease video market and discussing production ideas. It seemed like making the DVD had become just as much their idea as it was mine. "We'll put you in flowing, beautiful dresses," Sonja repeated to me numerous times. After six months conducting market research, meeting with potential investors, and giving lectures at universities where David watched me deliver speeches, they'd drawn up and insisted I sign a "Memorandum of Understanding," outlining specifics about the partnership.

A week later, David, the husband who specialized in marketing, asked me to meet him at the San Francisco Museum of Modern Art cafeteria, a place we'd used often to get together. I arrived first and settled at a table for what I assumed to be another marketing meeting.

David walked up, declined to get anything to drink, and sat down. "Sonja has an opportunity she'd like to pursue that might lead her to make a feature film."

"That's great," I offered as I sipped my cappuccino and took another bite of my scone.

"No, you don't understand," he continued, "We're pulling out of your project."

I stared.

Plates clattered. Patrons murmured. Forks clanked. Cars outside honked. My blueberry scone turned to dirt in my mouth.

"Here's all the research notes and information we've gathered," he'd said as he handed me a manila folder with my name written on it in bold black sharpie. "I can't stay. Sonja's waiting outside. We have to go."

My stomach dropped into the chair.

It was like having a boyfriend break up with you in a public place. A sense of propriety ruled and I was forced to maintain decorum in the polite museum eatery. "Oh, okay," a voice I recognized as my own said. "Sure. I understand."

Shocked, I politely followed David outside and voiced hello to Sonja. The late afternoon sun hid behind the horizon and twilight bathed our awkward ménage à trios as the five o'clock, just-out-of-work crowd shuffled past hurriedly.

I stood alone watching their backs walk away. I had no feeling below my waist yet somehow my legs started moving towards the parking garage. Gone was my usual brisk pace meticulously weaving through oncoming bodies, and I watched myself being jostled and jarred like a stranded bumper car. On the slow trek to my vehicle, I wrapped myself in abandonment that was just as familiar and ancient as a ragged green trench coat I'd gotten from a second-hand store to cover myself in the San Francisco fog. I folded myself into the well-worn driver's seat and headed for my silent studio apartment.

I'd gotten the idea to make a video when a producer for Home and Garden Television took my Learning Annex class. "Every woman here would have bought a video," she'd said afterwards. We'd started the project together, but after only a few months she left San Francisco to work in Atlanta and I was left with an idea, a sample script, two-thousand dollars of my own money invested in library music, and an ego committed to being a star. I looked for help and found Sandy Shore Films, David and Sonja, a husband and wife team who specialized in marketing and film making. With them I'd invested thousands more dollars and considerable more time. Now they were leaving me too.

Dumped and dejected, I grappled with what to do next. I asked the universe for a sign as to whether I was supposed to continue with the video project and if so, how. Applications for low-cost credit cards started appearing in my mailbox, and I took that as an affirmative nod from the heavens. I gathered women, hired a director and film crew, and pushed myself through hard work to silence the voices within that were apprehensive about taking on such a big project by myself, uneducated about the process, nervous about all the money I was spending, and fearful about producing something that could invite criticism. I had no close friends to talk to, and I had discontinued sessions with my therapist. I was approaching this phase of my life in the same manner I'd always lived—alone—pushing.

Late one night, about midnight, as I sat planning and strategizing how I could embark on a national tour to promote my video, my arm started tingling, and my heart raced. Certain I was having a heart attack at forty-two, I drove myself to the emergency room. Initial fright gave way to relief when all the tests proved my heart was in good shape, but I never thought to examine why I would be having a panic attack. Instead, I went to my doctor and complained about my anxiety, and she prescribed Wellbutrin, an antidepressant I'd taken in the past to help me quit smoking. I never acknowledged, nor could I manage, all the uncertain uncomfortable doubts and questions in my mind, but I could manage my pill intake. Fueled by adrenaline, caffeine, and Wellbutrin during the day, I found it hard to fall asleep so that same doctor prescribed the Trazadone I took nightly to shut off my anxious brain. The pattern to ingest something to help me feel better was reestablished, so what happened next was a natural progression.

Although I'd been a sober dancer for seven-and-a-half years, wine started to infiltrate my thoughts surreptitiously. I noticed the exquisite round goblet and thin sensual stem that held the inviting liquid. The frivolous animated demeanor of the dancers and customers drinking it also captured my attention. For weeks these images simmered in the far reaches of my consciousness, but I spoke about them to no one. It wasn't until I had dinner with a long-time acquaintance, someone who'd always drunk around me, that I voiced my private thoughts. "I've been thinking of drinking again. I think the reasons why I started drinking as a teenager are dealt with. I've had lots of therapy."

He seemed nonchalant. "Are you sure?"

"Yeah, I'm sure." I could feel the warmth caressing my skin from the inside out already. "What kind of wine is that?"

He considered himself a connoisseur and started to rattle off the wine's properties as he motioned the waiter over to order a half bottle.

When that bottle was finished we ordered another half bottle of something different. We had port after dinner.

Next, we went to a club where the dark lighting and pulsing music brought out the effervescent adolescent within me. I wondered aloud what exotic drink I should have next while the cocktail waitress threw out popular names. Like a contestant in a game show who's won the grand prize, "champagne cocktail" lit up my eyes, and a bell went ding ding ding in my brain.

It was easy to convince myself I no longer had a problem consuming alcohol when I took the first drink and scrunched up my face in disgust. Wouldn't alcoholics drink anything?

I decided to stick to wine and become a connoisseur myself.

Some people think booze gives them confidence, but it took mine away. I became aware of this when I went out dancing for fun, had a glass of wine upon arriving at the nightspot, then suddenly, self-conscious, hung on the sidelines of the dance floor trying to muster courage to jump into the mix and gyrate. I loved to dance. Sober, I'd done it for hours, but magically, as if the eight-and-a-half alcohol-free years never happened, I was awkward and hesitant all over again.

It was about nine months after I'd started drinking again that I walked away from the San Francisco Gold Club, then spent a glorious six months not being an exotic dancer.

Then my money ran out. Although I was extremely busy marketing my video and teaching Sensual Dance classes for women, I started traveling to Las Vegas because those clubs were open twenty-four hours a day. I could make more money working twelve or more hours in a row in Las Vegas than I could working seven hours in an evening shift in San Francisco.

From the outside, I still looked like vivacious Vixen, but I didn't want to play the game, so I needed a drink to be motivated to mime sensual ecstasy with anything resembling enthusiasm. I used speed to stay up all night so I could make the most money and alcohol to temper the jitters the speed caused. Younger bigger-breasted women intimidated me. I no longer had confidence to set my own boundaries and demand the customers or myself stick to them so I lost my own self-respect. In a pitiful attempt to be part of the on-going party the club atmosphere promoted, I'd sit at their table and drink with them, hoping they'd give me money. Seldom did I admit that I'd turned into one of those pathetic exotic dancers I once felt sorry for.

What had started this downward spiral was the film couple abandoning me, but what was more debilitating was that then, *I'd* abandoned me too.

At home in Berkeley I was making progress with my Sensual Dance Program but my ego was so fragile I never felt completely certain about my decisions. I lived on will power, exhausted from my schedule of producing and marketing the video during the day and week-long trips to Las Vegas to pay the bills. Two years of being isolated, afraid, and fatigued brought me to an emotional and physical bottom. I asked an acquaintance to attend a twelve-step meeting with me. My self-respect and confidence started returning as soon as I put the substances away.

A few years after this especially dark period I'd met Joe, and though I'd become an adult in my own right, my amygdala, the part of the brain that reacts automatically and is associated with memory and fear response, got triggered every time his words or actions touched an emotionally sensitive area. To defend from the excruciating feelings of being left by someone I felt so close to, my natural, first, unconscious reaction, was to get angry and leave first.

As reflexive as it was to move towards escape though, I wouldn't. Somewhere inside I knew that if it wasn't with this man, I'd have to explore these reactions with a different man. Changing men, or homes, or cities for that matter, wouldn't make my life better or eliminate my problems.

＿＿＿

Done with my walking route I return home. Yet I still don't know what to do. He hasn't left the house for work. My anger flares stronger. Again I think, *How dare he not want to talk. He doesn't care.*

I want to call my wise mentor to complain but can't talk freely with Joe in the house, so I leave again, feet still focused on covering as much ground as fast as I can.

After five minutes of walking while talking through the sequence of events and receiving much needed "poor you" responses from my mentor, I'm a bit calmer. I continue to whine though, my mind unchecked. "If only he'd change, things would be better."

I catch myself.

And laugh.

"Yeah right," I interject as she starts to tell me what I already know and am about to cop to. "The only one I can change is myself, blah, blah, blah."

I've walked so hard and fast I've walked right out of my flashback from childhood experience into my logical reasoning brain. The anger has boiled away.

My feet slow. My mind begins to see that at the bottom of the empty pot, in the hollow recesses of the shaped metal, I don't want to split from Joe. Perhaps, just perhaps, I caused the fight, or at the very least played a part in it. What did I do that could have contributed and how could I have done it differently? I let go of the hard alloy bit I've ground teeth marks into as if I was an untamed horse bridled and restrained, begin to relax, and use my now fully-functioning rational mind to be anchored again in the present.

My feet turn in the direction of home. I still won't be the one to make the first move. That's always him. He'll say "Give me a hug," and all I'll be able to do is reciprocate, but the door will be open for healing. As long as both of us stay, just for today, we have a good chance of finding our way back to each other. This really is the stuff my dreams are made of, even if it doesn't always feel like it.

I love Joe and I know he loves me, but he doesn't always show it in the ways I understand or need him to show it. He gives me what he needs just as I give him what I need. In other words, when I'm feeling blue, I want extra attention, so I give that to him when he's troubled. But he needs to be left alone to sort out his feelings so that's what he gives me. This is where our communication breaks down, our expectations sabotage our connection, and our misunderstood feelings get hurt. This is where our work as a couple will need to center. This is where we'll both have to step outside our comfort zones and learn to give someone else what they need instead of just what we think they need. This is where we'll need to learn better communication and yes, compromise. Sure, I've heard and read solutions to relationship problems in the past when I was desperately reading self-help books on how to make relationships work, but until I created the relationship with myself first so that I didn't have to leave myself, no matter what, even when I was confused or wrong, I couldn't stay and practice with someone else.

I need Joe. He's much easier on me than I am on myself. He'll often say, "You're fifty, give yourself a break," when I've succumb to societal pressure and forget my self-appeal philosophy. Though I've accepted myself and have done the hard work to grow my self-love, esteem, and confidence, current mainstream culture doesn't really want me to own or approve of my body. I'm constantly bombarded with half-truths and inundated with messages that tell me I'm not good enough the way I am. I can't turn on the television or read a newspaper without hearing about the latest way to shed those few extra pounds that in my advancing years and ease with myself have crept on. I see the same type of commercials as I did when I was twenty with young models who don't have any wrinkles to begin with telling me what products to use so I can look like them. Even back then I didn't look like they did, radiant and flawless as only film and filters can make you look. I know my external appearance doesn't determine whether I'm worthy or make me a lovable woman, yet I sometimes feel inadequate and want to look like those young women. This was especially obvious when at forty-seven I was preparing for my wedding. To say I wanted to look perfect would be inaccurate—I wanted to look twenty-one again.

≈

For the first nine months I was planning our wedding, I concerned myself only with details like where we'd have the ceremony and reception, which deejay and photographer to use, what flowers would best symbolize our love, and how could we afford to feed people in an elegant yet economical way. My first wedding happened twenty-three years previously, and the marriage was so short it's as if it hadn't happened at all. I threw all my time and creativity into making this one, the *real* one, memorable and unique. First I purchased blank ivory invitations and printed the inside with sumptuous rich script whose leading edges and tails curled. Working in Photoshop I added color to a picture of Rodin's sculpture, *The Kiss,* printed, cut, then pasted it onto the front of the invitations. I also designed and printed response cards on heavy cardstock, each one having an entire side with a different piece of art representing love that I planned to make into a collage and hang on the wall some day. I purchased cotton muslin, cut, hemmed, then tie-dyed each piece using either orange, yellow, or shades of blue, green, and red to make vibrant table runners to place over the top of white linen table coverings. My Matron of Honor, Amy, and I painted clay flowerpots that matched the table runners so we could put white azaleas into them for centerpieces.

One sunny morning I rode BART into San Francisco and stole Amy, whose own wedding invitations provided inspiration for mine, away from her job. We bought box lunches and ate them in a Chinatown park. Afterwards, we scoured the narrow streets for shops where I might find miniature glass frogs to use as wedding favors (I'd know the right ones when I saw them). As we walked, I resurrected the wonder I always had for the naked brown chickens hanging in Chinese shop windows while I chattered without restraint. "If I can lose five pounds (these were the same five pounds I'd wanted to lose my entire life) and do crunches for my stomach, I'll be set. My butt's more flabby than it ever was." Between my concerns about whether or not I should join a gym again or start running every day, Amy, herself an exercise enthusiast, found an opportunity to comment. "Why don't you just get a dress that fits your body?"

I shut up.

These were the same words of wisdom I'd spoken to others.

Almost a year had passed since Joe and I first discussed plans to make our ceremony unique, and now that initial thrill returned at the thought of getting a dress. Amy and I tried to plan some times to shop together, but her job kept her busy traveling all over the world. My mom was supposed to visit for a week and help me dress hunt, but before her departure my dad had an accident, and he needed her to stay in Wisconsin. Joe would've come with me but I didn't want to break the tradition of not having the groom see the bride in her dress before the wedding. Just as quickly as I'd gotten enthused to shop, self-pity wrapped its arms around me. Since Joe had come into my life I hadn't had to do much alone, and it wasn't easy to put on the pretense I'd once worn—that for something so significant being by myself was okay. I became melancholy, my mind quickly and easily regressing into feelings of isolation that years of being alone had acquainted me with, but just as quickly, within a day, because of a sober clear mind, I was able to see reason in the present that pulled me out of the past. I wasn't that solitary woman anymore.

A new friend had offered to go with me. In direct contrast to the huge commitment I was planning to make to Joe, however, I couldn't commit to a specific day and time for shopping with someone I didn't know well. My lone habits and daily routine were firmly embedded. Buoyed by the realization that I didn't *have* to be alone if I didn't want to be, I began the search for a dress—alone—empowered with a joyful spirit once again.

With only an hour to spare one late afternoon, after running errands, before I wanted to be home to greet Joe from his long day, I went into my first shop. I was overwhelmed by the number of dresses. I had an idea of what I was looking for but didn't describe it well enough because the sales lady brought me a yellow sequin number that I wiggled into and gawked at with fascination. In that dress I imagined myself as the conniving siren Joan Collins would play in a late-night soap. Although I wanted something similar to what I'd seen an actress playing Cinderella in the theater wear—an a-line skirt with a bustier-like top—this one did appeal to my inner girl who loved sparkles. I put it on hold.

A few days later, outfitted with time and motivation that had grown larger than my initial disappointment over shopping alone, I walked into two more stores. It was hard to tell what the dresses looked like underneath plastic, so I tried on some with plunging necklines, backlines, or both. I tried on some that were skin-tight but flared at the bottom like a mermaid's tail, that appealed to the former stripper within me but appalled the woman whose thighs had become less toned than they'd ever been. Some were snowstorm white. I envisioned ivory. Not quite matching my ideal but all beautiful nonetheless, every time I put one on I smiled at myself in the mirror and affirmed all over again that I was getting married. I had the saleslady hold a few as backup, and I kept searching. In each store I stood alongside women, girls really, half my age, with unmarred skin. The sales staff usually mistook me for the mother of the bride.

I was jealous of younger women. *If only I had those years back*, I silently wished, although I just as quickly had to confess that in my twenties I didn't know what marriage meant. Back then I'd been more enamored with the dress, presents, and being the center of attention than with my fiancé. I soothed my present-day mature mind with the realization that I'd lived through tough lessons and had earned every scar, wrinkle, and cellulite dimple I wore. I acquiesced to the fact that I wouldn't trade their fresh skin or naturally toned bodies if it meant retreating into my old ways of thinking.

The next week I stopped at a bridal rental shop close to a home Joe and I were considering buying. The shop was small and offered fewer dresses than any I'd been in, but the owner had me look through books of young girls modeling prom dresses and formals. These dresses didn't look like my vision either, but I used the pictures to describe what I was looking for. "Wait," she said, disappearing behind an overstuffed rack of vinyl sheathed gowns, emerging minutes later with a dress that didn't look like anything special. "We've had it for a while and no one's worn it. It's not the style young brides want."

The price was definitely within my budget so I tried it on. The owner helped me zip up the back and directed me to stand on a raised platform surrounded by mirrors.

I looked at my reflection and took in my inelegant ordinariness; matted hat hair, plain unmade face, and worn bra straps. Then I shifted my focus to the simple clean dress; a drop-waist bodice with thin braided straps and ornate silver beading, and an ivory satin a-line skirt layered beneath two panels of sheer ivory gauze.

My eyes moistened and began to sting.

The round woman with the cherub face spoke gently, "It's okay to want to feel like Cinderella."

I hadn't mentioned that I'd seen an actress playing Cinderella wear the same style.

When I'd seen the dress in the local play I liked it simply because I thought the style figure flattering. Now I had to acknowledge that although I'd read books like the *Cinderella Complex* and intellectually knew Joe wasn't a prince who was going to save me, I still harbored a small nugget of hope that all my woes would magically evaporate once we were married. At forty-seven I still wanted to be a princess and go to a Ball.

She fussed about me pulling the abbreviated train and hem straight and held the top a bit tighter at the back buttons. I guessed her to be in her late thirties and figured she'd helped hundreds if not thousands of prom attendees and hopeful brides. She was the next best thing to my mom being there—a fairy godmother.

More customers came in through the front door and she went to see what they wanted.

I stood alone, three different angles reflected back, eyes leaking. The dress was perfect. In a few short weeks a man would promise, "I'll stand by you always," even though I wasn't perfect. And I would do the same for him. Stress that had built up after months of wedding planning, living together only one year then moving eighty miles east for Joe's new job, and looking for a home to buy, was released. The search was over—for the dress—for the husband—for a home. Relief puddled my eyes as the hope I'd kept cocooned inside me burst forth from its silken wrap, unfurled in wisps resembling curls of exhaled smoke, and teased me with its promises. I envisioned a simple Tiara atop my head. I *was* Cinderella.

When the owner came back I blurted, "I'll take it."

I stepped out of the dress carefully, hung it up, and changed back into my clothes. I put the dress, *my* dress, in its plastic protective wrap and took it home. The next day I called the tailor.

"If you cried when you tried it on, then it's the right dress," Amy said.

Now I just had to make the rest of me right.

I had a forty-seven-and-a-half-year-old body, which meant I had a forty-seven-and-a-half-year-old face. My teenage years had brought on horrible acne that I'd tried to combat with tetracycline, but it lasted into my twenties until I took Accutane. Now I had scars, rosacea and broken blood vessels on my skin. While working as a dancer, dark lighting erased these blemishes, along with ten years or so from my age, so I never thought about how to be gentle to and nourish my aging skin. I'd only been concerned with how it looked from a distance to others. I'd even used painful botox injections, and sometimes my face burned when I used glycolic acid facial products to exfoliate and stave off wrinkles.

Having found my wedding gown and taken care of most of the wedding details, I had time to hang out with my new friend Lani, an esthetician. She taught me that antioxidants, the buzz-word for food, were present and essential in face products. She read the ingredients list on the products I was using, pointed out the harsh chemicals that would aggravate my sensitive skin, and said I needed face primer to fill in pores and lines before applying foundation. We spent an entire day matching makeup shades with my skin tone, testing products with provocative names like "Sexy Sweep" and "Dr. Feelgood," enjoying lunch, and engaging in a feminine ritual I'd never been given the gene for—shopping.

"Brighten, tighten, and lighten. A BLT but without the calories," the fresh-faced specialist chimed decisively as she demonstrated an under-eye repair product.

We burst into laughter. It was charming, just like the heavily made up nineteen-year-old cosmetics clerk, and a little ridiculous, which made it more fun.

"Brighten, tighten, and lighten," I repeated throughout the day for a giggle.

From the flawless face of the young woman standing before me, who had no idea what it's like to have dark under-eye circles, I bought the two–step cream and pencil under-eye repair. I spent money on extend-lash mascara, lip gloss, eye shadow, and Brow-Zing, something Lani said I needed in order to shape and deepen my brow color but that I, quite honestly, had been doing just fine without while using my cheap pencils from the drugstore. Chatting and laughing while trying on eye shadows, lip shades, and talking about makeup brushes, I felt girly. Although I had expected to feel envious and insecure when surrounded by all the young women in the cosmetics section of Macy's, I was surprised to find myself having a good time.

Lani also told me that old cosmetics have a lifespan and grow bacteria so I needed to throw mine out. Similar to unworn clothes I hoped to fit into again or jewelry that never left the soft felt-lined drawer of the ornate wood box on my dresser, the antiquated face paints were buried treasures. Every time I'd see them again anew, I'd exclaim with joy.

The red and copper lipsticks, blue and purple shadows, and too-orange blush/brush packages were reminiscent of past attempts at glamour and helped me create a different persona. As a dancer I'd needed the colors to mask my vulnerability and create an illusion. While playing dress up for risqué events like the Exotic Erotic Ball, these pigments helped me hide my identity. But I no longer needed to conduct my activities under cover, just like I no longer needed a stage name. I was planning to stand in the exposed afternoon light in a dress fit for a princess and invite witnesses to peer closely into my naked heart. With fond memories, I bid the old makeup adieu.

Using my new light-toned day-appropriate cosmetics and mom's help with hair styling, I glowed as, may I dare say it, a middle-aged bride, on my wedding day. My waist was bigger than it once was, my hair shorter, my face more lined, but I was getting married to someone a few years older than I who had his own waist and lines. Along with my bouquet of one white gerbera daisy, a classic symbol of beauty, one yellow/orange rose symbolizing friendship and desire, one pink rose to show feelings of admiration, and one lavender rose to signify enchantment, I carried within my heart the miracle of love, the mystery of a life still to come, and the fulfillment of a dream.

I'd debated about having my father walk me up the aisle.

The tradition is rooted in the days of arranged marriages, and I was a modern woman who'd even discussed with Joe having just the two of us walk down the aisle together. When I read that today a father giving away his daughter is a symbol of his blessing, I reconsidered. My parents had waited a long time to see me in a happy relationship.

I found comfort in and embraced other matrimonial traditions as well. I wore my mother's crystals purchased by my father for her in 1963 as "something old" representing a link to my family and the past. My wedding gown was "something new" that represented hope for good fortune and success. I learned that "something borrowed" usually comes from a happily married woman to lend some of her good fortune and joy to the new bride, so I borrowed my sister's wedding garter that was so stretched out from hanging in my brother-in-law's car for seventeen years that I had to wrap it around my thigh twice. The simple headband I wore contained little blue crystals for "something blue," a symbol of love and fidelity. In my left shoe I kept a sixpence from 1959, the year my parents were married, to attract the same wealth to my marriage they had in theirs.

Adorned with meaningful symbolism and traditional good-luck charms I held onto my seventy-three-year-old father's arm as we walked towards Joe, who waited in his black tuxedo. My eyes focused only on him while my father steadied me past eighty guests, half of whom had traveled almost three-thousand miles to attend. At the end of the rows of folding chairs in the lodge that after the ceremony was to be converted for the dinner and reception, in front of the arrangement of two-foot high white flowers positioned on a white plastic Greek column, beside the minister, stood Joe—smiling. All thoughts of my appearance vanished.

Getting to know Joe over the two-and-a-half years we were together before this day, I'd learned he had all the qualities on my preferred man list—except two. He had glasses for reading (to me they symbolize intelligence). He didn't smoke. He was sensitive and expressed his emotions. He valued mine. He had dark hair. He liked animals. He loved to dance. He continued to work on his own personal growth and evolution to be the best Joe he could be. He didn't abuse alcohol or drugs. The only items he didn't have from my list when we'd first met were external and didn't really matter—long hair and boots.

Yet, even, or especially, in the early stages of our relationship after we'd moved in together, to protect myself from loving him too much, my mind had wanted to hang onto things about him I wasn't fond of. He didn't turn lights off when he left a room. He washed dishes one at a time with the water running instead of filling up the sink like I did. He picked out minute details in the home that I glossed over. He was prone to snuff his nose rather than to blow it. Fortunately, my body admitted I needed him and approved long before my conscious mind was able to.

In the blank, black, subconscious night, my mind couldn't rationalize, project, interject, analyze, or create irrational fears and insecurities about being close to another human being. My left foot searched out his leg, his warmth, a token of him under the covers for connection and to reassure me I wasn't alone. I'd turn my body around from its most comfortable right-side sleeping position and encircle his back, clutch his chest, conform to fit him instead of asking him to conform to me, which is what my intelligence wanted in the daylight. The same way I'd fallen into unconditional love with my cats, watching, listening, and wondering about their nose twitches and dreams as they slept, I fell deeper in love with Joe while watching his involuntary eye and lip spasms and body jerks while listening to his gentle snores. During sleep his tranquil face exhibited the innocence of a child before it'd grown into a man with fears, worries, and scars.

Events from our early days flood my mind. On lazy Sunday mornings after we'd started having sleepovers, I'd listen to him with quiet lips and open ears when he told stories of his childhood and life before me. When he'd gotten a new job and was fearful his first few days as many of us are when we make a change, I supported his mixed emotions and devised the "Joe Cheer," usually done in the nude, and continued to resurrect it when he needed an emotional boost and a laugh.

His patient observation of my insecurities also flitted through my awareness. When we'd started living together bedtime caused me anxiety. I'd stand by my side of the mattress, fidget, rock from one foot to the other, and have silent conversations with myself. *It's cold in here. It'll be even colder tonight. I'll probably have to get up to use the bathroom. I'd like to put my long underwear on. They're not cute.*

Next I'd go to the dresser and look for something sexy. I'd start to put on lingerie I never usually wore but then hesitate and stand in the middle of the bedroom, half in half out of the outfit as I got colder. *What if he doesn't want to have sex? Do I just sleep in this? This'll probably just ride up around my waist. If I wear it, will he feel obligated? Am I supposed to feel obligated to initiate sex? Are we supposed to have it every night? I like skin-to-skin contact but I also like being warm. Am I supposed to be naked?*

After deliberating for a week and discussing this dilemma with a few friends, I opened my mouth and asked him, "Is it okay if I wear my flannels?" I wanted to crawl into bed in comfort wearing my ten-year-old flannel pajama bottoms with the saggy butt and hole in the knee that were so stretched even washing didn't help them shrink back into shape.

"Of course," he smiled.

I wore those thin faded-pink bottoms for two years during the winter months, and he'd promised to marry me anyway.

With time he'd become my best friend, my lover, my hero, my teacher, and my student. Eventually, my overly analytical, nitpicking mind agreed with my body that I needed him.

What rushed at me now as I clung to my father's arm and approached this persistently loving man who stood firm, was his rugged maleness that I'd initially been attracted to, his sincere brown eyes, boyish innocence, full head of dark hair, mustache that betrayed his youthful look with silver, and his unique masculine aroma.

I took my place by his side.

Focused on the minister and her words, I felt no nervousness. I was in a safe zone encircled in the same fluffy heart from the 1950's *I Love Lucy* series opening credits that I'd always fantasized about.

Borrowing from Native American wedding traditions where water is used for purification and cleansing, we passed a bowl and towel between us, washing our hands, symbolic of releasing old errors, limited thoughts, and memories of past loves.

My heart rejoiced.

Adopting another Native American wedding tradition, we drank from a wedding vase to represent and affirm individuality but also to signify that we were willing to share the same vessel of life. First we each drank from a side spout on the end, and then turning to face guests, we drank from the common center vessel at the same time.

Some spilled.

We laughed.

My heart—and face—beamed.

After the minister spoke, I repeated vows with a voice that wavered. I pushed a white-gold diamond-encrusted ring on his finger as a single tear eked out from underneath my waterproof mascara.

Amy handed me a tissue.

Joe looked into my eyes, repeating his vows, and pushed the diamond wedding band on the ring finger of my trembling left hand. His hand held mine steady.

The minister pronounced us man and wife.

We kissed.

Our friends and family clapped.

We ate, toasted, and danced our first song to a classic melody so simple yet complete it causes my eyes to swell with emotion *every* time I hear Joe Cocker sing it, "You are so beautiful to me."

After that we danced more, cut wedding cake, and formed a conga line snaking and jiving through the hall to The O'Jay's 1973 hit, "Love Train."

By the time we'd gotten married, Joe and I had been in transition for a year and a half. We'd moved in together and eight months later made a frantic effort to unpack boxes and hang pictures before his parents came to visit. A mere two months after that he accepted a new job, and I started repacking. After a week-long visit to Philadelphia to meet his seven siblings and their spouses and kids for the first time, less than thirteen months after we'd moved in together, we moved to the California central valley. There only three months, but long enough to learn that the landlord didn't like to make timely repairs, and only three months before the wedding, we'd started looking for a house to buy. Two weeks after the wedding we moved our belongings, most of which hadn't been taken out of boxes for seven months, into our own home.

Suddenly, after all this chaotic busyness, my mind had no unpacking or repacking to focus on or control. I had no wedding details to put my attention on and energy into. I had no part-time catering job on the weekends, and my coaching business wasn't established in the new area. Similar to the confusion

I'd had about my identity when I'd quit dancing, I didn't know who this new married Susan was.

I'd created an entire life around anything *but* domesticity, yet here I was focusing solely on it. I scrubbed, lined with contact paper, put our dishes in, and kept food stocked in the cupboards. I made sure meals were on the table, laundry was done, and that Joe's shirts and pants for work were ironed and in his closet. I cleaned windows and doors. I felt obligated to get our home in order and keep it perfect for Joe. He was paying all the bills. I had never been supported financially by a man and subsequently felt inadequate because of it. I also felt rushed to finish my book and create my own business so I could contribute money to the household. I didn't have time to write, however, so I heaped derogatory adjectives about myself on my already burdened shoulders. When I slowed down long enough to think about it, I lamented becoming a housewife—a label I loathed—and complained about being overwhelmed. Amy again spoke words of wisdom, "You're supporting your man."

Yes! Yes! My mind could grasp this, but liking a concept and being able to relax into it were totally separate notions. I couldn't enjoy the creative aspects of homemaking like providing sumptuous, economical, healthy meals and making curtains because I still had a hard time seeing the value in it. It was in my rebellious youth that I'd adopted the belief that I never wanted to be as dependent on a man as I interpreted my mother was, and subsequently, I'd rejected her talents. If I was now engaging in the same activities she did, well, then I was rejecting myself too. This was part of the Cinderella dream, but it was divergent from everything I'd ever known as an adult woman. Joe didn't care that I wasn't paying half the bills; all he cared about was that I was happy. "Do what you want," he'd say, but how did I know what I wanted? I'd always pushed to support myself. I'd been so driven, out of desire, yes, but also out of necessity.

We don't know what Disney's Cinderella did after the Prince found her with the glass slipper, other than live happily ever after, but this Cinderella had years of unchecked anxiety masked as ambition as well as unexpressed sensitivity. Joe's support was allowing me to soften, and I became like an old faucet that needs a new washer; an anxious mixture of sweetness and sadness escaped in a steady drip. When I read a newspaper report of someone dying, I'd break down in sobs. I'd see a commercial or watch a television show where two people were reunited, and I'd tear up. When I read or heard about the mistreatment of animals, I'd cry. If I heard a story about an average human committing a heroic act, I'd let flow the sweet tears of rejoicing. I'd hear about a distant friend of a friend of a relative that had an illness, and I'd go to Joe and hug him with a twisted red face. "You're just a big mush ball, aren't you," he'd soothe, as he'd hug me back. The path that Joe had paved to my heart was now clear and smooth and all kinds of sappy, sweet, sad stories and events traveled it to my yielding nucleus. Just as my body's insatiable lust for physical release and sweets had consumed me for a time before coming into healthy balance, so too now the last bits of unexpressed emotion that I'd once needed movies to help me release, poured out.

$\backsim$

I like this sensitive vulnerable Susan, but when we get into fights my first reaction, still, even after a few years of marriage, is to erect a dam and toughen up. Feeling deserted and discarded is a scary place my subconscious mind never, never, absolutely *never* wants to experience again.

The only living creature who's never hurt or abandoned the sensitive child within me was Dinky, the kitten in chapter two who'd helped me become responsible to myself. Throughout her lifetime she'd fulfilled many roles. She'd been my sick baby; I clutched her close while she'd peed all over me when a child scared her at the vet's office. She'd been my comfort; her paw reached out at night to cover my hand while I slept. Like a loyal family member she'd always been there when I came home from a night of work too exhausted to talk. I oftentimes saw her as a wise matriarch. For many years, I fed her special food trying to outsmart kidney failure and had her undergo surgeries to remove bladder irritations and growths in her mouth.

I euthanized her at sixteen years of age because she couldn't be propped up with medicine any longer, but she'd been caring enough to stick around until Joe came into my life. Though she didn't live long enough to see our new home, I missed her and felt her presence regularly.

Some time after we settle in our home, a dirty gray cat appears on our lawn. It sits perfectly poised as only proper cats can, back legs down, slender front legs straight, as if it is a regal aristocrat sitting on an elevated throne. It voices an obvious yet thin cry that seems to question whether it has the right to actually make noise. Its short white fur, though dingy, sports splotches of orange and gray, but it is so matted it reminds me of coarse sheepskin. One eye opens half way. It's missing part of an ear and the piece it does have looks charred. It opens its mouth and lets out a second, barely discernable meow.

I get some dry food and water and put them by the side of the house. I'm normally not afraid of cats but I'm hesitant to get too close to this one. It tears into the food.

"Is this your cat?" Joe and I ask a neighbor who slows down while riding his motorcycle by our house.

"Her? No. She's not ours. She's a neighborhood cat. She lived in the house next to us but when the wife kicked the husband out, she kicked the cat out as well. Comes round to our house sometimes. Every time the guy comes back to visit my brother, they joke about her. My brother says, 'You better take your cat,' and the guy says, 'That's your cat.' And they go back and forth like that."

"Have you seen her ear?" I ask. "It looks awful."

"Yeah, there's an old male around here who mounts her sometimes and chews on it," he laughs.

I stare.

"I try to chase him off when I see that happening," he continues. "She's an inspiration. Too stupid to die. When we're feeling down, she comes 'round and we see that others are suffering as well. Once she got ran over and the guy across the street took her to the vet and fixed her up."

My heart tears.

I turn to Joe. "I have to take her," then I go inside to get the large portable carrier I'd used to transport Dinky and her son for sixteen years. I don't want to pick her up, she looks so mangy, so we coax and scoot her into the carrier.

In the vet's waiting room, she lays on an old towel and I open the cage door, reach tentatively, and stroke her head lightly. She purrs.

"It's okay, little one," I speak softly again and again as people bringing well-cared-for pets walk in and out of the office.

They take her into the back room, and I wait patiently until the vet returns. "The growth on her ear is cancer and we'll have to amputate it but she can live this way as an indoor cat."

My heart smiles.

"She doesn't have leukemia, but the tests are inconclusive about diabetes."

My heart hopes.

"There's another test we can run, but we won't get the results until tomorrow."

The bill is already totaling more than the amount Joe and

I have agreed on so I call him, and we increase what we're willing to spend.

I leave her overnight. She has ear mites, fleas, and probably worms or worse, and the only place I'm comfortable keeping her is in the garage, but I don't really want her there either.

Pulled between my heart that has grown in an accelerated, cartoonish way like Jim Carey's character, the Grinch, in *How the Grinch Stole Christmas*, and the practical reality of our financial limitations, that night at home I tell Joe, "If the test indicates she has diabetes, I'll bring her home for one safe warm night in the garage and then put her down."

The vet calls my cell phone the next day. "The tests are still inconclusive about diabetes, but there is one more test we can run."

The little girl within me who wants to rescue this cat and who doesn't know or care about being responsible with money wants to throw every available resource at the problem. The adult within me wrestles with her. The rebellious teenager within gets angry. I abhor reaching a conclusion based on money, but we've already spent over five hundred dollars.

I call the vet back and tell her I'm on my way.

I love cats—unconditionally—wholeheartedly. Joe calls me the cat whisperer, and at times throughout the years I thought Dinky was part human, and I was part cat. I identify with their nature to be independent and understand their desire to bond and be close only to a chosen few. They're my compatriots— my soul mates of the animal kingdom.

Without forewarning I'm transported into the body of this wretched feline. *Lonely. Lost. I scratch at the door where I'm used to being inside, but there's no answer. Scratch. Scrape. Meow. Meow. Scratch. Scrape. Don't understand. Confused. Cold. Ear throbs. Scratch. Scrape. Meow. Meow. Hours. Days. Ravenous. I leave the familiar door, hesitant to walk away from safety, but sooooo hungry. My throat hurts. A world that was once full of fun surprises is now scary. Cold. Hungry. Alone. Fend for self. Navigate. Watch out for predators. Alone. Something moves. Tummy growls. Instinct. Pounce.*

My eyes swim in a salty release, and I maneuver my car carefully to the side of the road. I weep without restraint and hug my stomach as I rock alone in the driver's seat. Just as I'd identified with the homeless man in Ghirardelli Square, in the cat's abandonment, I feel my own abandonment—from others—as well as myself.

I call my wise mentor. "It's … It's … It's Susan," I manage to spit out between intermittent breaths and blubbering. My sobs and gasps continue until her words and caring attention have an impact. I calm some. "It'll be too hard on my emotions to bring her home for one more night," I reluctantly, eventually, admit.

At the vet's office they have me wait in a little room with a glistening silver table and stark mauve walls that match my mood. It's been less than a day since I've seen her, but when they bring her in, her appearance startles me. Her mangled ear, matted dirty fur, and half open eye give her a belligerent streetwise edge that reminds me of homeless youth I'd seen begging for food in black leathers and silver studded chokers on the streets of Berkeley.

I feed her free packaged treats I've gotten from a bowl on the receptionist's desk. My heart, like a porcelain vase nicked in just the right place, shatters as she gobbles the tiny morsels. I take the towel the vet has used to wrap her in and using it as a shield, hug her. The voices outside the tiny room increase my isolation. My shoulders and chest convulse with heavy sobs.

"It's okay little one," I speak towards her—but for myself.

When the treats are gone, I grab more.

The vet's assistant enters, "She's such a good cat. She just slept peacefully the entire time." I try to comfort myself with what I told Joe, "She was literally crying out to us to help her. She was hurting."

Afterwards, I stay with her lifeless body a few short minutes calming myself with what the living tell themselves about the dead; she rests peacefully in heaven.

Two days later I drive by the house of the man who'd stopped on the motorcycle that day, and when I see people outside, spin my car around and pull up at their curb. I start telling them about her prognosis but when I get to the part of the story where I've facilitated her passing, the man's older brother, a weathered, brown, though not unhandsome man in his forties, walks away.

"She was his friend," the man I know says.

My heart that within the last few days has begun to mend feels the nick in just the right place and again splinters. I try to explain how much I'd agonized over the decision.

"He'll get over it," he says. "He just needs time to process."

I get in my car, drive around the block until I'm out of sight of their house, and park. My stomach is weak. I feel wrong.

I call Joe, but he doesn't answer his phone. I call my sister, but she isn't home so I talk with my brother-in-law.

"You did the right thing. The poor animal was suffering," he says.

I grab onto his words. I drive to the grocery store, drag myself through the aisles to buy the few items I need, and return home.

I sit at my computer pouring forth words in a letter of explanation. I read, change, reread, edit, and then print. I walk out of the house with the page, hear loud rock music coming from their house, interpret it as a sign of mourning, and go back inside.

I know what it's like to lose someone you care for. The night I'd chosen to gently stroke Dinky's aging body while she passed, I'd gone home after, eaten a large bowl of ice cream, next a grilled cheese sandwich, then more ice cream while watching *Ratatouille*. The wounded child wanted to drown herself in food. My hole had been voracious and wanted to consume just like their hole was vast and needed to fill itself with waves of sound.

I want to let them know I feel their pain.

I want them to absolve me of any wrongdoing.

I walk outside again and stand at the edge of my house. I turn back. I re-read the letter and make small editing changes.

I walk outside again and stand at the corner of my house looking towards theirs. I become fearful of what I might encounter if I approach a house where I don't know the occupants.

I return to the inside of my own home again. I re-read the letter and make small editing changes again.

I call my mom. "You should be angry with them for allowing an animal to get in such a bad way," she tells me forcefully. My mind can see her logic yet still the hurt remains.

Joe brings me a bouquet of flowers. "I know it was hard to let the cat go," he says.

The next morning, Saturday, he and I take the letter to their house and put it in the mailbox.

Long after the incident with the cat stopped keeping me up at night, long after I'd gotten over the anger I experience at Joe in the beginning of this chapter, I go for an afternoon walk. Infused with energy on a bright sunny day, I make it a few blocks from our home. A small green car speeds by, and a woman's voice escapes the window and belts me. "Cat killer."

My shoulders stiffen.

As if I've stepped in a dirty puddle, memories about the cat splash around me. Momentarily, I feel guilt and remorse. Then, disbelieving, I laugh out loud and dial Joe, the first person I think to call, the only person who, I'm learning, will still be there the next day even if I argue with him. The only person who I'm learning to be there for the next day.

"I probably won't sink to her level," I tell him, "but if it happens again, I know what to do."

"What's that, baby doll?" he asks.

"Yell CAT ABUSER!"

He laughs.

I relax.

It was while writing the second draft of chapter one, which was originally only seventeen pages but then expanded to be chapters one and two and almost sixty pages total, that I experienced my first anxiety about putting my story out into the world. I hadn't intended to expand my thoughts, but editors told me they felt cheated by the original lack of story and friends told me they wanted to know more about relationships. It didn't go—I hadn't gone—deep enough. My husband told me to trust their words.

I prayed for help and it was as if a dam broke open, the words pouring out and rushing to be first on the page. They wrote themselves. Feelings that had only appeared in my aura and intentions, visible to others through strained facial expression perhaps but never to myself, burst through.

As if I'd held my breath for decades, the sensitive me I'd stifled and swallowed now gushed forth in a large stinging sigh and I became alive, and reactive to everything—my husband's gentle snores that when we were first together had unnerved me but now, *usually*, lulled me to slumber, anytime my cat merely *thought* about opening his mouth, the train whistles that were commonplace in the far away distance that I at one time had been used to.

I bought an herbal combination that was designed to relax not only my mind but also my internal organs. They didn't stop my cerebral midnight movies though, so I'd lay in bed soft and pliable waiting for the sandman, hoping to be rescued from my insomnia liked I'd hoped for relief from my heartache in the pages I was reliving.

I rose at all hours with words in my pen that had to be written. I'd race to the table telling my husband, if he was awake, not to talk to me so my pen didn't dry up, and I'd write the shitty first draft all writers swear by. Then I'd try to edit those words and this is where the difficulty started. Still trying to make order out of disorder, still hoping to get it right, get it perfect so someone, anyone, at least one person would be interested, helped, soothed, I'd agonize over sentence structure, paragraph meaning, comma placement, embarrassing my family, or even myself.

I read Erica Jong's *Fear of Fifty* until 1 a.m. trying to make myself sleepy, but I'd get interested in her story and never fall asleep. I'd been liberated by her ever since I'd read *Fear of Flying* in my mid thirties, and I found similarities and camaraderie as I read about her early years of insecurity, analysis, and struggle to find her voice. Through her words I gained more courage, and I continued to write.

Again, I listened to my husband when, haunted by self doubt in the middle of the night, I'd wake him up to ask, "What if it (the book) is a stinker?"

He'd offer the wisdom of his years, "Then you'll do the next right thing."

When I did sleep, I'd have disturbing dreams, and in my waking hours I'd try to dissect these psychological snapshots.

One of these dreams involved Anthony whom I was engaged to and lived with at twenty-eight, but I was calling him "Joe." I couldn't comprehend why this duo-dream man, part past, part present, left me.

Hacking free from dream tendrils that snaked around my subconscious, I pulled myself from bed and went to my husband who was making his breakfast in the kitchen, hugged him and said, "Don't leave me."

Returning my tight embrace he responded matter-of-factly, "Where would I go?"

I'd be comforted for awhile and would continue to write the life that had been so disorderly in its early years, it had become the new order.

WISDOM

Just as people have eyes to see light with and ears to hear sounds with, so they have hearts for the appreciation of time. And all the time they fail to appreciate is as wasted on them as the colors of the rainbow are wasted on a blind person or the nightingale's song on a deaf one.

Brian Ende
Momo

True intimacy with another human being can only be experienced when you have found true peace within yourself.

Angela L. Wozniak

"Do you remember Kyle?" my mom asks over the phone.

I pause for a moment, "Of course I remember Kyle," a bit more politely than my first thought, which is *Duh! He was such a menace in my life that I devoted pages in my book to our relationship.* I'd never told her specifically about the drugs and hitting that occurred when I was nineteen, only that it'd been an awful time. I continue, "A few years ago his brother sent me an e-mail after finding me on the internet, and then Kyle sent me a message too. I thought about writing back, 'Are you still hitting women?' but I never answered him."

"He died in a motorcycle accident," she says. "There's a wake announcement in the paper."

I get chills. "What? When?"

"All I know is there's a service for him and his wife this week."

I go to my computer and google his name and some details. I learn that a group of motorcyclists left a bar in the middle of the afternoon. ... Country roads. ... Coming over a hill. ... Speeding. ... In front of others. ... Hay truck turning. ... Unable to avoid crashing. ... No helmets. ... Thrown into roadway. ... Wife run over by SUV. ... Motorcycle in ditch. ... Pronounced dead at scene. ... Cocaine found on both of them. ... He was fifty-one. She was forty-two.

In the e-mail a few years ago, he'd seemed proud to write, "Still partying like I used to. Play hard. Work hard."

For days I feel the thud of body on pavement, then a ton of car crushing down. I could have been on the back of that Harley Davidson. True, our relationship had happened thirty years previous, but my life could have been forever entwined with Kyle's—till death do us part.

It'd been a time when all the future held promise. Unfortunately, it was also a time when I held naïve ideas about life and questions I thought were answered by focusing on something outside myself. But looking for answers and comfort in external sources can only lead to calamitous results, even death. If it's not a physical demise, then it's certainly an annihilation of emotion and spirit. For what is living but experience, feeling—vulnerability to life—and to love. Hiding in a bottle or a needle or a job or a material object or excessive shopping or another person's approval, basically anything external, I cut off my true nature. For so long though, I didn't know how to take the focus off activities, people, objects. I didn't know to ask myself, *what helps me feel good about me?* I didn't know how to conduct myself in a way that guaranteed I could lay my head down at night and sleep peacefully. I didn't know how to be my own friend.

Kyle hadn't been my friend.

Joe and I were friends above all else.

That's how it had started. That's why it continued.

Joe and I had both been timid, like school kids experimenting. As we'd crept closer to *that time*, when our petting became more passionate and the kisses furtive, we'd wondered separately how our sexual relationship would evolve. We were two middle-aged adults trying to learn a new way, and our anxiety was high. A few months into the relationship, after our first night out dancing to rock music, as he drove me home, Joe turned to me and exclaimed rather loudly, "What about sex?!" Reacting, it had been on my mind too, I turned to him just as quickly and said back just as loudly, "I guess we'll have it!"

Sure, I'd had sex before, but none—*absolutely none*—of my sexual experiences leading up to being with Joe prepared me for respectful, available, physical intimacy. In the early stages of our relationship, as related in chapter nine, when I tried to do a striptease routine I'd done so often that I could have performed it sleepwalking, I broke down, feeling awkward and embarrassed. Regrettably, even after being married for a few years, I was still awkward, actually more so, because deep-seated beliefs around behavior, sexual and otherwise, were now hardwired into my brain: The male is always in charge. Good girls don't initiate sex, act like they want it, or ask for what they need.

I know, I know. This view has supposedly changed in the world today. It had even changed in my life when I was a dancer but indoctrinated beliefs can be so strong they need repeated scrutiny. Part of this internalized belief, truth, was that good girls, good married girls, good married girls that talk about God or who pray and meditate, didn't take control of their sexual satisfaction. Good girls kept a clean home, called their mothers often, kept food in the refrigerator, made soup... Good girls appeared perfect from the outside no matter what they felt on the inside.

However, at one time I hadn't been a good girl. Inside the club I'd been a bad girl, according to society's collective morals, and another part of my belief was that bad girls can do whatever they want. The only problem with that thinking though, is that when I labeled myself as bad, everything I did was bad. It had been easy to approve of my actions when I was in a "bad" place, but years later, outside the "bad" club atmosphere, I discovered I harbored derogatory views of myself and my sexuality; there was a negative association with past carnal liaisons. Those actions hadn't made me bad, what happens between two consenting adults isn't good or bad, right or wrong, but there was a small kernel of dogmatic belief that said sexual power was wrong, damaging, a sin. This belief was nestled so deep inside that even I didn't recognize it until I was writing this book. It had become part of the forbidden feminine that along with emotions like anger and self-care before other care, misconstrued as "selfish," I'd been conditioned to think unladylike.

Like a tiny gnat that buzzes around your head intermittently annoying you even though you can't see it, the memories of my past freedom tainted my vision of myself. There was still a dichotomous split inside me that I wasn't aware of when I was a dancer because it had worked for my life then. It'd been okay to think of myself as bad, it had appealed to the rebel within me, but I was no longer living on the fringes of acceptable society. I was involved in community activities and standing up as a leader in our neighborhood. I was no longer living a "bad" life, but it didn't work to simply think of myself as "good" either. My antiquated belief system dictated that good girls had rules and inhibitions. That didn't work for my marriage. That didn't work for sex. Sex is messy. Sex is losing one's self in the moment, and I could no longer do that with this man if I adhered to some fabricated role in my head. Thinking of any part of myself as bad reinforced dishonorable feelings about my choices, similar to how labeling myself good caused me to feel virtuous yet stifled in my choices. Using either of these labels took away my freedom to decide what works for me as an individual. This wasn't choice. Real choice empowers. Labels disenfranchise and defeat. While I wasn't Vixen any longer, she still lived within me and I could claim the sensual freedom she'd enjoyed if only I could learn how to integrate it into my marriage. This would be *true* female sexual empowerment.

Although the atmosphere of the strip club had circumvented my inhibitions and encouraged my bravado, it had been false empowerment. The sexual encounters I'd had while working as a stripper left me physically satisfied, sure, for the hunger within myself had been temporarily abated; but I didn't go away stronger, able to build on the experience I'd just had. I'd been an animal. Animals act instinctually, procreating merely for survival without regard to the other participant. I didn't feel that the men I'd been with were holding me up and supporting me like Joe was. Even the guy in Las Vegas I nicknamed Pizza Boy because I could call him up and he'd come over and deliver, whose youth and exuberance were an aphrodisiac feeding my body and ego, even with him, after he'd leave and I'd fall asleep smug, certain, and proud of myself for taking charge, I'd felt like a little something was missing—a little something wasn't present that I needed, though at the time I was unable to put my finger on it.

Now I had it.

With Joe.

A complete package: love, trust, companionship, partnership, and support.

Unfortunately, the brain is the biggest sex organ, and while my body knew all the mechanical maneuvering, my brain still had more moves that weren't complimentary to the kind of intimacy Joe and I were creating. My libido had always been driven by physical as well as emotional separation; distance created tension, and that tension I connected to desire. Consequently, my desire revolved around emptiness, desperation, frustration, and longing. In addition to men like Geoff, who didn't even live in the same country, the bad boys, the ones who kept me wondering, worrying, the kind I would never tame, reinforced those negative feelings around desire. This was a ridiculous way to search for love, a form of self-abuse. I'd even sought out abusive types of sex. For a brief time, I'd skirted around the edges of sadomasochism; although I never ventured into dungeons or ritualistic degrading sex practices, the fiery Russian spanked my left hip so hard once during intercourse that it left a bruise that I wondered would heal completely. That black, green, and purple patch on my skin remains forever burnt into my memory. Still, today, it makes me ponder the lonely woman who confused pain with love.

Being with Joe, I harbored no jealous, resentful, distressed, impetuous—basically black—emotions. More pointedly, right from the onset of our lovemaking, I felt light and experienced something I never had before—happy orgasms. When we were intimate, after I'd climax, I'd break into laughter. Writing it now makes me smile. This is the tone of our love and our life—happiness, joy. I've heard orgasm referred to as a little death, but on the contrary, this laughter, this love, was all consuming, a physical manifestation of being alive that resembled a field of purple and yellow wildflowers stretched as far as the eye can see.

It didn't take long, though, for my brain to attempt to block this lightness of spirit. Although I was in the relationship I wanted to be in, I was anxious. While I had never consciously thought that perpetual longing for a relationship was ideal, staying single was more familiar to me, therefore, more comfortable and safe. My military dad's deployments and tours of duty to foreign lands had introduced a cycle of happy—leave—sad—yearn. Then my experiences moving from army base to army base as an adolescent reinforced the same cycle of happy—love—leave—sad—yearn. Even though my mind told me I *really* wanted to be close to Joe, my brain was hardwired to be comfortable with distant love—imagined love—and yearning. This had been my pattern, my experience that turned into, distressingly so, belief; *Love is elusive and will ultimately end. I will never have the kind of relationship I want.* Because this was my internal mantra, albeit, subconscious, I'd unconsciously recreated that my entire adult life. First, at the tender age of eighteen, I'd yearned for Sam when he moved to Washington State after driving me to Wisconsin to live with my parents. In my thirties and into my forties I'd yearned for Geoff from England, and during those years that we were on again, off again, I'd yearned for the man who lived three hours north of me in Nevada City, whom I only saw once a month. In between these relationships I'd had encounters with men who were substance-addicted and, therefore, emotionally unavailable. As Vixen, I'd been with people who weren't really known to me, or I to them. I was good at responding, enacting, acting.

But I wasn't acting any longer.

I was feeling.

This man whom I loved and really wanted to be fully connected with was feeling awfully close—too close—closer than anyone had ever been to me. There was no tension. And without that tension, I didn't feel comfortable and safe. And people can only fully relax when they feel comfortable and safe. And people can only experience true intimate and connected physical pleasure when they're relaxed.

For some time though, I didn't even know what was happening with me. While it was distressing to watch myself push away from Joe, my reactions caught me by surprise, and all I could do was observe. Sometimes in the middle of foreplay, saddled with the tempestuous torrent of my brain, I'd start thinking about electricity bills, laundry, groceries, pet care, anything, unable to remain in and focus on the pleasurable feelings of my body. Sometimes I'd giggle like a nervous schoolgirl. This was particularly upsetting because I'd done that with men at the strip club trying not to offend or anger them while playfully warding off their advances. I didn't want to group Joe with the men from the clubs.

Sometimes I'd stiffen and memories of my ex-husband from twenty years previous surfaced because he'd been disrespectful while grabbing at my breasts and crotch outside the bedroom. Sometimes I'd lie passive, expect Joe to do the work, and then wonder what was wrong with us. Lovemaking didn't feel natural, and when I couldn't do it, I blamed him. I'd get angry with our infrequency, yet I wouldn't approach him. Then I'd feel hurt when he didn't approach me.

It benefited us most when I took the focus off him and concentrated on myself; just as I'd found benefited me most in every situation that I had dilemmas in, concerns about, or worries over. It benefited me most when I surrendered to the situation as it was and looked deep within my heart for answers to the questions: How was I going to own my body—fully—completely—respectfully? What did I find attractive within myself? What did I find sexually alluring about myself? What would ignite my passion? What would make me want to fuck my best friend? I pondered these uncomfortable questions while I took a good look in the mirror.

Just as I'd sat and watched bodies when I was trying to find out what "normal" people looked like, I again observed others. I noticed other married women and saw that while some seemed casual, some spent time on their appearance and looked quite beautiful. I reasoned that this helped keep lust and attraction alive. A friend whom I'd noticed wearing makeup for the first time in her forties told me, "I don't want people to remember me as plain." I now realized that I didn't want my husband to have that continual plain image of me either. Our pets and my phone clients didn't care what I looked like so I never fixed myself up during most days, but perhaps it made a difference to my husband. More importantly, I realized it made a difference to *me*. It didn't really take that much effort to apply a dab of foundation and a hint of mascara and eye pencil, the greatest benefit being that it helped me feel attractive for myself.

I had to start talking. One piece of advice that had been given to me numerous times before we'd gotten married was "just keep talking." Honest communication seemed to be the key factor in any good relationship. Just as I had to be willing to stand without a stage and in the glaring daylight as Susan Bremer, recovery person, former stripper, I now needed to be able to stand naked within this relationship and expose my emotional and psychological vulnerabilities.

This was easier said than done. In order to remain open and willing, to be patient and to trust that giving of myself and my emotions to another was safe, I needed help.

~

Admitting to saying prayers isn't easy for me. I have a visceral reaction when I say the word "God" because my voice brings a concrete reality to the male God of my upbringing. Mom blames my Vermont College education on my inability to agree with her brand of religion, and while college did educate me about how religions were created and patriarchy evolved from an era when women, matriarchy, held power, I'd had negative, shameful associations with God and the church from an early age. Although one of my earliest church memories is as an excited child at Christmas telling the story of Jesus' birth and getting a brown-paper goody bag filled with peanuts and candy afterwards, what stands out stronger is that once during an afternoon Lenten service, as part of our parochial school day, we children in the fifth grade sat listening to the minister who stood high above us on a pedestal. Perhaps he was discussing fears, the topic escapes me forty years later, but I distinctly remember that in one sentence he referred to the boogey man.

I laughed out loud.

Mortified that the chuckle had escaped and echoed through the silent sanctuary much longer, I'm sure, than it actually did, I clasped my hand to my mouth and shut my eyes. When I opened them, the minister's punitive gaze bore through me.

While in my teen years, getting up early on a weekend to go to church was a chore, so after I turned eighteen I exerted my independence by staying home on Sunday mornings although I was breaking the fifth commandment; *Honor Your Father and Your Mother.* Even if I woke up those mornings before everyone left for church I'd stay in bed until they were gone. One such morning I got out of bed a few minutes after everyone piled into the car for the ten o'clock service. My rumbling stomach and castigating mind needed to be silenced. On the counter sat a cellophane-wrapped paper plate of homemade cinnamon rolls. I devoured them. While I sat full and numb at the kitchen table, a commotion at the back door let me know my parents and sister were home.

"Oh!" my mother said when she saw the empty paper plate with little moist indents where frosted delicacies had once been. "I took those out for us to have after we got home from church."

While they busied themselves making eggs and toast, their disappointed faces resurrected the guilt of not going to church in the first place that I'd tried to stuff down with the sweets, and heaped more shame upon my already remorseful countenance.

Still, there was a part of me that hoped God and the church could be a saving place. At nineteen, when I returned to the Wisconsin Synod Lutheran Church, desperate for help and guidance to leave and stay away from Kyle, the pastor's verbal condemnation that I was a sinner resurrected guilt and shame. I fled his office as soon as I could.

At twenty-five I went back once more. I looked to God and the church for acceptance and relief because I felt there was no backing out of the marriage I'd committed to even though I was having serious doubts about spending the rest of my life with my fiancé. I thought I needed to accept my lot in life and move forward—like a martyr—a good girl. After the wedding, still uncertain about a lasting love and terrified of commitment, I walked away from my new husband as well as the church.

I'd only known God in the context of the Lutheran Church, but when I took on the monumental task of creating, producing, marketing, and distributing my DVD single handedly, I'd walk the Berkeley Hills for exercise and sought God again, this time without a formal church. I visualized and prayed earnestly, albeit, for only what I wanted—international recognition and stardom. These hadn't materialized in my life so I abandoned God again.

Twelve-step principles emphasized the need to have a Power Greater Than Myself to surrender to. Initially I cringed whenever someone referred to their higher power as God so I got stuck on Step Two of the twelve steps; *Came to believe that a power greater than ourselves can restore us to sanity.* My only vision of a power greater than myself had been young Jesus on the cross with shoulder-length brown hair. I'd rejected this image and had no image to replace it with, but I was desperate. I kept my ears open, heard others talk about their own struggle with the concept of God, and held onto Julia Cameron's acronym for GOD in *The Artist's Way; Good Orderly Direction.*

It was while sitting in a small candlelit meeting one night that an image of a very old man with white hair and a long white beard, wearing vibrant purple and blue robes, popped into my mind. This vague cross between Merlin the Magician from Disney's *Sword and the Stone* and Mickey Mouse's robes in *Fantasia* comforted me and became my vision of my Higher Power. This wise, patient, loving, elderly gentleman replaced the punishing God of my youth and freed my conscience so that nightly, like I'd done as a little girl, kneeling at my bedside, hands folded and head lowered, I could talk to my God. This new vision continues to expand and today incorporates eastern spiritual philosophies as well as western. It even led me and my husband to attend a lecture series at a church where the speaker, Mark Gungor, humorously told stories and gave permission, quoting biblical passages, for married men and women to have great sex. During that seminar I laughed enthusiastically in church along with everyone else in the packed pews.

With help from meditation, prayer, and introspection, I realized there were a few elements my brain had to explore in order to further relax during sex with my husband. First, there was the atmosphere. I never concerned myself with atmosphere in the past because sexual encounters just seemed to spontaneously combust, but now I recognized that I needed to practice what I taught others to do in classes and on my DVD. Next, I admitted that I needed to feel sexy for myself before I'd *ever* feel that with my husband. I used to put a lot of energy into getting ready for work as a stripper playing to the image that society has set as a standard for sexy, but honestly, sometimes I didn't even know what sexy was anymore. I wasn't wearing skin-tight costumes, wasn't whipping my long hair (I didn't even have long hair), and I wasn't svelte or rock hard with a flat abdomen. I needed to discover what excited the woman within who was now grayer, more curvaceous, and who'd accepted that she was of middle age.

Also, I've read that women need fantasy to fuel their sexual passion but I'd never been one to fantasize during sex. I'd seen women's porn movies steeped in romance and mystery made by Candida Royale, and I just wanted them to get the nonsense out of the way and get down to the sex—the naughty sex—the dirty sex. Here was another clue to my inability to relax during sex. I'd been conditioned to think of sex as dirty, but what was dirty about making love with my husband in our bed during the daylight? There was nothing forbidden, naughty, or secretive about that. Sex had always been taboo, something to be kept hidden, in the dark, not spoken about in polite mixed company, something to be ashamed of even. While shame helps establish private behavior versus public behavior and provides a protective barrier around intimacy (it keeps most people from procreating in public, for example) shame that inhibits intimacy within a loving, mutually respectful relationship is deleterious.

What we weren't ashamed about though, was eating. There was nothing taboo about eating—or spending too much money on food.

Our birthdays are only twenty-one days apart, and we've

developed a habit of doing one grand thing in between the two dates, so this year we made reservations for an extravagant dinner date. In order to feel just as sumptuous as the meal we were going to have, underneath the slimming black-pinstripe slacks I wore delicate, black-lace, boy-cut panties that rode high on my cheeks. I selected a thin, pleated, black-gauze blouse over a black-lace shelf bra I'd always thought sexy because of the way it held my breasts, and I left the top buttons of my blouse open so a whisper of what was underneath peaked through. I painstakingly applied eye shadow, eye pencil, brow tint, mascara, blush, and lipstick to adorn my face, and dabbed myself in my favorite perfume, Shalimar.

As we sat across from each other he fed me juicy shrimp while I licked the marinade from his fingers. He licked his lips slowly as I withdrew a spoonful of garlic mashed potatoes. He motioned me over to his side of the table and after I situated my dinner plate, water glass, and utensils, and we appeared for all purposes to be enjoying dinner side by side, he slid his fingers down my stomach and lower, to my center, then brought them back up again nonchalantly and placed them in my mouth. I purred and snuggled close to him.

Oh wait! That was my fantasy. And it *was* taboo.

The reality is that I wasn't that bold. We sat across from each other the entire time and ate our own dinners. The reality is that we ate three courses and went home stuffed and fell into bed. We'd enjoyed each other's company and conversation, but we were in public, and I didn't voice my desires or orchestrate them.

The reality also is that I didn't need to change what I found sexually stimulating and erotic. I just needed to approve of my sexual proclivity and merge that with the sweetness I saw our love to be. Sex, physical intimacy, when engaged in too soon, can block emotional intimacy in a relationship, but I didn't want the emotional intimacy we were building to be a barrier to our physical intimacy. I now wanted the emotional intimacy to be a bridge to physical intimacy.

A few days later, underneath my old clothes, I put on the same lingerie I'd worn for that luxurious dinner and approached my husband. It wasn't perfect. Deepening a healthy sexuality that worked for us as a couple would take time, but we had to start somewhere. We figured we had the rest of our lives to practice.

While shame was a barrier to exploring and celebrating my sexuality in a monogamous marriage, which in itself is troubling enough, I was also beginning to see that shame was such a natural part of me that even when I did something my brain realistically knew I had a right to do, such as speaking my truth, making a request, or putting forth an opinion, it infiltrated my thoughts and inhibited my response. Shame mixed with and got all tangled up with fear, similar to my first experience as a young child when I was more afraid of disappointing my parents than the terror I felt about jumping into the pool.

I first noted this when I realized that I was afraid to make phone calls asking retailers about past due money owed me from purchasing my DVD. I had the right, it was a business deal, but yet I'd cringe and postpone it until I couldn't put it off any longer. When I sent a few sample chapters and a proposal to Ben Fong Torres, whom I'd once interviewed with for a copy-editing job, asking for his opinion on my book proposal, I was afraid to open his return e-mail, convinced he'd berate me for writing what I wrote, afraid he'd condemn me for writing him at all.

When I submitted six-hundred word articles for consideration in the local paper, I again would postpone opening the e-mail from the editor, worried that, she too, would lambaste me for voicing an opinion. No matter how diplomatic and cordial I'd been in my dealing with customers, vendors, or people whom I considered more knowledgeable than I, I was afraid the recipient would think me foolish, wrong, or unreasonable. I identified this dreadful feeling in the center of my stomach as intrinsic shame, and I concluded it belonged to yet another internalized belief that said I wasn't supposed to speak up for myself, or even to speak up at all.

This self-knowledge was disturbing and I wondered: Wasn't I ever going to stop being the little kindergarten girl who felt everyone was laughing at her? Wasn't I ever going to stop being that little child who was terrified of jumping into that pool but more terrified of displeasing others? Wasn't I ever going to stop being the new girl who had no friends and who just wanted everyone to like her? Wasn't I ever going to stop needing others' approval?

The unfortunate answer to these questions is "No," because I, myself, had never approved of the awkward little girl, lonely adolescent, self-conscious adult, and self-absorbed stripper even though they lived within me. And because I hadn't approved of them, I'd denied their existence and in the extreme, distanced, even defended myself from them. But, if I held them tightly, validated their fears, celebrated their gifts, and approved of how well they'd coped and gotten me to this point in life, they could release not only the shame they held for themselves and their past actions, they'd be free to bring their greatest gifts to the woman I am today.

The little girl, although awkward and shy, is also playful. She's the one who enjoys lying on the floor laughing while the dog licks her face and who loves creating Christmas card pictures in Photoshop. The lonely adolescent is the one who reaches out to other women, empathizes with their struggles, and offers suggestions to help them get the love they want. She also continues to push me towards work I'm passionate about. The self-conscious adult is the one who will always be aware of personal boundaries and be considerate of others. The self-absorbed stripper will keep herself physically fit and sees the need to enjoy her body and continue to explore how to feel more pleasure in it. This self-scrutiny and willingness to embrace *all* facets of my personality and to understand my past actions, like chiseling away at a piece of rock to uncover the form within, chips away at internalized shame. Embracing all parts of me brings to the mature adult woman I am today approval of who I am today.

With self-approval comes the confidence to take risks. Learning how to maneuver the results of those risks instills competence, teaches self-reliance, and builds esteem. I like the thought of increasing self-esteem as I age. I'd rather rejoice in a healthier sense of self and confidence on the inside than chase an idealized image of a perfect outer self that doesn't really exist. I'd rather think of myself as having wisdom lines and choose role models for aging gracefully and with style.

As I've started to look with loving eyes at the women I encounter who are old, I mean, really old, late eighties and nineties, and wrinkly, not face lifted, not botoxed, the women who don't dye their hair any longer, I've found multitudes of women who wear their age magnificently. While visiting my mom for a week in Wisconsin (her cancer has been in remission for years and she's as active as ever), I accompanied her to the Cousin's Breakfast, a gathering of older female relatives that occurs once a month. The last woman to arrive caught my eye. Her solid white hair, infectious smile, and the wink she gave me highlighted her blue eyes that sparkled in the fluorescent diner light and took my attention away from the many wrinkles she wore with sophistication. Her attractive face smiled often and betrayed her ninety-plus years. Mom told me later she's had two hip replacements and gets cortisone injections in her fingers regularly so she can continue to play the church organ. A vision of the symbol-clashing bunny from the old energizer battery commercials flashed through my mind, and I now have an image of myself when I say, "I plan to be very old, very wrinkly, and very wise."

But I'm not there yet. Each day I strive to inherently feel that my worth is based on my talents, skills, and contributions to life instead of my appearance, which is just a subtext of who I am. It helps to surround myself with people who have similar values and ideas, but that isn't always possible.

Although my memories of Las Vegas aren't pleasant, most of them are about working in strip clubs, I do want to be present at a baby shower for a friend who lives there, so I drive to this place that draws addicts in vast numbers: gambling addicts, sex addicts, drug addicts, and alcohol addicts come from all over the world to party in Las Vegas. My sober sensibilities don't relish the thought of returning, but I know I don't have to be anywhere near the old clubs or the infamous Las Vegas Strip.

It's grand to see my friend, Jolene, her husband Brian, and our friend Trina, who's arranged the event and flown in from Tucson. The three of us had worked as dancers at the Gold Club in San Francisco. The last time we'd all been together was my last night working, seven years previous, when we ate dinner.

Jolene and her husband have lived in Las Vegas for years. When she moved there initially, she'd worked at Olympic Gardens, but much had changed in the Las Vegas Strip clubs from when I'd worked there with Stacy in my early dancing days. Most clubs advertised as Gentlemen's Clubs, but some required their patrons act more gentlemanly than others. Olympic

Gardens had turned into a less-than-gentlemanly club. Jolene wasn't comfortable with men wanting to manhandle her for a mere twenty dollars a song so she'd returned to a profession she'd dabbled in briefly on her many exploits around the world as a young woman in the stripping industry—prostitution.

I envied her junkets and the high fees she charged as a call girl, or escort as she preferred, upwards of ten-thousand dollars a day, but while I lived with that envy during my financial despair, I never joined that line of work. My internal beliefs would not permit me to sell my sex for money. I had considered staying in the sex industry and becoming a dominatrix, I didn't have to let strangers penetrate me in that profession, but I never did that either.

When contemplating both these jobs, I'd reflected on my stripping career and admitted it had interfered with my love life by plying me with men's attention and a false impression of acceptance and admiration. If something so simple as showing my body and making it available for eyes as well as the occasional hand affected me negatively, then these other two careers would more seriously mess up not only my love life, but also my sex life as well. It was interesting to hear the few stories I was privy to though, and knowing Jolene helped me feel like I still lived outside the normal society my inner teenager would always rebel against.

Besides myself and Trina, a few other women, escorts themselves, come from out of town to stay at Jolene's. A very personable blonde from Michigan arrived before I did and pitched in to help with the pre-party shopping and decorating. Once I'm there, a second woman arrives in a huff, introduces herself by her escort name, and asks for a ride to a grocery store some miles away, all the while keeping her sunglasses on. A girl from New York shows up the next morning but doesn't offer to help.

Jolene is a fun affable woman who opens her heart and her home to everyone so it's no surprise that the women who come for the baby shower are an eclectic mix of prostitutes (former and current), sex worker's rights advocates, even a university teacher (Jolene has a masters degree from a prestigious university) along with a woman who's been a business client of her husband.

Immediately after the baby shower, when most of the guests have gone, Jolene's water breaks. My brain buzzes with excitement and awe as we women mill around unable to do much but whisper and exclaim about the timing. Jolene had stated, while opening gifts, the only one missing was her little bundle of joy and she was ready to have him materialize.

The midwife arrives and attaches the fetal monitor to Jolene's stomach, and from outside her downstairs guest-room door we can hear a strong heartbeat: whoosh, thump, whoosh, thump, whoosh, thump—the baby becomes alive. Never in my life have I heard such a loud affirmation of life. My heart swells and eyes tear. Childbirth isn't something I'm ever going to experience first hand.

None of us want to leave our posts on the living room sofas, but the contractions are slow to come so a few hours after midnight we try to sleep.

The next morning my legs continue to cramp from the long drive a mere forty hours earlier so I decide movement will be the best medicine. While walking, I call my mom to tell her the news. "Jolene's water broke right after her shower ended. She wasn't due for three more weeks," I exclaim. While she's commenting, an incoming call beeps through on my cell phone. I press flash to take it.

"Brian just emerged from the bedroom exclaiming, 'We're going to the hospital,'" Trina rushes.

I blurt into the receiver, "Are we all going to the hospital?" It has become a vigil.

"If you go, you'll be the only one," she says quickly. "Let me ask Brian," and then the phone is silent before I have a chance to say anything else.

"Yes," she comes back on to relay breathlessly as I hold the phone to my ear while running back to their house.

The car is idling in the driveway, Jolene is in the front passenger seat, and the driver's door is flung open. I climb into the back, and Trina runs to grab my purse from inside the house. I sit awkwardly, half on and off the seat, straining to be closer to the front. Brian rushes out of the house, hands me his computer case, and jumps in. He holds Jolene's hand as he backs out of the driveway and directs to me, "Check in my wallet in the side compartment for my driver's license."

Happy to be of use, I find it and tell him so.

With a weak voice Jolene requests, "Check in my wallet in my purse for my ID card." Eager to help, I search for it but can't find it. I check again. And again. She assures me it's there somewhere even though I never see it.

We aren't turning back.

Interjecting myself in the opening between the front seats as well as I can from the back seat, I take Jolene's hand when Brian lets go of it so he has both hands for the steering wheel. I lean as far forward as I can to be of as much support as I can. Jolene squeezes my hand, and her head rests against mine, exhausted after twelve hours trying natural childbirth with nothing but soothing bath water to ease her pain. Though feeling like an imposing intruder in their very personal moment, I also feel honored to be involved in that same personal moment. Her gentle moans and heavy breathing filtered only by her golden hair that falls against my face and neck, reverberate through my head when the contractions come.

Brian speaks encouraging words as he tries not to speed but still to get us to the hospital as fast as possible. I want to support her with words also, but I don't know what to say. I can't say the words he's said. That would be stealing.

We speed by the Las Vegas strip, it's glitz and fanfare subdued in the November daylight, memories of darkened nightclubs, disrespectful men, and too much alcohol wafting over me.

When Jolene breathes heavy with pain, I increase my breath too.

Brian pulls up to the front entrance of the hospital, and I help Jolene out of the car. I sprint ahead and push through the front doors while Brian gets her to a chair. No one looks up to read the urgency in my wide eyes. *Where are the attendants in white pushing wheelchairs like I always see in the movies?* I wonder. I feel helpless as I try to find someone to ask where to take her but am too polite to interrupt the front-desk clerk and her customer. Brian comes in after moving the car to the parking lot, and I throw up my hands in exasperation.

"Go sit with Jolene," he commands and relieved to be told what to do, I go to my friend who sits naked under a thick white hotel robe that has fallen open in the public hospital lobby. I close the robe at her legs and start rubbing her shoulder.

"Don't touch me," she quips. "Just hold my hand."

I take her hand.

Brian comes and leads us to the admitting area for maternity.

Hospital personnel take her through double doors and out of our sight.

The midwife arrives, and we three sit silent listening to the drone of a news reporter on a local television station.

They call Brian back to be by her side.

We two sit silent listening to the drone of a news reporter on a local television station.

We hear moaning.

"That's her," the midwife notes. "They have to check her out before administering the epidural."

My only experiences with childbirth have been watching comedies like *Friends* when Jennifer Aniston's character gives birth and *Nine Months* when Julianne Moore's character gives birth simultaneously with Joan Cusack's in a slapstick scene where one father desperately tries to film the event. Giving birth in real life sounds like no joking matter.

Somewhere in the back, Jolene moans again.

"I wish they'd work faster," the midwife muses.

A nurse comes and gets the midwife.

I sit silent listening to the drone of a news reporter on a local television station in my day-old garments without even my usual ball cap to hide my greasy hair. My chapped lips, grubby teeth, and unwashed face increase my isolation, as couples, dirt-free and relaxed, walk into the maternity reception area ready to be admitted for their scheduled c-section.

After an hour I decide to find them. I'm holding onto Brian's computer case and Jolene's purse, and I don't want them to forget about me. Besides, surely it must all be over with by now.

Staff buzz me into the secure delivery area and tell me which room to go to. (Later I learn they thought I was the mother.)

I open the door to her room slowly and am immediately assaulted with the booming whoosh, thump, whoosh, thump, whoosh, thump of the baby's heartbeat magnified through the fetal monitor. Next I hear Jolene's voice. I tiptoe around the curtain blocking the door and see Jolene straining upward in the reclining bed, breathing loudly and pushing—breathing loudly and pushing toward her feet that are in metal stirrups. The midwife looks at me. Brian gives me a nod then returns to his paperwork. Trying to be unobtrusive I stand as close to the door and as tight against the wall as possible.

"I have to pee," Jolene says with urgency as soon as the contraction stops. "It feels like I have to pee," she repeats a second time.

"Scooch down to the end of the bed and we'll get you a bedpan," the nurse replies.

I press my back even tighter against the wall. *This is intense. Body functions are private. I'm out of place. I wouldn't want a friend watching me go through this. This is a family moment. I'm intruding. Wow! What an experience. Can I stay? Do I want to stay? I'm intruding. I don't belong here. This is intense. It's interesting, but really not my place. I can't stay. It's too intense. Should I stay? I might miss something. I'm not even helping. I have no place here. Do I leave the bags here? Should I interrupt? Why am I here?*

Carrying their personal belongings with me, I quietly back out of the room.

Brian comes out to the waiting room an hour later (although it felt like forever) and reports that Jolene has finally been given the epidural and is doing well. He takes their possessions and after getting a slice of pizza from the cafeteria, leaves again.

I feel obligated to stay. What if she has the baby right after I leave? Also, Trina phoned and told me I need to wait because she'll be bringing the young girl from New York with her and dropping her off at the hospital on her way to the airport. I'll have to give her a ride back to the house later. We all want to be present when the baby comes.

Throughout the afternoon, clean sparkly women from the house and guests who've traveled for the shower from California and Arizona arrive at the hospital before they make their way back to McCarran International Airport to fly home. I feel like Cinderella, but this time the feeling isn't positive. Contrasted to their fresh faces, I feel dirty and displaced. Also, I know I can be just as beautiful, just as clean and presentable as they, if only I'm given the chance. And I'm exposed to, or more accurately, forced into, their conversation. While they talk of places they've been and people they know in common, I catch myself feeling jealous. I'm covetous of their money and independence. This secret envy disturbs me.

They all start talking about the same customer. One of the women is flying overseas to be with him for a few days, at his request of course, and is lamenting how it takes too much energy. It sounds as if he demands her complete, undivided, non-stop attention, the same as he requires of every woman he pays to be with him. She's trying to figure out how to leave a day early from their "date" while keeping all the money. Others join in because they've had similar experiences with the same man.

I shift in my seat. My rear end aches from sitting in uncomfortable chairs. My legs ache from driving, then standing excessively over the course of two days. My knees ache from inactivity.

They have to put up with him because of the money.

My skin aches from lack of hygiene.

They talk about him callously.

My jaw aches from unconsciously clenching it. My cheeks and nose ache from the grooves worn into them by my glasses.

They joke about him.

My eyes ache because I'm seeing my greed reflected in these women. My brain aches from their conversation.

These women are hard—unfeeling—they have to be. While I don't know each woman's story, I know their collective story. The entire business is based on manipulation, lies, giving up of one's self. I know the loneliness, the emphasis placed on the money for comfort—as well as distraction.

Suddenly I'm back in the Las Vegas strip clubs where I feel pressured to be nice, say things, do things even, that I don't want to do. I don't want to think of those days when I'd been fearful of not having enough money. It was while drinking again and working in Las Vegas that the desperation I felt was palpable, evident in my eyes and on my face to everyone but myself. I'd played the game, tried to manipulate. I'd lied, skirted the rules, and hid from management as I rubbed up against men, and let them rub me. I was thrown back into the midst of that energy, manipulative energy, secretive energy, negative energy. To be in that world I'd have to shut down again. Disconnect from myself. Erect armor.

It's late, seven or eight at night, and I've been sitting for seven or eight hours. I'm raw from lack of sleep and the lack of empathy they have for their customers.

There are now only three of us left: myself, the girl from New York I'm to drive back to Jolene's house, and another woman who's meeting up with a colleague soon for a two-woman date with a client at the Bellagio.

The Bellagio is a luxurious hotel I've never stayed in although I had dinner there once. I adore luxury. I adore beautiful clothes. The most extravagant floor-length coat I'd ever seen was in a Las Vegas shop, and its memory floods my senses. I would look like somebody important in that coat. Others would see me in it and exclaim over its—and my—beauty. Just like those Nancy Sinatra boots had made me tall and special when I was five, wearing that coat would signal to the world I was special. I'd felt like a princess, Cinderella, trying on the black and spotted brown fur coat trimmed and mixed with rich eclectic hues of denim and suede. The saleslady had professed it a bargain at two thousand dollars, and I'd schemed in my head how I could get the money. To this day, I lust after its memory. It was something Steven Tyler would wear. I thought him elegantly eclectic and gracious. His autograph on a twenty-dollar bill and my time spent with him was a highlight of my dancing career. If I went into their profession, I could have that coat.

I had to walk.

And talk.

I called Trina, who was sitting at the airport waiting for her plane to board and whisk her home to Tucson.

"Why am I here?" I ask. "How did I end up here?"

"You just jumped in," she recalls. "You were the only one to offer. I know Brian really appreciated it. He was freaked."

I had.

I'd jumped feet first. I'd immersed myself without hesitation into the pool of life, decidedly different than the stalling I'd done when I was five trying to muster courage to jump into that pool that had been as bottomless as my trepidation—decidedly different from the way I'd avoided relationships and experiences in my adult isolation. I'd jumped feet first into the situation, the moment, without any concern for my comfort. It was a selfless gesture I wouldn't have made in my younger days because I couldn't give up a self I didn't have. The woman who'd never had the soft spot for herself couldn't have a soft spot for others, but now she had one not only for babies, but for all kinds of people and circumstances.

Once the commotion dissipated though, I was sitting in two-day worn underwear, sporting two-day, unbrushed, fuzzy teeth and fuzzy skin exposed to fuzzy memories that I'd just as soon forget.

I end the call with Trina and tell the girl from New York I can't stay any longer.

Back at Jolene's house I shower for a long time.

I sleep fitfully that night, wake up at three in the morning, throw the last remaining items I haven't packed already into my suitcase, and get into my car before the sun comes up and clears away the darkness from my spirit.

Barely twenty miles away from Jolene's home, my legs already ache. I have five hundred miles and nine hours left to drive. The pain will only get worse. I eat Tylenol as if they're butterscotch candies and drink black coffee along with Starbuck's sugar-laced Frappuccinos to keep my eyes open.

I drive fast to be where my inner child, rebellious teenager, self-centered stripper, and all-knowing adult can be safe and celebrate their gifts instead of squash them to please others. I drive fast to get back to the sunlight and the me who's moved on from those days of dark self-subjugation. I drive fast to get back to the place where I'm no longer hopeless and to get to the roots that I've planted. I drive fast to get back to the life I've created that allows my true nature to bloom. I drive fast to get back to the place where I'm happy and where I'm somebody very, very important. I drive fast to get back to the comfort of my warm safe home where I'm known intimately. I drive fast to get home to my cats and my dog and my husband who comes home to me every night. I drive fast. I get home at one in the afternoon, crawl into my warm pajamas, and sleep peacefully for the first time in four days.

~

The original version of this book didn't have a section on approval but after writing for a while I realized there had to be something beyond acceptance because that can seem like resignation. You can accept something but still be unhappy about it. You can accept without approving but you cannot approve without accepting. The original version of this book also didn't have a chapter labeled wisdom and when I thought about writing it, had to seriously contemplate, *What do I know about wisdom? How do I measure it?* In my quiet moments, I like to think I have some, but often my mind isn't quiet.

Webster's first definition for wisdom is an "understanding of what is true, right or lasting," and my computer dictionary states "the quality of having experience, knowledge and good judgment" as its primary definition. Swami Vivekananda writing in *Karma-Yoga and Bhakti-Yoga* posits, "Wondering is thus the first step in the acquisition of wisdom."

Based on these qualifiers, I can assure myself I have some wisdom and that I have all the tools to acquire more. I'm alive. I'm sober. I ask questions of myself. I explore the consequences of my actions before and after I make them. I make informed decisions. I embrace my self, my body, my mind, and my spirit. I know that no matter how much I get distracted by material things—sensations, experiences, thoughts, feelings, and words are all I can really possess in this world.

I liken myself to the voyagers in the 1959 adventure film adapted from the novel by Jules Verne that I watched as a child, *Journey to the Center of the Earth*. I've been a Scientist of the Self and have descended deep into my center, have had progress and setbacks and have encountered skeletons. But the collections of bones I've bypassed, stepped over, and have maneuvered around are old outdated parts of me that point in the directions I *shouldn't* go instead of like the *Journey's* actors who encountered a skeleton pointing in the direction they *should*. And instead of being outfitted from the beginning, I've had to pick up along the way the tools necessary to build friendships, accept responsibility, embrace commitment, trust with impunity, communicate honestly, respect without judgment, and love myself unconditionally. As I've found these tools and have thrown them into the worn leather bag of my psyche, I can pull them out again to inspect the hard dark lumps within my core, to gingerly brush away the debris and dust to unearth the gems beneath, and to explore the recesses and shadows of my character. I've used these tools to become aware of, and to understand the "me" that had hidden in dark passageways, eventually accepting and approving of my body, my sexuality, my life, and my journey. It is mine. It is all I will truly ever own.

Perhaps I can only measure wisdom by how far I've come.

EPILOGUE

When I'd made this appointment to get head shots for my Self Appeal business with the same photographer I'd used to get bachelor-party photos, I hadn't thought about "playing," but the thought of capturing alluring photos now excites me. I already have some terrific pictures I'll be happy to have when I'm old and wrinkly, and it'd be nice to have more to treasure.

At first I'm awkward. My long locks are gone. Unlike the tight spandex and body-hugging vinyl I'd chosen in the past to highlight my female curves, the jeans and tailored Bebe baby-blue satin top I now wear I've chosen carefully to hide the parts of me I think have gotten a bit *too* curvy. As I run my hands over my waist smoothing my top down and feeling womanly definition, I loosen a bit and tap into the sensual moves born of practice that are stored deep within me. I half close my eyelids, tilt my head back, and purse my lips.

It's easy—familiar.

Suddenly though, like shifting winds in a storm driving the rain in the opposite direction without forewarning, something within pummels me unexpectedly.

I stop.

"Do whatever you want," the photographer urges. "A strip-tease even."

I want to. I enjoy having the attractive photos even if only to know they're tucked away, but as this patient Cyclops stands firm watching my every move, I feel unduly scrutinized. How can I reveal myself, even if only pretend, to this stranger? That's what *he* wants.

I'm reminded of Ana Nicole Smith's drunken slur at the American Music Awards that all the media played when she'd died. "I feel like Ana Nicole Smith saying, 'Like my body?'" I confess.

"You're not like her. Don't you ever compare yourself to her. She's a gold digging slut!"

His venom surprises me. In that instance, however, I do feel like her. And it feels sad.

Just as I'd looked into that mirror fifteen years ago and seen the tanned seductress with spiced cocoa lips and deep aqua eyes that reflected lust and silver club lights whom I didn't know, I now look into the camera lens that mirrors someone I do know.

My sensuality isn't for him. It isn't for display or for sale.

"I … I can't do this," I stutter. "It's not working."

"Take your time," he soothes. With the camera held to his face he stands diligently. His business is waiting for the right moment, look, gesture. He's adept at catching the best looks of nationally- and internationally-known celebrities, and here he is at my disposal—as if I'm the celebrity.

I pause.

I think.

I don't need some static pictures taken by a stranger to mirror my beauty back to me. I see it in the loving eyes of the many people I have in my life today. In a flash of realization, I finally understand. *I'm multi-dimensional.*

"No," I say a little louder, a little more firmly.

I gather my few makeup articles and hair spray, slip them into my tote, put on my coat, and pay for the session. I walk out of his studio doors and into the sun, the light reflecting from my wedding and engagement ring diamonds drawing my attention, the light from my life drawing me home.

www.ingramcontent.com/pod-product-compliance
Lightning Source LLC
Chambersburg PA
CBHW021042090426
42738CB00006B/152